# FABLED SHORE

## *From the Pyrenees to Portugal*

### ROSE MACAULAY

OXFORD UNIVERSITY PRESS

1986

Oxford University Press, Walton Street, Oxford OX2 6DP

Oxford New York Toronto
Delhi Bombay Calcutta Madras Karachi
Kuala Lumpur Singapore Hong Kong Tokyo
Nairobi Dar es Salaam Cape Town
Melbourne Auckland

and associated companies in
Beirut Berlin Ibadan Nicosia

Oxford is a trade mark of Oxford University Press

First published 1949 by Hamish Hamilton
First issued, with Raymond Carr's introduction, as an
Oxford University Press paperback 1986

British Library Cataloguing in Publication Data

Macaulay, Rose
Fabled shore: from the Pyrenees to Portugal.
1. Spain—Description and travel
2. Portugal—Description and travel
I. Title
914.6'04824   DP42
ISBN 0-19-281483-X

Printed in Great Britain by
Richard Clay (The Chaucer Press) Ltd.
Bungay, Suffolk

# THE CENTRAL SCHOOL OF SPEECH AND DRAMA

## UNIVERSITY OF LONDON

**Please return or renew this item by the last date shown.**

The Library, Central School of Speech and Drama,
Embassy Theatre, Eton Avenue, London, NW3 3HY
http://heritage.cssd.ac.uk
library@cssd.ac.uk
Direct line: 0207 559 3942

# CONTENTS

# FABLED SHORE
## from the Pyrenees to Portugal by Road

Each division on this border represents Twenty Miles

**Top map:**

FRANCE

Pyrenees

ANDORRA

R. Ebro

AROZ
ULLDECONA
TORTOSA
AMPOSTA
Poblet ×
MONTBLANCH
BENICARLO
NISCOLA
PUERTO DE
LOS ALFAQUES
Vg. de San Jorge
VALLS
Centcellas
TARRAGONA
VENDRELL
VILLANUEVA Y GELTRU
VILLAFRANCA
DEL PANADÉS
R. Llobregat
NOYA
MARTORELL
TARRASA
LLOBREGAT
BARCELONA
ARENYS DE MAR
BLANES
SAN FELIÚ DE GUIXOLS
PALAMOS
LLAFRANC
BAGUR
GERONA
FIGUERAS
BELCAIRE
PALS
C. Norfeu
CADAQUÉS
ROSAS
PORT BOU
SAN MARTI
AMPURIAS
TORROELLA

CATALONIAN SHORE

**Bottom map:**

R. Guadalquivir

VELEZ RUBIO
LORCA
BAZA
GRANADA
GUADIX
RONDA
MALAGA
MANAKE
TORREMOLINOS
MOTRIL
ALMERIA
MARBELLA
ESTEPONA
SAN ROQUE
LA LINEA
GIBRALTAR
ALGECIRAS

C IAN SHORE

PORTUGAL

SPAIN

Top map

Bottom map

1st. Class Roads ——
2nd. Class Roads ——

ev

# ACKNOWLEDGMENTS

I SHOULD like very gratefully to thank Dr. J. M. Bastista i Roca, of Barcelona and Cambridge, for his kindness in looking through and making suggestions for the bettering of some of the Catalonian section of this book, and also for giving me introductions in Barcelona. I am grateful to Mr. Bernard Bevan, lately Information Officer of the British Consulate-General in Barcelona, for much information, kindness and help; to Miss Massey, of the same department, for valuable assistance in Barcelona; to Mr. W. C. E. F. Leverkus, British Vice-Consul at Cartagena, for his information and advice; to the Patronato Nacional del Turismo at Madrid and the Secretariado Nacional da Informacâo at Lisbon for very kindly supplying me with photographs; to Señor Antonio Marquet of Barcelona, and the Instituto Español in London, for also helping me with these; to Mr. R. B. Neumegen, of Messrs. Offley, Forrester & Co., for information about sherry at Jerez; and to Professor Edgar Prestage for lending me the most recent researches of Portuguese scholars into Prince Henry the Navigator's towns on Capes Sagres and St. Vincent.

ROSE MACAULAY

# ILLUSTRATIONS

# FOREWORD

BY RAYMOND CARR

ROSE MACAULAY'S *Fabled Shore* has ceased to be a description of Spain as it is, a sort of guidebook for superior persons. It has, like Richard Ford's *Handbook for Travellers in Spain* become a classic to be read in its own right. It describes her journey along the Mediterranean coast from the French frontier to the Portuguese Algarve in the late forties. Then the Francoist tourist slogan ran 'Spain was different'. It was. Now it is—more or less—like the rest of Western Europe. The last of the invaders—tourists from the sun-starved north, successors of the Greeks, the Romans, the Goths, the Moors and the French—have seen to that. Miss Macaulay—like all of those who find untenanted beaches and a simple village hospitality and then come home and write about them—bears her share of the blame for later desecrations. A few months after the publication of the *Fabled Shore* my wife and I set off in Miss Macaulay's tracks. In her undiscovered fishing ports of the Costa Brava there was already a sprinkling of other English visitors in sandals and clutching back numbers of the *Statesman* and the *Manchester Guardian*, putting stars in the margins of her pages. They were the scouts of an invading army.

In the late forties the physical and emotional scars of the Civil War—it had ended in 1939—were still visible. She finds the vanquished still bitter and picks up rumours of the still active anti-Francoist maquis. The victors are engaged in the rechristianization of Spain, rebuilding the churches burned down in the Cvil War by the 'Reds'. The roads which shook off Miss Macaulay's car bumpers were still pitted with shell holes. Village boys to whom a foreigner was 'a quaint baboon, an ape, an owl' pursued and pestered her and in an attempt to escape their attentions she gave up wearing her hat. A woman alone, driving a car, was a phenomenon; it called forth 'the usual interested crowd pressing round my car and the usual fifty children climbing on the running boards'; it provided the theme for countless conversations with Spaniards for whom such behaviour was 'not our custom'. Today it would not raise an eyebrow, when abortion on the National Health Service is a major issue for Spanish feminists. Women are no longer turned out of churches for wearing short sleeves. In the Catalan town of Figueras there was no petrol to be had; now it is one of the first stops on the road for a sizeable portion of Spain's thirty million annual tourists. In the whole of her journey Miss Macaulay encountered only one other British motorist. Benidorm, now a horror landscape of sky-scraper hotels with their fish and chip bars, their discothèques where the Scots live it up as if in Glasgow on a Saturday night, was still a fishing village frequented, so Miss Macaulay asserts, by smugglers. Perhaps it was a sign of things to come that the only drunks she met 'were one or two Britons'. Torremolinos, Mecca of the package tour agencies, then boasted but a single hotel.

If a description of a vanished age was all there was to *Fabled Shore* it would only be of interest to the social historian, or as a description of the Odyssey of an English eccentric in her fifties, a compulsive sea-bather, tramping up hills to visit monasteries and castles in a temperature of 101° in the shade, or driving along dusty roads wondering where the next petrol pump might be. She is of no avail to those searching for secluded spots along that now ravaged coast; in Denia where expatriates drink themselves into hazy afternoon stupors, Miss Macaulay found only the memory of the English raisin traders who had vanished in the Civil War. *Fabled Shore* offers something much more valuable than holiday hints. It has a true feel for the Spain that had not been submerged by the tourist avalanche of the 1960s that helped to finance Spain's industrial take-off, for something that the yobbos of Benidorm leave unmolested because it can make no appeal to their drink-sodden minds: the Spain of History. In 1897 Murray's bowdlerized edition of the

Ford's *Handbook* set forth the true capital asset of Spain: 'In historical and artistic interest Spain is second only to Italy . . . and it possesses a character and originality of its own by which all intelligent travellers have been irresistibly fascinated'. 'It is' writes Miss Macaulay 'this sense of ancient history that gives Spain its peculiar, its extraordinary savour and character'.

This irresistible fascination can only be transmitted to the reader, the sense of ancient history retrieved, by a learned traveller. Rose Macaulay is learned. She studied the standard works on Spanish architecture before she set out; she has the geographers and historians of classical antiquity at her finger tips. She remembers that the youths who pester foreign ladies are descendants of the Turdentani described by Strabo. It was the sailing book compiled by a Greek mariner in the sixth century B.C., in the version of the late fourth-century Roman poet, Rufus Festus Avienus, that set her out on her travels. It is most refreshing that she expects her readers to understand and enjoy Latin without the benefit of translation.

Learning alone does not suffice to create a great travel book. There must be enthusiasm and empathy—the capacity to *feel* the past. This is Rose Macaulay's supreme gift. Tarragona to her 'seems as full of Roman ghosts . . . as Ampurias is of the whispering shades of Greeks bartering and strolling in their stoa above the sea, watched by dark suspicious Iberians from beyond their wall'. Tarragona was, she writes, to the Emperor Augustus what Brighton was to George IV; where Scipio wintered the army that was to drive the Carthaginians from Spain, where the poet Martial sought to escape the company of 'brutish Celtiberians' who seldom wore togas and proved incapable of providing intelligent social life. She seeks in vain, in the dust and heat, for Carteia, founded by Phoenicians and later a colony of the half-bred offspring of Roman legionnaires, where Pompey was betrayed and Crassus hid. She cannot find it. A pity. Were the 'substantial remains' Ford found in the 1840's those of the lost city of Tartessos, once rich and mighty? Like so much of pre-Roman Spain, that city has 'slipped into the realms of myth'. After a dissection of Pytheas, Pliny Pomponius Mela, she plumps for the traditional site at the mouth of the Guadalquivir. Modern Cartegena has disappointed many travellers but she sees in her mind's eye 'the elephants of Carthage trumpeting up and down the steep streets'.

Rich in classical reference, she is less strong on Moorish and medieval Spain, and even fades out altogether in more modern times. Cadiz is, for her, a possible Carthaginian successor of the lost Tartessos. She sees the city that was to Romans what Paris was to nineteenth-century Britons, a city of rich food and dancing girls of easy virtue. She does not mention that it was in Cadiz that a handful of Spanish patriots in 1812 gave Europe the word 'liberal'. Sagunto is, for her, the fortress where the Celtiberians, abandoned by their Roman allies, perished rather than surrender to Carthage. It is not a city where General Martínez Campos brought out his troops to declare for Alphonso XII, great-grandfather of the present king. Modern history is, for her, mostly a sad tale of destruction. The liberal anti-clericals of the 1830's reduced to uninhabited ruins the monasteries that the plundering soldiers of Napoleon, last of the barbarian invaders, had spared. Yet it is, one feels, the neglected and decrepit state of much of Spain's historic past that constitutes for her their charm. It is in these neglected buildings—many now since restored—that the ghosts of the past materialize.

Blind spots she has, but she harbours none of the absurd prejudices that disfigure the works of 'the outrageous Ford' as she calls him. She understands the sentimental Latin piety, 'the riot of bad taste, of crude tawdry and simpering vulgarity' that puts plaster Madonnas in Romanesque churches. Ford found the baroque architecture, in which Spain is so rich, unpalatable. For him the baroque portal of the Palace del Marques Dos Aguas in Valencia is 'grotesque', a fricasée of palms, Indians, and serpents. For Rose Macaulay it is splendid. She bemoans the destruction by nineteenth-century urban improvers of the

Valencia of the seventeenth and eighteenth centuries; now it is the magnificent nineteenth-century architecture that is going down before the bulldozers of speculative builders. Ford found Murcia, capital of 'this Dunciad province', full of baroque and therefore dull. Not so Rose Macaulay. It is enchanting, so is Lorca: so is Jerez.

'One villa', said Ruskin, who built his own villa overlooking Coniston water, 'can destroy a regiment of hills'. The Costa Brava, Miss Macaulay writes, 'is still in the main a succession of little fishing ports and untenanted caves and rocks . . . if it should ever become, as it would long since have become in Britain were such a coast conceivable in Britain, a continuous chain of luxury hotels and villas, I should not revisit it'. The Costa Brava has not been vandalized by speculative builders as has her deserted Murcian and Andalucian shores; but you can no longer get a dinner and a room for ten shillings surrounded only by Catalans on holiday. Her finest prose is evoked by her imagination peopled by the ghosts of the past, by what has not vanished: the streets of Lorca, the Cartuja of Jerez, the ruins of Ampurias.

THE CURVED gulfs, the promontories, the shore stretching along the sea, the hills standing close above it, the high towns lapped by the waves . . . the sea walls guarding the ports, the way the marshes and the lakes lie, and the high wild mountains rise. . . .

RUFUS FESTUS AVIENUS (late 4th century)

IL FAUT visiter les pays dans leur saison violente, l'Espagne en été, la Russie en hiver.

THEOPHILE GAUTIER (1845)

BEING ENTERED *Spaine,* he must take heed of *Posting* in that hot Country in the Summer time, for it may stirre the masse of bloud too much.

JAMES HOWELL (1642)

THE GRAND object of travelling is to see the shores of the Mediterranean.

SAMUEL JOHNSON (1776)

# INTRODUCTORY

A GREEK mariner from Marseilles compiled in the sixth century B.C. a topographical sailing book of his voyage from the Lands of Tin in the northern seas, down the western coast of Portugal and round the Sacred Cape, and so along the southern coast of the Iberian peninsula, through the Pillars, and along the Mediterranean coast to Marseilles, his home. The later part of this sailing book, from the Tartessos region (near Cadiz) to Marseilles, had great detail, describing each bay, each cape, each port, for the benefit of those Greek merchant mariners who adventured and trafficked down that far and fabulous coast to the Pillars of Hercules, and beyond these into the dark and questionable Atlantic where the silver mountains stood back from the Tartessian shore. From this sailing-log, or rather from some later Greek version of it, the late Roman poet, Rufus Festus Avienus, made, towards the end of the fourth century A.D., the poem that he called *Ora Maritima*—dull and prosy verse enough, but fascinating material; to those making part of the same journey, every line has interest. And from Avienus I had thought to borrow the title of this travel book. But it did not go down well with my publishers, for the booksellers believed that their clients would take it for a girl's name, and when they came to read the book, be profoundly disappointed and return it. So I renounced *Ora Maritima* for a title less deceiving. *Fabled Shore* is a true description of this long strange coast and its haunted hinterland, to which Homer sent Odysseus voyaging, where, in the regions about Tartessos, dark Tartarus was placed, and the Elysian plains, the abode of the blest, 'at the ends of the earth, where life is easiest. No snow is there, nor great storm, nor ever any rain; but always Oceanus sends forth the breezes of clear-blowing Zephyrus.' That, as Strabo observed, is obviously Iberia. As to the Islands of the Blest, they lie opposite Cadiz. And it was in the Cadiz region too that Herakles killed Geryon and drove away his cattle. Herakles indeed was the hero of all this shore; he sought the Hesperides and their golden apples off it; and he it was who clove in two the bridge of land that joined Africa to Spain, so that to this day its two halves are called the Pillars of Hercules. Indeed, most Greek legends were at one time placed in that far western land that stretched, mysterious and unknown, beyond the Pillars and the familiar Mediterranean, along the fabulous Outer Ocean to the Sacred Cape.

That part which is washed by the Mediterranean as far as the Pillars of Hercules [wrote Polybius] is called Iberia, while the part which lies along the Outer or Great Sea has no general name, because it has but recently been discovered, and is inhabited entirely by barbarous tribes, who are very numerous.

The Massiliot sailor and I made (except that he went further and in the opposite direction) the same journey, he by the sea road, I by the land. I had the best of it, for I saw inland cities that he never knew. But all the way down this stupendous coast I trod on the heels of Greek mariners, merchants and colonists, as of trafficking Phœnicians, conquering Carthaginians, dominating ubiquitous Romans, destroying Goths, magnificent Moors, feudal counts, princes and abbots. History in Spain lies like a palimpsest, layer upon layer, on the cities, on the shores, on the old quays of little ports, on the farm-houses standing among their figs, vines and olive gardens up the terraced mountains. Ghosts from a hundred pasts rise from the same grave, fighting one another still; dig a little deeper, dig below the Moor to the Goth, below the Goth to the Roman, Carthaginian, Greek, Phœnician, and in the end you get down to the Spanish, who were there before history began, and will be there after history, defeated and routed at last by this strange land, dissolves in impenetrable mists.

It is, I suppose, this sense of ancient history that gives Spain its peculiar, its extraordinary savour and character. Other Mediterranean shores too have history, and are haunted by classical ghosts; but the French shores and the Italian have made more concessions to to-day; they keep their ghosts well under. Or, anyhow, the French do: few ghosts haunt the Corniche road between Hyères and Menton, though the mountains of Provence know some. In Great Britain our history is thickly covered up; it never runs wild about the place. We prize and pet and guard it, as the Spanish do not; we make a great to-do about a fragment of a Roman wall, and think a tenth- or eleventh-century church something quite out of the way. Spain grows Roman walls and basilicas and tenth-century churches like wild figs, leaving them about in the most careless and arrogant profusion, uncharted and untended, for travellers to stumble on as they will. It is a lordly attitude, not to be emulated by such comparative parvenus as ourselves, nor by such professional antique-owners as the Italians. It has the drawback that buildings we should here cherish and fence off and proclaim as national monuments are in Spain too often left to moulder away in neglect, like many of the monasteries which once dominated and ruled the country round them, and now are ruins, sombre in their abandoned desolation, or, like hundreds of former churches, they have become parts of farm buildings, their naves and apses shelter for cattle. The efforts of cultivated authorities can do little now to salvage all the ruined and obsolescent glories of Spain. Yet such obsolescence, such ruin, has its own splendour: to come on San Pere de Roda looming shattered on its Catalonian mountain, San Miguel de Culera, the Cartujas near Jerez and at Porta Coeli, so lovely in their desolation, as much utterly one with their background as ancient mouldering trees, has a breath-taking excitement that the carefully ordered trimness of our own Tintern or Fountains or Glastonbury cannot give.

Similarly (or obversely), the riot of bad taste, of crude, tawdry and simpering vulgarity, which is the frequent modern contribution to the ancient magnificence of Spanish (as to Italian) churches and cathedrals, does little to spoil them; it is a palimpsest, the stamp of nineteenth- and twentieth-century Latin devoutness, on churches whose ecclesiastical authorities are usually of the people themselves, and provide quite naturally what the people like. Our own cathedral deans and chapters, those cultivated and tasteful antiquarians, may shudder at the tawdriness; but this is a people's church, the people pray in them (or, alternatively, make bonfires of them), and the people's taste is notoriously shocking. Anyhow, and whatever the reason (which may lie deep in childhood associations), I cannot but feel amicably towards the painted plaster puppets who simper at us, guileless and amiable dolls, from those tremendous Gothic and Romanesque backgrounds. The Catholic Church, like Spain, can afford such sugar-icing.

Travelling about Spain and Portugal, as anywhere else, one is following in the tracks of innumerable other tourists, whose comments, whose tastes and distastes, whose experiences and points of view, cannot fail to excite surprise. They vary greatly, of course, in instructiveness. Some few are indispensable as travelling companions; others are more wisely consulted at home, or even neglected altogether. One must have with one, naturally, one or more guidebooks; much as these omit, they do put in a lot, including the obsolete hotels, and including the plans of towns with all the streets named after the last clique of generals, statesmen and liberators but one, so that they are not only useful as plans but as guides to recent local history. I had with me Baedeker, who told me everything that occurred to the railways on which he travelled, how here they crossed a road, there skirted the sea, how from one bend he saw a castle, from another a mountain range. Baedeker seldom alights from his train, except in cities, when he begins his excellent description with 'Proceeding from the station . . .' The smaller places he is content to mention and dispose of with 'Quitting Blank, the train next passes Dash.' But he is full of indispensable information, and so are the

Blue Guides; it is interesting to note how they and Baedeker occasionally show their independence of each other by differing on facts or dates. I had too the inimitable Murray, the first edition, by the learned but irate Richard Ford, who inveighed so bitterly and at such length against the inhabitants of the country he travelled in, their treachery, their superstition, their cowardice and their backwardness, but more bitterly still against the French, for he had by no means yet got over the Peninsular War. In spite of these antipathies and contempts, and in spite of having travelled a century ago, with quadrupeds for transport (horses on the level, donkeys to climb hills), Ford is an interesting guide and full of information.

Besides these general guides, I had with me a few more specialized books about particular regions, or particular aspects of the scene. I had Señor José Pla's indispensable *Guia de la Costa Brava,* which describes with loving minuteness every cove and playa of the author's native coast, from Port Bou to Blanes, where the Costa Brava ends. I take it that Señor Pla had a boat, and landed on all the beaches which cannot be reached from the road. Lying in the car for reference (it is very heavy) I had the massive and learned *Historia del Ampurdán,* by Señor Pella y Forgas; and also two small and learned works on Ampurias, and two excellent books about architecture, Sacheverell Sitwell's *Spanish Baroque* (without which I should have missed a good many examples of this elegant importation, and much delightful *azulejos* decoration both in Spain and Algarve) and Bernard Bevan's *History of Spanish Architecture,* which is particularly good in its comparative groupings, analyses and syntheses of styles. To instruct me in the doings of some of the past invaders, I had books about the Greeks in Spain, the Romans in Spain and the Iberians in Spain; no Carthaginians in Spain (but they did not really leave much to look at), nor Moors (except Washington Irving's *Alhambra*), because we know about Moors already, and anyhow most Moorish architecture books have to be rather large, the Moors having been in Iberia for so long. Finally, I had my log-book, Avienus's *Ora Maritima*. The only trouble with this as a guide is that most of the capes, rivers and towns no longer bear their Roman names, which, together with some changes in the shape of the coast, tends to make identification sometimes difficult, and a matter of dispute among learned historians.

When I got home, I fell to reading the other books, the learned books and the tourist books, the intelligent books and the silly books, the critical books and the gushing books, so that now I know about the tourists of all periods in Iberia. I was pleased to note that a great number of them, both British and French, had been stoned by the Spanish, as well as stared at. I was pleased not from malice but from pride, for I had myself only been stared and shouted at, except for a few boys on the ramparts of Peñiscola who had thrown down two or three harmless tomatoes at me, which I thought moderate from a notoriously xenophobe people. Actually, I encountered much friendliness.

But what I mainly found peculiar in the nineteenth-century tourists was the extreme interest that many of them displayed in the personal appearance of the female Spaniards, who always seem to me to be among the less interesting objects in any landscape. I mean, of course, not especially the female Spaniards (who are usually handsome), but the human population of any country. This is, no doubt, my personal limitation of taste, which finds buildings and landscape more æsthetically pleasing than the animal creation. But many visitors to Spain seem to have been almost as much interested in gazing at females as are the Spanish themselves; they are for ever darting, with an ardour almost Byronic, after bright eyes and flirted fans, and delight to compare the complexions, shapes and walks of ladies all over the peninsula. Indeed the ladies, and also the gentlemen, look very well, and much better than most ladies and gentlemen elsewhere, except in Italy; but still less well than the curve of a little fishing port round a crescent beach, or than the golden stone baroque façade of a Romanesque church, or the palm-grown plaza of some small white tile-domed town, or the sweep of a pastel-hued mountain-side up from a blue bay to the ruined citadel on its crest, or a terraced garden of olives, oranges and figs sprawling sweetly round an ancient sun-baked farm built in the great apse of a long-abandoned convent or church. It is these things, and a thousand more, that make the exquisiteness and the poetry of Spain. But let the susceptible nineteenth-century tourist catch sight of a shapely female form, and all the glories of landscape and architecture were forgotten. A notable exception was Augustus Hare, who always sought seriously after beauty. We seem to-day to be less susceptible, and twentieth-century tourists are able to travel Spain in less emotionally ardent mood.

All the same, one of the most interesting and interested tourists in Spain was Théophile Gautier, who went there over a century ago. Gautier regarded going to Spain as a considerable enterprise, set about with hardships and perils. 'Une enterprise périlleuse et romanesque. . . . Les privations, l'absence des choses les plus indispensables à la vie, le danger de routes vraiment impracticables, une chaleur infernale, un soleil à fendre le crâne, sont les moindres inconvénients; vous avez en outre les factieux, les voleurs, les hôteliers. . . .' Despite all these inconveniences, his accounts of what he saw are often exquisitely apt, and he is one of the few tourists whose journey is worth following in detail, for he had sensibility to and great pleasure in beauty, and could paint it in vivid words. He also, like so many writers, felt hardships deeply. Anyhow, one may feel gratified that they were his, not ours. In our time, a journey about Spain is not perilous, though it may be, and indeed cannot but be, romantic. There are few privations, no absence of things indispensable to life, the infernal heat of the sun did not cleave my skull (but then I like heat, in moderation), there are fewer *voleurs* than in England, and the *hôteliers* are on the whole more agreeable.

There may be plenty of *factieux,* but they do not bother foreigners, only one another. There are, it is true, some roads still *vraiment impracticables* for cars, parts of which seem to have been irrevocably pot-holed by the chariot wheels of Romans and Carthaginians and barbarous Visigoths, and never adequately repaired; but these are, among major roads, the minority; no doubt in Gautier's day they were worse, and anyhow he drove not on rubber tyres but in vehicles as bone-shaking as the chariots were.

Were I to mention a hundredth part of the good travel books about Spain and Portugal, it would take more space than I can command. But however much one reads about this strange and fascinating peninsula, however trodden its cities and its roads, it seems still, to each fresh and eager tourist, to have a wild virgin quality, as if oneself were its first ravisher for centuries.

It was an odd thing: during the summer months that I spent in the peninsula I encountered scarcely any travelling compatriots, and saw only one G.B. car, and that was at the very end. Possibly the other English were all in France, Italy and Switzerland, where I hope they were happy, but I cannot believe that they were as happy as I.

## CHAPTER ONE

## CATALONIAN SHORE

LEAVING the Catalan mountains of Roussillon for those of the Ampurdán, one knows that it is already Spain. The small dark frontier guards in olive-green uniforms and shiny black cocked hats are of another century; they have grace and beauty rather than apprehension; they pore over passports with interest and absorption and apparent surprise at what they find there. 'British Subject' . . . is that, they inquire, a name? Perhaps they find the handwriting of British passport officials obscure. It takes time; but they are pleasant and friendly, and when they have digested the passport and driving licence, and, with interest, searched the car, they wish one good fortune and a happy visit to Spain, which they hope one will enjoy, and one is away.

The road, the old Roman road from Gaul to Tarragona, sweeps up from Port Bou in wild and noble curves, lying like a curled snake along the barren mountain flanks of the Alta Ampurdán, climbing dizzily up, darting steeply down into gorges and ravines, above deep rocky inlets where blue water thrusts into rock-bound coves, and small bays of sand where it whispers and croons in its tideless stir. Points and capes jut boldly through thin blue air above a deep cobalt sea; rocky islets lie offshore; the road dips down to the little bay of Culera, where once throve a little fishing port, where now is an almost abandoned village, pounded to pieces by the bombarding naval guns of the civil war, which ranged down the Catalan coast with their capricious thunder. Here, in a quiet valley behind the quiet village of San Miguel de Culera, moulder more ancient ruins, those of a great Benedictine convent, one of those great monasteries to which Ampurdán gave its feudal allegiance through the Middle Ages. There is a cloister left, some broken arches, a few columns and capitals, three Romanesque apses; they and the church are twelfth century, built on the ruins of an older, probably Visigothic, convent and church: they have an air of having been there from the earliest Christian times, brooding, remote, fallen, but still dominating those bare, pine-clad hills where little vines sprout like cabbages out of the stony mountain sides.

The first beach of any size is that of Garbet, shut between two points and much frequented by Catalan *veraneantes*. Cross the Punta de Gates, and there is another wide bay with the road running close above it. On this July day it was very smooth, iridescent, turquoise with bands of cobalt and indigo further out; it is a most lovely bay, or rather a series of tiny bays. These Catalan bays, with the blue and green boats drawn up at the sea's edge and the brown nets spread out on the hot sands to dry, while bare-legged women sit and mend them, have a grace and beauty far more pictorial than the fishing beaches of Provence, or even those of Liguria; they suggest an antiquity still more remote, a tradition more unbroken. So did boats and nets lie, so did Iberian fishermen wade and lounge, Iberian fisher-women cobble and gossip on the hot sands, before the Greeks sailed down this coast from Phocæa five-and-twenty centuries ago.

The road, bending inland, runs into the old town of Llansá (the Roman Deciana). Llansá is charming. High above its plaza stands its fine Romanesque church, San Vicente, partly destroyed, like so many Catalan churches, by the anarchists in 1936. Two kilometres from the town is the little port, Puerto de Llansá, a crescent of sandy beach full of fishing boats (sardines are the main haul), shut at its southern tip by a rocky island and a castle, so that the little bay is smooth and sheltered like a lake. On the beach just above the nets and boats is a small white inn with green shutters, the Miramar, with tables and benches on the sand outside it. Here I spent the night; from it, on that hot July evening, I bathed in the smooth curve of sea, that lapped about me as cool and warm

as silk, while stars came out, and the great rock jutted into
still water against a rose-flushed west. Afterwards I dined at
one of the little tables on the sandy verandah, among the local
fishermen and a few Catalan visitors. The *patron* and his
family were charming. They had seen, it seemed, few British
passports; anyhow, they and their acquaintances who were
dining there pored over mine with absorbed interest. They
sat and gossiped and drank coffee at the little tables till long
after midnight; *vieja costumbre española,* shared to the full by
Catalans. It includes, naturally, late morning rising; my inn
got stirring about half-past eight, and I got my coffee about
half-past nine, after an exquisite early bathe in the still, limpid,
opal, waveless sea, to which I stepped carefully down the sands
between the drying nets. At ten I took the road winding
above silver-blue coves and rocky shores round the deeply indented bay that holds Puerto de Selva in its southern crook.
Vines, olives, figs, cactus and aloes filled the hot morning
with their aromatic breath. Puerto de Selva is, to my mind,
almost the most attractive little port of all the Costa Brava.
Sheltered by the crook of the point behind it, and by the great
jut of the Cadaqués peninsula that pushes out, vine-leaf
shaped, north of the Gulf of Rosas, the little port lies on one
side of the inner curve of a horse-shoe, facing west to the
opposite shore and hauling in nets full of sardines. Above it
on both sides of the bay tower great bare mountains, their
faint evanescent colours shifting with each turn of light and
shadow, so that they are here opal, there transparent indigo,
there again faint rust; it is like the shifting colours on a dove's
breast. The houses round the port are gaily and freshly
painted white, their doors and shutters a vivid blue and green;
they wear balconies with tubs of geranium, blue convolvulus
and plump-leaved sprawling shrubs. Some people prefer and
would restore the less gaudy rust, moss and ochre colours, with
which the town camouflaged itself against bombardment during the civil war, producing an effect of melting into its
mountain background; and indeed this must have been very

lovely. But so also is the vivid white and blue that dazzles on the luminous air. The camouflage, it seems, was not very effective, for Puerto de Selva suffered much damage from bombs. Like so many Catalan villages, it was bombed by one side and had its church destroyed by the other, thus getting the worst of two worlds. The interior of the church has been rebuilt: over the altar is the legend 'Radix salva. Erecta in ruinis A.D. 1944. Salva Porta.'

Two miles inland from the port is the still more ancient village of Selva de Dalt. The woods which gave village and port their name have long since been destroyed; now only little vines scramble over the lower slopes of the great hill flanks. Selva was hot, tiny, and smelt of figs. Its little lanes were blocked with donkeys and great loads of grass, and trailed off into hill paths. One of these led up the mountain on whose top towers the great ruined Benedictine abbey of San Pere de Roda. A car, they told me, could get up the mountain to within two kilometres of the monastery, and one would finish the climb on foot. A donkey, said Murray, would make it in an hour and a half. I dare say it would; but I had no donkey; it was very hot, and very steep; I renounced the enterprise and turned my back on Selva.

But the shadow of this mighty ruin haunted me, and haunts me still. I should have seen it. Instead, I read all about it in books by Catalans—how it was one of the major Benedictine foundations, which wielded feudal power over the country for miles round, sheltering the villages of Selva and Llansá and encouraging the fishing in the ports because the monks loved fish. The monastery was abandoned in 1798; the monks wearied of their lonely life on the mountains, and came down to the cheerful plains, nearer the fish, moving finally to Besalú. The deserted abbey was sacked and plundered of its doors, windows, pillars and stones; it fell into ruin, long before the dissolution of the monasteries put it into the hands of the State. To-day it broods in sombre Romanesque magnificence, a pile of broken walls, Byzantine arches, square towers, solitary on the bare mountain, looking down over Ampurdán and the sea. Not even Poblet or Ripoll is a more tremendous relic of the monastic grandeur that dominated eastern Spain during the *Edad Media*.

From Selva a rough road jolts inland across the vine-leaf promontory to Cadaqués. The coast, which has here at present no road (it is said that there is to be one), is indented by one lovely small bay after another, only accessible by foot; coves, caves, beaches and points, rocky islets, little harbours, none so well sheltered as Puerto de Selva, except Port Lligat, which is shut round by an island and is smooth and still, like a lake; among its three or four fishermen's cottages the square white house of Salvador Dali stands out. Lligat has a fascination not incongruous with Dali, and not quite of this earth.

The first port to be reached by the road from Selva is Cadaqués; a very pleasant and beautiful place, with its wide open plaza on the sea, shaded by mimosas and planes, the white town with deep blue doors and windows, the long curve of beach with the coloured fishing boats drawn up, the magnificent church standing high and sheer on the top of a pile of houses and narrow streets. Cadaqués is an historic port; in its bay the French, through the Count of Foix, met the Catalan admiral, Roger of Laurier, to negotiate peace after the French invasion of 1285. Barbarossa's squadrons took and sacked the town when they raged down that coast in 1543. Cadaqués has always been exposed to the people of the sea, as well as to storms, strong currents and winds that have made the lives of its fishermen hard. It is remote; until the making of the roads from Selva and from Rosas, it lay isolated in its bay at the tip of this easternmost spur of the Pyrenees. It is said to be still archaic, behind the times, in spite of the recent incursions of *veraneantes*. Archaic or not, it is a lovely place, white and clear and curved like a crescent moon. They fish for pearl in the bay. The church, Santa Maria (undamaged both by republicans and rebels), has a fine Romanesque-looking exterior, but inside is dated 1662, and is a gorgeous riot of baroque. It was in the porch of this church that I first read the placards which, all over Spain, warn señoras and señoritas what they must wear in church. 'Señora! Señorita! You present yourself without stockings? In a short dress? With short sleeves? You go into church? Stop! Stop! If you go thus into church, you will be turned out. If you go thus indecorously to confession, you will not be given absolution. If you have the audacity to approach the Blessed Sacrament, you will be refused in the presence of all.'

Apart from the sex unfairness of this (for it seems that señores may wear what they like), what strikes one is the profound difference of attitude between the Roman and the Anglican Churches, the one making church-going an occasion, a mystery, to be approached *en grande tenue,* in especial clothes, the other easy, casual, laissez-faire, go-as-you-please, come-as-you-are, come in your working and playing clothes, bare headed, bare armed, bare legged, just as you happen to be. (Vain hope, for how seldom do we come at all!) To surround religious devotion with pomp and ceremony, awe, stockings, voluminous ceremonial clothes, has much to be said for it, though the stocking requirement must keep many women from church; in these fishing ports stockings are seldom seen; the women mending nets on the beach and marketing in the town never wear them; they may keep a pair for church, but to go home and put them on when the bell clangs for a service must be difficult. On the other hand, those who do go to church thus decorously attired, thus set apart from their secular workaday selves, must, I suppose, feel very blest and spiritually prepared. As, no doubt, church-goers in Victorian England used to feel, processing churchward on Sunday mornings in top-hats and Sunday frocks. The Anglicans, who have dropped so much, have dropped all that; 'come as you are, my dear people,' is now the vicar's vain and coaxing plea. What English vicar would dare to placard his church door with 'Ladies! Stop! Stop! Change your clothes or you will be turned away!' The same difference in attitude lies, I think, behind the so careful guarding of Spanish churches, so that between one and four, when caretakers and sacristans are having their midday meal and their siesta, you will find every church and cathedral locked against visitors; very disappointing for those who are passing through in the afternoon and cannot wait. In England, cathedrals and churches stand casually and negligently open to all comers all day until dark; you may wander about them, stockingless, in mid-afternoon. The difference may, in part, be due to fear of the ancient Spanish tradition of ecclesioclasm, which has done in the past such irretrievable hurt to churches. But there is, I think, also a difference in attitude; the Holy Mysteries, the Heavenly Sanctuary, too hallowed for unguarded approach, as against come-and-go-as-you-please.

From outside the Cadaqués church one looks down a sheer precipice of a wall over the moon-like port and pale-blue bay set with fantastic rocks. A flight of steps takes one down into narrow streets, clean and steep, and so into the broad, delicious plaza, which was this afternoon bathed in soft and luminous brightness; it seemed a serene and happy place. At one side is the curve of sea; at the other restaurants and café tables. A waiter came and talked to me in charming American; he had, he said, waited for ten years in New York (and I remembered reading that many Cadaqués men emigrate to America, because life in Cadaqués is hard). 'They live very good there,' said the waiter, on a wistful note. 'Sure thing, they live very good.' But it seems to the casual visitor that life in Cadaqués too might be good; the place has an exquisite tranquillity, dignity and grace.

Leaving it reluctantly, I took the coast road for Rosas. It is a good road, winding up and down great olive-grown and rocky mountains, whose rust-coloured slopes sweep down to blue bays. I believe these mountains are the Sierra of Rosas, the eastern end of the Pyrenees. Above the olive zone they tower, barren and noble, in the magnificent uselessness of uncultivated mountain lands.

The road dips down to the sea at the lovely little bay of Montjoi. From here one may—indeed one must—walk to Cape Norfeu, and get, on a clear day, one of the most glorious views of the Costa Brava—all down the Gulf of Rosas as far as the Medas islands and Cape Bagur, and inland across the Ampurdán to the high Pyrenees.

Leaving Montjoi, the road sweeps round the bay of La Pelisa and curls north-west, dropping down from the heights into Rosas Bay, between bamboo groves where the cicadas ziz and churr without stop in the July heat, making the sound of a thousand saws. A great azure gulf opens at one's feet; the Gulf of Rosas; one slides down into the port, along a road where boats are building, smelling of tar and sweet timber; and here is the long bay beneath the mountains, where the Greeks (having lost their southern Spanish marts to the Carthaginians) anchored and traded two thousand five hundred years ago, and, at the gulf's southerly end, made their settlement of Emporion. The gulf was sheltered—'portus effuse jacet nullisque flabris æquor est obnoxium,' wrote Avienus. Yet not so sheltered as all that, for the day I was there a little breeze was ruffling the sea.

There is, it seems, no certain proof that the town now Rosas was founded by the Greeks. The Greek settlement of Rhodus (probably an offshoot from Emporion) may have been not on the site of the present town, but near it, and now buried beneath the silting sands. Traces have been found. 'Here too,' says Strabo, 'is Rhodus, a small town belonging to the Emporitans. . . .' And Scymnus, writing in the fifth century B.C., says that Rhodus was founded by the Massiliots after Emporion. But just where in the gulf it was, both they and other writers leave tantalizingly vague.

Rosas does not emerge much into history until the Middle Ages, when it was part of the domains of the Counts of Ampurias, who kept the Ampurdán in such a continuous bustle, and may well have disturbed and buried ancient sites beneath the weight of the fortifications and castles that they threw up all round Castellón de Ampurias. Under these so militant and enemy-conscious counts, Rosas was a naval port, anchoring the squadrons that guarded the trade of Castellón and the river Muga, to which came merchants from far Mediterranean and Adriatic ports. Rosas lay under the dominion and shadow of the great Benedictine convent of Santa Maria, which, greatly ichthyophagous like all monasteries, encouraged the fishing industry all up the coast to Cape Creus. The city encircled a walled and fortified abbey citadel, of which remains are still to be seen. Suchet blew it up in 1814. Fish and coral brought the town prosperity, and revived it after its many assaults and destructions, for through centuries it was a centre of the storms that always raged over Ampurdán both from within and without. A tough and adventurous seafaring population was reared in this dangerous city; often in recent centuries they have fared, like my Cadaqués waiter, out of their own exquisite sea across the wild dark wastes of the Atlantic to try new lands. Some, like him, have returned, to talk American to tourists in the plaza, or to sail their fishing boats about their blue and jade and silver bay, and to lounge on the sea wall beneath the trees, as I did now, looking down the long bay that the sinking sun turned to a great rose, looking at the white, west-facing town delicately flushed, and across the bay to the opposite coast, where Castellón de Ampurias rises on its hill among the shadow-blue plains of Ampurdán. Rosas is lovely, though it has not the remote outpost charm of Cadaqués. I drove along the short coast road to the point where the lighthouse stands, and beyond it to the point of Poncella (view, as Baedeker would say; and a view indeed it is). On the hill-side above the faro is the ruined castle of La Trinitat, smashed up in 1808 by the French. I began to climb up to it, but was stopped by a sentry; probably it bristles with guns that foreigners may not see. I returned to the town, and took the road to Castellón de Ampurias, five miles west.

Once the capital of Ampurdán and the residence of the counts, Castellón stands on the river Muga, under three miles

from the sea, surrounded by reservoirs and marshes. It stands
on a hill; a fine mediæval walled city, with a fourteenth-
century church, castle, moat and bridge. The church—or
rather cathedral—is magnificent; a tall square-pinnacled tower,
arcaded in three tiers, with fine buttresses and gargoyles, a
broad nave of seven bays, west door sculptured with alabaster
apostles, rich retablo and high altar. It is one of the most
pleasing Gothic churches I saw in Catalonia. Close to it (I
think joined on) is the castle, with its moat and its steep
fortress walls brilliant all the way up with flowers and green
plants. The streets are fascinating; you come at unexpected
corners on some broken arch that may once have been part of
a cloister, or of some chapel of ease; in them fig trees grow
and goats graze. Coming to Castellón from the shore where
the Greeks trafficked and made their settlements, from that
golden shore, classical, Mediterranean, pagan, urbane, is to
step into feudalism, into the rough, turbulent life of Gothic
barbarism, where wild counts and dominating abbots and
their retainers fought one another and defended their cities
from assault. Everything seems built for defence or for prayer;
and even the churches are forts. There is nothing Greek about
these walled and castled cities.

I had to get on to Figueras, five miles further, where there
would be petrol and oil (both scarce in the country north of
Barcelona). Figueras, the capital of Ampurdán, and, after the
fall of Barcelona in the last months of the civil war, for a
short time capital of Republican Spain, is noisy and crowded,
its narrow streets a maze, through which I and my car were
guided to an hotel by a kind youth who was studying English
and collected stamps; for both these hobbies he found me
profitable, though, for all I understood of what he said, he
might as well have talked Catalan. He collected and introduced to me his instructress in English, a smiling little spec-
tacled lady who conversed with me in the street, but seemed
to understand the remarks she made to me better than those
I made to her; with me it was the other way round. She said,

'You make long stay in Figueras?' I said, one night only. She said, 'You will be a week staying, yes.' I said one night. She said 'Yes, one week. You like Figueras.' I said it was beautiful. She said, apologetically, that she could not quite understand my English, which was not, was it, of London. She said some more, in the English of Figueras, and we parted with mutual compliments and friendship. I like the people of Figueras. But not the church clock, which made the night unquiet by resonantly striking every quarter. Wakeful and fretful, I began to understand the Spanish passion for church-burning. But, in the case of Figueras, I was mistaken. I saw the church in the morning; a fine fifteenth-century building which had been destroyed by the church-burners and was being very beautifully rebuilt; the new part included the bell tower which so sonorously disturbed the night; the old one, I was told, had not struck the night hours. Perhaps sleepless nights in Figueras had been planned as a form of reparation for sacrilege, and I thought it served Figueras right.

Some of the old church remained; part of the nave, the base of the tower, the sculptured figures over the west door. San Pedro must have been a magnificent church. I was shown over the ruins and over the new building by an intelligent priest; he gave me a booklet about its history, which related also much of the history of the town. Figueras was the Roman Juncaria, and stood on a Roman military road; it was destroyed by Saracens in the early Middle Ages, and rebuilt, further from the road, a plain and humble town which the inhabitants called Tapioles; in the course of time it became Ficerias, Figariæ, Figueras. To-day the ancient name is only preserved in one district, called Tapis. Tradition says that St. Paul (so busy in Spain) visited Juncaria, landing at Emporion, and preached the Christian religion there with immense success, which produced later several martyr saints. The Saracens destroyed Figueras and its first (probably Visigothic) church; after the reconquest it was rebuilt, with the help of the San Pere de Rosa Benedictines. This Romanesque church was burnt down, with the whole town, by an incendiary count of Ampurias. With its indefatigable powers of recuperation, Figueras built itself and its church up again, the latter in the purest Catalan Gothic of the fifteenth century; austere and tremendous, its severity lightened by its graceful *campanario*. There were later disasters and attacks, and the *campanario* was scarred by French bullets; but the church remained standing for nearly five hundred years, its longest period yet. Then, on July 21st, 1936, the Figuerenses began to set fire to churches; 'surgió la chispa necrosificadora, el espiritu satanico de destrucción y de ruina . . .' the mob broke into the parish church during Mass, seized benches and chairs, and set them ablaze. What a conflagration! Flames leaped to the roof. 'The faithful, livid with fear, retired into a corner of the church, believing their last hour to have come,' but they were allowed to go without molestation. The flames consumed nearly everything; what they left was looted or destroyed.

Mysterious madness which ever and anon attacks the Spanish, driving them to these strange pyrrhic frenzies! It seems the reverse side of religious devotion: in Anglican England we have little of either; in consequence our churches and cathedrals remain standing, though somewhat sparsely filled. It was odd to picture the cheerful Figuerenses at their fiery work, seeing them so peaceably and gaily employed in their broad market square on this July morning eleven years later. Indeed, this morning market was a lovely sight—a brilliant orchard of gay fruits piled on stalls—oranges, peaches, apricots, greengages, melons, tomatoes; and behind each stall a smiling buxom woman selling, before it other smiling buxom women buying; had they, I wondered, eleven years ago tossed pictures and images on the bonfire in San Pedro as now they tossed oranges and apricots into straw bags, and with the same zest? From all accounts, yes.

Meanwhile, the new San Pedro goes up apace, and will be beautiful. If it lasts another five hundred years, it will be lucky. The ancient castle of San Fernando, north-east of the town, was blown up in 1939, a last explosion of the Republicans when Franco's army marched in. Figueras is a pleasant capital; it has broad ramblas and narrow streets, and is difficult to find one's way out of. It had no petrol. They told me at the garages that petrol north of Barcelona was chancey; one might find some pump which had just got its quota, or one might not. La Escala, they said, might have some. They spoke as embittered men: the Ampurdán, one gathered, was being starved of petrol to feed Barcelona, which drank it with gluttonous profusion.

My mind was now set on Ampurias; I hurried out of Figueras, with my basket full of fruit and pots bought in the market. It was another hot and shining day. My way to La Escala and the coast ran through fifteen miles of level country, along a jolting road, past little ochre-coloured mediæval villages and farms, across the river Fluvia, and so through Vilademat to the little port of Escala, at the southern end of the Gulf of Rosas, whence a short road goes through woods to Ampurias. I arrived in La Escala in a propitious hour: petrol had just arrived, and there was a queue of camions at the pump in the street leading down to the shore, and a busy woman working it. (Most petrol pumps in northern Spain, as in France, are worked by women; further south, not; in the south women are not, I think, supposed to meddle with anything to do with motoring; they stick to donkeys.) The little port was crowded with beautiful fishing boats, great and small; I think it was a holiday, for it was gay with music and coloured paper festoons. Fantastically shaped rocks jutted up about the sea. Señor Pla says Escala is the chief fishing centre of the Costa Brava, and that the fishermen have a hard life, for the port faces north, and in winter gets the tramontana and the icy winds from Canigou and Provence. This, says he, has made the *escalanes* a rather sad, pessimistic people. Fortunately it was not winter when I was there; on that July morning La Escala was blue and exquisite, though its rock-strewn bay was ruffled by a breeze. The town did not look sad and grey, as my book said, though it does lack the brilliant whitewash and paint of many of the harbour towns. At nights the fishing boats go out with lights, the whole Gulf sparkles as with fireflies, and is very exquisite. Tiny coves of rock and sand surround the town to north and south; that morning they were pale jade and aquamarine, the waves lapping against jagged rocks.

The short road to Ampurias crosses a bridge just outside La Escala and runs through a sandy pine-wood. The ruins lie above the road, back from a bay of delightful sand and jutting rocks, the bay where Gnaeus Cornelius Scipio landed with his squadron to fight the Carthaginians, 'at a place in Iberia called Emporium,' says Polybius. 'Starting from this town, he made descents upon the coast, landing and besieging those who refused to submit to him along the seaboard as far as the Iber . . .'

The Emporium where Scipio landed in 211 B.C. was already over three centuries old as a Greek settlement, and illimitably older as an Iberian village. Somewhere about 550 B.C. Phocæan sailors and traders from Marseilles, cut off from the southern coast by the iron curtain of the Carthaginian conquest, made here, in the shelter of this Gulf of Rosas, and close to a small native town, a trading settlement. They settled first on what was then an island, where the almost ruined little mediæval village of San Martí now stands, guarding that buried town of Paleopolis, and a temple of the Ephesian Artemis which must have stood there. This first settlement is still unexcavated. The second, Neapolis, made a few years later, on the other side of the little harbour and buried from sight for many centuries, only yielding up occasional treasures to casual searchers, was first systematically excavated by the Barcelona archæological society forty years ago; interrupted by the civil war, the work is now again in progress. Neapolis has been revealed, layer below layer, each period identifiable by its fragments of pottery and sculpture and its coins, from the Visigothic town superimposed on it by the barbarian invaders, through the Roman city of splendid and ornate buildings, market places, temples and rich villas, the Hellenistic city that preceded and merged with the Roman, the Attic town of the fifth century, down to the earliest levels, the level of the sixth-century Massiliotes who founded the settlement and of the Iberian town joined to it; of those earliest towns there is little to show now. Neapolis was, when Strabo described it in the first century A.D., a double city, divided by a wall. . . .

because formerly the city had for neighbours some of the In-dicetans, who, though they maintained a government of their own, wished for the sake of security to have a common wall of circumvallation with the Greeks, with the enclosure in two parts, for it has been divided by a wall through the centre; but in the course of time the two peoples united under the same constitution, which was a mixture of barbarian and Greek laws.

Livy's account is more detailed.

Even at that time [195 B.C., when Cato landed there with army and fleet] Emporiæ consisted of two towns separated by a wall. One was inhabited by Greeks from Phocæa (whence came the Massilienses also) the other by the Spaniards: but the Greek town, being entirely open to the sea, had only a small extent of wall, while the Spaniards, who were further back from the sea, had a wall three miles round. A third class of inhabitants, Roman colonists, was added by the deified Cæsar . . . and at present all are fused in one mass, the Spaniards first, and later the Greeks, having been received into Roman citizenship. One who saw them at that time would wonder what secured the safety of the Greeks, with the open sea on one side and the Spaniards, so fierce and warlike a people, their neighbours on the other. Discipline was their protector against their weakness. . . . The part of the wall which faced the interior they kept strongly fortified, with only a single gate, and at this one of the magistrates was posted as a continuous guard. At night a third of the citizens kept vigil on the walls. No Spaniard was admitted to the city, nor did the Greeks themselves leave the city without good cause. Towards the sea the gates were open to all. Through the gate which led to the Spanish town they never passed except in large bodies, usually the third which had kept the watch on the wall the night before. The cause of going out of the town was this: the Spaniards, who had no experience with the sea, enjoyed transacting business with them, and wanted both to buy the foreign merchandise which they brought in their ships, and to dispose of the products of their own farms. The desire of the benefits of this interchange caused the Spanish city to be open to the Greeks.

The remains of the walls, huge and massive, with their single gate, are of the fifth century B.C. By then, Emporion had Greek works of art, Attic vases, the famous statue of Asklepios and other Athenian objects. Emporitans grew richer and more cultivated; by the fourth century, the Hellenistic age, their town was enlarged and beautified, a long, crowded rectangle of crossing streets and open squares, villas with mosaic floors, tombs, temples, statues. There was the temple of Jupiter Serapis, surrounded by a spacious colonnade, the door giving on the sea. There was a stoa, or market-place, with shops within the pillared ambulatory without, where buyers and sellers walked, chaffering and bartering in Greek, Iberian, Latin, all the dialects of the Middle Sea. And through the city the winds from this sea, and the sound of it, murmured always.

The Romans came; Emporion wisely allied itself with Rome, as a defence against Carthage. Romans colonized the Hellenistic town, making a city behind it far larger, richer, finer, than Emporion itself. There were beautiful houses, grand temples, rich mosaic floors, cisterns, plumbing, baths. The name was now Emporiæ, for there were three cities, the Roman, the Greek, the Iberian. Recent excavations of the Roman town have discovered its great wall, built by Cæsar, on the base of an older wall of the cyclopean type. There have also been exposed a gymnasium, and a large elliptical amphitheatre. Emporion under the Romans had advanced far from the early cramped Greek town. In the third century Frankish pirates attacked the coast and destroyed Neapolis; its inhabitants abandoned it, and settled in the Roman city, which was presently Christianized; there was a basilica, and a Christian burial ground. Then, in Rome's decadence, arrived the barbarians, and the Visigothic town superimposed itself on Emporion. It became the seat of a bishopric.

Then, by the ninth century, Ampurias disappears from history; it has been conjectured that it was sacked and destroyed by the Norman pirates who raged up and down the coast, though some historians blame the Saracens. Villanueva, in his *Viaje Literario a las Iglesias de España,* quotes a record from the archives of the monastery of Santa Maria de Roda— 'The pagans came and sacked the whole town, and the pirates laid waste the territory; its inhabitants and peasants were in large numbers taken captive, and many others, abandoning their farms during that time because of the oppressions of the wicked pirates, emigrated elsewhere.'

A common story all down that perilous coast. Ampurias was apparently abandoned; and, after some attempts by its counts to revive it, they retired inland to Castellón de Ampurias, and the sea town gradually sank deeper beneath the silting sands, and was forgotten, to wait a thousand years for its unburial. The guidebooks of a century ago, such as Ford's, count Emporion a complete loss, but for the 'miserable ruined fishing hamlet' on the hill close by; all that the Baedeker of 1901 says is that the name of Castellón de Ampurias 'recalls Emporion, an ancient Greek colony on the Gulf of Rosas.' Later English guidebooks only give Ampurias a few lines.

Ampurias to-day is a place inexpressibly moving in its beauty and desolation. Along the intricate criss-cross of the streets that run between the vanished houses, cypresses darkly and necropolistically stand, and fig trees sprawl stickily in the sun. The columns of arcaded porticoes and of temples rear broken stumps against sky and sea. You may wander through the city among ghosts of Greek traders, Iberian vendors, Roman gentlemen lounging outside their villas or gossiping in loud Roman voices in the agora, simple Visigoths knocking down heathen statues and drinking deeply of the wines of Ampurdán.

Across a sandy stretch of land to the north the tumbled, ruinous little pile of San Martí climbs its rocky hill; beneath it sleeps forgotten the old, the original Paleopolis. In front of Ampurias the sea whispers and creams; its tang breathes about the ghostly city like a song. Before Herodotus wrote, Greeks lived and traded here; before Rome was a republic, this little Greek mart was doing business on the shores of the gulf that sheltered merchant ships beneath this great spur of the eastern Pyrenees. Now, along the massive wall above the sea road, red oleanders sprawl. A model of the Asklepios statue presides serenely over that broken desert of little streets. In the western corner, close to the Roman city, on the site of a ruined convent, stands the little museum, where some of the Ampurias finds can be seen—mosaics and vases, pottery of all the periods, fragments, some most lovely. Most of the important things are in the Barcelona archæological museum, and some at Gerona; but this little branch of it has kept some valuable finds, and also some interesting and pleasing model reconstructions of buildings. It is an unpretentious, rather charming little place.

From Ampurias one goes a few hundred yards along the sea road to San Martí, the walled hamlet on the hill that was once an island. It is the quietest mediæval hamlet imaginable; but for one gay-tiled villa, the houses, inhabited by a few peasants and animals, seem all tumbling or tumbled into ruin. Its square-towered church crowns the steep streets. Why the village is in such dilapidation, and how long it has been so, I was not able to discover. I wandered about its empty, stony streets, and spoke with a few people outside a tumbling house; a peasant was driving a donkey cart piled with grass up the street; by the gate there was an ancient well. The counts of Ampurias used long ago to frequent this fortified town on its hill; but they retired inland to the safer fortress of Castellón, and San Martí was abandoned to peasants and pirates.

I ate my lunch in the pine woods below the high, steep walls, then went back to Ampurias to spend the afternoon among its whispering centuries of ghosts. Leaving it at last, I drove back along the wood road to La Escala. From there a new road, made during the civil war, runs south for a few kilometres down the rocky coast of coves and capes as far as El Milá. But to explore these coves properly one needs a boat. The gnarled grey rocks jut out into a cobalt and azure sea with, in profile, the mute ferocity of couching beasts, sheltering between them here and there white coves of sand, above some of which a few cottages sprawl, and in and out of which fishing boats slip. A stormy sea among these fantastic wildcat rocks must be an affair of sound, foam and fury; that July afternoon the Mediterranean was a suave and cooing murmuration of blue doves. But my road turned from it inland towards Gerona.

It was a bad road. As a road there was nothing to be said for it, except that it ran through good scenery and passed fine mediæval towns. It was rough and jolting, like so many of the roads that lead to important cities in Spain, roads that shook my car continually to pieces. The pot-holes on the Gerona road were perhaps caused by Roman chariots thundering along them from the coast; or perhaps the Romans had found them thus and made them worse. No doubt they cursed. Then 'twas the Roman, now 'tis I. It was also, no doubt, the rough and turbulent counts of Ampurias, who, throughout the Middle Ages, thundered about Ampurdán, making such disturbances as they threw up castles and palaces and forts, and attacked anything they met which did not submit to them. The bishops of Gerona (often the cousins or uncles of the count) may also have done their share.

Anyhow, and whosesoever fault it was, the road from La Escala to Gerona, via Belcaire and up the Ter valley, is execrable. My front bumper was jerked off, beginning a long series of such decadences. Throughout the nearly four thousand miles of road that I covered in the peninsula, I learnt that cars are not so firmly held together as one had hoped. One piece after another is liable to drop from them; there is a sudden intimidating clatter, and it will be either a bumper or an exhaust pipe or (more perilously, for I was once all but over the edge of a very steep mountain precipice) the steering axle, that, still attached at one end, has broken its bolts at the other and is clattering with a noise of machine guns along the road. If these objects, which I detested, but which were, it seemed, essential to my car's structure, action, and well being, could be fastened on again with straps, I fastened them on with straps, until I reached the next garage. If they could not (like the steering axle) be fastened on with straps, or otherwise replaced by amateur effort, I left the car on the road and walked or got a lift to the next garage, to bring back mechanics with the necessary tools. It was not always quite easy to explain to the mechanics what the necessary tools would be. I had a Spanish motoring phrase book with me, but it said few of the things that I wished to say. It said, 'Have you a really trustworthy man on whom I can rely to clean my car?' and, 'My car has fallen into a ditch. Do me the favour to send an ox (two oxen) to extricate it,' and (more vaguely and pessimistically), 'My car has discomposed itself. I have left it in charge of a peasant —— kilometres from here.' (Fortunately I never acquired this peasant, since my car locks.) Once arrived at a garage, even without one's car, one can explain what has gone wrong by indicating similar appliances on other cars and remarking 'Esto no marcha,' 'This part does not go,' or 'This thing has fallen off.' Spaniards are very helpful, kind and intelligent about cars. If they see a woman changing a wheel on the road, they leap from their camions or their cars and offer help; it is, I suppose, one side of their intense and apparently universal astonishment that a woman should be driving a car at all. All over Spain, except in the more sophisticated cities, my driving by was greeted with the same cry—a long, shrill cat-call, reminiscent of a pig having its throat cut, usually wordless, but sometimes accompanied by 'Olé, Olé! Una señora que conduce!' For Spanish women do not drive cars. I was told this many times, and indeed, observation confirmed it; I saw not a single woman driving all the time I was in Spain. Why not, I sometimes asked. 'It is not the custom here. Spanish ladies live very quietly.' One man, more analytic, explained, 'You see, we Spanish do not live in this century at all, nor in the last, but several hundred years back. We hear that in England women do the things men do, but in Spain it has never been the custom.' This is not true: the peasant women work in the fields and drive donkey carts everywhere; what he meant was señoras. And, apparently, so few foreign señoras are seen driving that they are still regarded as prodigies and portents, much like a man suckling a baby. This, together with the intense Spanish interest in people, and particularly in women, makes it impossible for a woman-driven car to be allowed to pass without comment, as a harmless foreign oddity, as we more sophisticated, live-and-let-live English let foreigners and their strange habits go by without turning the head. In Spain, all heads are turned; and there is a disconcerting outcry. If any student of national psychology can analyse and explain this ancient Spanish custom (one gathers from all travellers that it is ancient) it would be an interesting investigation. The demonstrations sound mainly astonished and derisive; some times rather inimical; always excited and inquisitive. Strange ambivalence of the Spanish! If their curiosity is sometimes partly hostile, their helpfulness to foreigners in difficulty, and their flattering compliments to females (even elderly females such as myself) are delightful and admirable; we can never rival or repay them.

But on the Gerona road that evening I needed no help; I tied on my bumper to a headlamp and proceeded to jolt and bound along.

I came to Belcaire, three miles along this vile road: a fine fortified town where the counts of Ampurias had built themselves an imposing palace or castle; its ruined walls and towers magnificently crown the little city—the old Roman Bedenga. Both in Roman and feudal times Belcaire was full of stir; the counts made it a constant resort, as they galloped so destructively about Ampurdán. All those noisy Frankish aristocrats, who supplied members of their families for every place, lay or clerical, that would give them feudal powers over the natives of Spain—one pictures these Catalans like storm-troopers, or Black-and-tans, rushing about the Spanish Marches fortifying mountains, plains and cities, fighting Moors, Norman pirates, and one another, massacring Jews, marching north to give battle to the Franks of Provence or Toulouse, never tranquil, always tough, strong and devout. Their Romanesque churches were superb, even before the year 1000, even while the *terror milenario,* the knowledge that no building could outlive the Day of Judgment, kept architecture simple and austere. This danger point safely passed, Romanesque flowered into its full Catalan beauty. And their castles, both before and after *l'an mil,* were noble and grand, as we see them in ruin to-day, for castles were what they understood and did well; 'necesse est edificare castela . . .' the lords of the Spanish Marches always knew that, and in time their castled land came, by the Franks beyond the Pyrenees, to be called Catalonia for that reason. It was the Frankish counts who set the tradition of the small Catalan walled town as we see it still to-day—high, ochre-brown citadels, many of the houses arcaded and terraced (perhaps from the brief Moorish influence?), tiled roof climbing above tiled roof to the solid, fortress-like church that crowns the pile, with its heavy nave and apse and square tower—embattled churches, with belfries like watch towers to observe and clang the warning news of approaching foes. All have a family look as to colour and shape; all are beautiful; all look mediæval, though of which century one could not say without nearer inspection. Many have castles. Belcaire is such a citadel; so are Ulla, Verges, and the other towns that ennoble (this has to be the word) the valley of the Ter, and, indeed, most of Catalonia. To follow a road that runs through them is to travel through the dark turmoil of history, through what Gautier called 'cette obscure tourmente qu'est le haut moyen âge.'

I reached Gerona before dark. The approach to it is startlingly beautiful; it stands high above the river Oñar where it joins the Ter; its houses seem to climb precipitously, river-washed, up the steep slope of the hill. It is brown in colour, narrow-streeted, mediæval. The Gothic cathedral dominates it with stupendous splendour, standing at the top of a long and lovely seventeenth-century flight of golden stone steps. Except the long avenue and steps at Guadix, I know of no more beautiful approach to any cathedral or church; it beats Tarragona, because there is more space in front of it, and the baroque curve of the flight is lovelier. I believe that the effect of the outside of Gerona cathedral is not too well thought of architecturally, the nave being too large and too bare; but I admired it. Inside, the tremendous span of the single-vaulted nave is magnificent; its effect is heightened by the sombre darkness that nearly all Catalan churches affect, and to enter which from the dazzling radiance of the Spanish sunshine is like groping one's way from a burning shore into a deep cool cave.

Gerona, the Roman Gerunda, had a church and a bishopric from the first years of Spanish Christendom. One of the earliest bishops was Narcissus, Gerona's tutelar saint. Tradition gives the foundation of the present church to Charlemagne, in 786, when Gerona was taken for a brief time by the Franks from the Moors. When the Moors got it back again they used it for a mosque, letting the Christians worship in what is now the lovely fourteenth-century collegiate church of San Felíu (but what it was then is obscure). The cathedral was rebuilt in the early eleventh century when the Christians finally captured the city, rebuilt again and added to through the fourteenth, fifteenth and sixteenth. Guillermo Boffiy's famous nave, the widest in Christendom, was designed in the fifteenth century. Its spacious breadth makes a remarkable effect of tranquil strength and lack of fuss. That it was a great engineering feat is proved by its unshaken resistance to the storms and shocks of battle which have raged down the centuries round Gerona, a city with at least five-and-twenty sieges in its history.

There are interesting things in the cathedral (which I saw next morning)—a fourteenth-century retablo, covered with enamel and silver plate, a shafted wood and silver baldacchino, a few good tombs. To the north-west are the Romanesque twelfth-century cloisters, with very charmingly sculptured capitals, like the Elne cloisters in style. One is reminded again of the unity of Catalan culture on both sides of the Pyrenees. As beautiful is the Romanesque cloister of San Pedro de Galligans, the tenth or eleventh-century Benedictine chapel built against the city walls. The cloisters are of the same date and style as those of the cathedral. They now house a museum. In San Felíu's chancel walls there are some beautiful Roman bas-reliefs.

Apart from churches and museums, there are things to see all about Gerona, and I spent an agreeable day seeing them. It is a fascinating city; the crowded streets and houses, girdled by their ancient walls, rising above the running river (unlike most Spanish rivers in summer, it did run), and above these the steep fortressed hill to guard the town. No wonder every one has always tried to take Gerona. To the Romans, it was rather a place of strategic importance and a loyal city than a pleasure resort such as Tarragona; but they resided in it a good deal. The Moors fought for it again and again; under the Franks, it was head of a countship; ecclesiastically, it clung tenaciously to power, and fought that of the counts with grim determination. The present bishops of Gerona must look back with some wistfulness to the grand feudal state kept by their mediæval predecessors, their wealth and wide lands, their trains of slaves and concubines, their noble libraries, their great monasteries (though the abbots often gave trouble), the dues they extorted from their vassals, even the wars of envy and fear waged against them by the counts of Barcelona and the kings of Aragon, who pursued, as a rule, a policy definitely anti-clerical. The lives of bishops in Ampurdán now, alas! move on more restricted lines.

Leaving this noble city in the evening, I jolted back to the Mediterranean, this time (but no more smoothly) by another road, that crossed the Ter at Torroella de Montgri, and, in this magnificent-looking mediæval town I stayed the night, in an extremely pleasant old inn in the arcaded plaza, which calls itself the Nuevo Hotel. Torroella is a city of historic importance in Ampurdán history; above it on a mountain stands, grand and forbidding, the empty shell of a tremendous battlemented castle, built at the end of the thirteenth century by King James II of Aragon and Barcelona, as a royal challenge to the feudal domination of the counts of Ampurias. Torroella had once a port that served Gerona; the sea, now several miles away, was then at its gates, and the Moors landed there in 1178 to sack and slaughter the monastery and monks of Ulla. The counts of Ampurias, one of whose hobbies was diverting the course of rivers, out of greed, spite, irrigation, or merely to make a change and feed their sense of power, diverted the river Ter twice; the second time the wash of sand thus caused gradually choked and closed the gulf and port, and Torroella became a harbourless city, its cargo trade largely passing to the little port of Pals. Torroella lost importance and wealth, but was thereafter less exposed to the incursions of pirates (Saracen and northern) who harassed all this coast. Torroella, unlike Figueras, has had few modern developments; it has remained, in appearance, wholly mediæval, though in the nineteenth century it was deprived, for some senseless reason, of its magnificent towered walls.

The narrow streets, the arcaded plazas, the ancient churches built against the walls, the great fortress that crowns the hill above the city, seem to brood over centuries of unquiet history; violence and feuds have raged in these streets, here royal power has waged war with baronial and conquered, here the liberties of a community have been striven for and won, here the warning horn of the sentinel was wound in the intimidating night watches to tell Torroellans that pirates from the islands had been sighted on the sea. Wealth has flowed through the city gates, corruption and tyranny have reigned, fortune has ebbed and departed. Torroella has suffered plague and loss; the population dwindled away and emigrated; poverty followed the rich days. But it became, like Figueras, Pals and Palamos, a royal city, free from feudal lordship and tyrannies. It wears a fine air of freedom to-day, and has much local pride. The landlord of my inn took me round it after dark, showing me the church (the one which had not been destroyed by the *rojos*) and the house and garden and patio of Conde Roberto, the lord of the manor. It is a beautiful patio. But my landlord had something still finer to show me; he led me round the outside of the house, and there, high in the wall above us, was a lit window, and in it sat illumined a Madonna and Child, with two little angels fluttering about them like moths round a lamp. The effect was bijou and charming. The Conde Roberto, observed my landlord, was a gentleman extremely devout. The engaging simplicity of Latin piety never ceases to please those from chillier and more sophisticated lands. I tried to imagine, say, the Duke of Norfolk installing a similar window and figures in a wall of Arundel Castle, and lighting it up at nights for the benefit of the citizens of Arundel; but imagination faltered. One would, I think, like Conde Roberto very much if one met him.

We returned to the inn, where, at one end of the spacious ground-floor room, dinner was being cooked. We ate it at the other end; it was very good. Most of the diners were, I think, Torroellans who had come in for a meal; handsome, lively people, with the free Catalonian air. I woke next morning to sounds of chaffering and gossiping in the broad, tree-shaded plaza under my windows, and looked out on the morning market. It was the prettiest sight; piles of brilliant fruit,

oranges, melons, pears, cucumbers, scarlet pimentos, heaped
in baskets under awnings against the grey walls of houses and
shops. I went out and bought fruit, then back to the inn for
coffee. My bill for the night, dinner and morning coffee (including a filled thermos) was thirty-five pesetas, or ten
shillings. The dignity, kindness and charm of the Torroellans,
the ancient beauty of their city, make the most harmonious
blend.

From Torroella I visited La Bisbal, where they were dancing the *sardana* for the Fiesta Mayor. Then coastward to the
fishing village, gaily-coloured and bleak, of Estartit, with the
Medas Islands lying offshore like strange ships; then, the Ter
re-crossed, southward for Pals and Bagur. Pals, once called
Monte Aspero, five miles from Torroella, a walled town
standing cinematographically on a hill, is of startling distinction in ruin. Its remarkable tower, the Torre de las Horas, is
all that is left of the ancient castle destroyed in the fifteenth
century; its magnificent walls, broken and ruined, still have
many of their round towers. Some archæologists maintain that
the Pals walls are finer than those of Tossa de Mar, and that
the town should be made a national monument, to prevent its
complete decay (not that Spanish national monuments are
always preserved from this). From the hill of Pals one gets a
wonderful view of the Ampurdán plain and of the long bay
of the Platja de Pals.

These untouched survivals from the depths of the Middle
Ages strike on the senses with a shock of what is nearly fear;
atavistic fear, tugging at the deep roots of ancestral memory.
There are many good reasons for the stark, untrimmed
mediævalism of so many hundreds of small Spanish towns—
long poverty, lack of the money which made England destroy
and destroy, rebuild and add in (usually) atrocious styles;
smallness of population, which made the adding of new houses
to old towns, like an encircling rash, unnecessary; lack of that
restless drive towards change that makes so many Europeans
perpetually at odds with the life they know, perpetually

impelled to grasp at and achieve the new, as women grasp at new fashions in dress. The Spaniard, fundamentally perhaps more at odds with the life he leads, tends to go round and round it in circles, splashing it up in torrents of foam and spray; but he seldom proceeds horizontally or vertically to something new. Even the Catalan, by race and geographical position more cosmopolitan, more one with European culture, certainly more progressive and adventurous, than the rest of Spain, is tied, politically and economically, to peninsular tradition and history, and shares the inheritance of the conditions which produced Spanish Middle Age towns. Catalonia was a perpetually armed and embattled stage set for wars and assaults, feudal filibustering, invasions from the looting and slaughtering barbarians, the people of the sea; cities were built strongly, when possible, on heights, walled and towered, closely crowded houses steeply climbing above narrow streets; they had, and keep, the armed, defensive look of sentinels on guard. In the most restless and turbulent baronial periods of English history, towns were seldom built like these formidable walled piles, which have the awful fascination of dark towers in a dream. They seem symbols and types of the deep mediævalism in the Spanish soul; a mediævalism most utterly evident in Castile, but which has its place too in the less urbanized and progressive regions of Catalonia. These small Spanish towns differ greatly from the *villes closes* of France and the walled hill cities of Italy; they are less gay, more sombre, cleaner (a heritage, probably, from the Moors). Catalonia has little baroque; those seventeenth- and eighteenth-century façades which, further south down the coast, were continually added to Romanesque and Gothic churches, with charmingly incongruous effect, like a cavalier hat with feathers worn with a suit of mail, are only rarely found in Catalonia; the fortress-like solidity of those stern exteriors remains, as a rule, unsoftened and unadorned. There is more interior baroque, as, for instance, in the Cadaqués church, where it gambols and capers inside Gothic walls.

Walking about such towns as Torroella and Pals, one does not come on late Renaissance or baroque doorways enlivening those deep and ancient *Edad Media* streets.

Pals is a survival; and one must sympathize with the archæologists who are trying to ensure that it continues to survive. Whether or not its fabric disintegrates, what it stands for in the Spaniard must, it seems, for good and ill, endure.

Pals stands in a land barren and devastated long since by the sea barbarians, sparsely inhabited. Legend says that the invaders were apt to seize the dwellers near the sea and carry them away captive. Its woods were burned down two centuries ago, its plains are swept by the tramontana. The road curls seaward and arrives at Bagur, which is a mile from the sea, and through its narrow streets the sea air blows. They say that Bagur was one of the towns created by the flight of the coast dwellers from the invading Norman pirates who destroyed Ampurias and so much else in the eighth or ninth centuries. The castle that crowns its hill is of the tenth century. They say (I mean Señor Pella y Forgas, the erudite historian of Ampurdán, says) that the people of Bagur were, from the first, indomitable, content and noble, addicted to smuggling, emigration and coral-fishing, and of inflamed passions. I was so unfortunate as to make no acquaintances among these dramatic, almost operatic, beings, during my brief exploration of the town. The town is elegant, white, full of trees and arcaded houses, said (surprisingly) to be inhabited by American Indians. The feudal castle that dominates this pretty town belongs to a different world. From the castle one looks across a mile of barren country to Cape Bagur and the sea that washes its sheer cliff, and north and south along the jagged line of indented blue, and to the town of Palafrugell five miles to the south. The loveliest little bay of the Costa Brava, Fornells, is three miles away; the road wriggles up a mountain and down again to a sandy, forested cove with a group of white houses on the sea's edge, shut round by pines, olives and carob trees. The playa of Aigua Blava is across the creek; in the deep blue-green curve of sea between the two shores fishing boats lie and rocks jut. It is a cove exquisite for bathing; sheltered, pine-fragrant and smooth; indeed, if one had to make a choice of a summer home on this coast, this cove of Fornells is perhaps the most enchanted. Nothing except a gay throng of bathers disturbs its peace; between the sea and the little creeks of white sand and the shadowing pines and the paths that climb the wooded mountain-sides, the mellow days slide by like sun-warmed apricots that burst with ripeness, the nights, chirring with crickets and lapping waves, lit by an amber moon and huge bright stars, by glinting fireflies among the trees and the candling of the fishing boats in the bay, the nights must surely be like purple figs for sweetness.

If one had a boat—and one would have to have a boat—one could sail it all down the coast, in and out of the little creeks and coves, to the bay of Tamariu among its tamarind trees, to San Sebastiá and Llafranc, landing on the islands and exploring each cove and each fishing port, with the invaluable guidance of Señor Pla. You cannot do such exploration by land, unless you have many weeks to spend climbing and walking along the cliff paths (if you have the weeks, you could not spend them better). There is no connecting road between these little bays; the roads to them (when there are any) radiate out separately from the town of Palafrugell; they are, one and all, so charming when you reach them that they are worth the two or three miles of jolting dust. Calella is a tiny port whose shores are crowded with brilliantly painted boats and a jumble of fishing tackle; behind them the circle of houses stands white and balconied, often arcaded, with blue and green doors and windows, brown nets up to the open doors, gay clothes flapping from the windows. The scene and colour have great beauty and animation, with the sea slipping and lapping on pale brown sand, the fishing population busy with nets and boats, little brown boys gambolling in the water. From dawn till dark an artist could paint the lovely scene, until the sunset stains it rose and deep gold, to fade quietly away into the blue shadows of evening, the purple deeps of night. Describing Calella, one describes (roughly) so many little fishing ports down the Costa Brava that one may take one's choice; but each has its special and individual quality.

There is only one drawback for foreigners on these lovely shores, as elsewhere in Spain: the inhabitants stare and point. A foreigner is 'a strange outlandish fowl, a quaint baboon, an ape, an owl,' and must endure a pursuing mob, who lay aside all other occupations for the pleasures of the chase. 'Muy mal educados,' some disapproving elder may apologetically comment on the manners of her young compatriots, and will sometimes attempt, vainly, to call them off. 'We live in a past age,' another will explain. 'We do what perhaps you did several centuries ago.' Perhaps we did; certainly foreign visitors used to complain that they had been pelted with vegetables and pursued with cries. We have now grown out of this agreeable pastime, and permit sari-wrapped and bare-legged Indian ladies and Polish counts in crimson cloaks and floating hair to walk by without a turn of the head. And it is doubtful if, at any period, the English ever felt that intense interest in people that takes the Spanish (and Portuguese) from any occupation to stare and pursue. Particularly their interest is in women, and more particularly in a woman alone. The fact of her sex, and the fact of her aloneness, seem to the Spanish at once entertaining, exciting and remarkable, as if a chimpanzee strayed unleashed about the streets. For Spanish ladies do not travel about alone. It has been said that foreign gentlemen are less regarded, and this is so. But they are by no means immune; and the way in which the children duck and run when their quarry turns round to look at something, like dogs when one stoops to pick up a stone, suggests that some one has cuffed them in the past. It is the national sport, and one should be glad to give so much innocent pleasure. Should you show vexation, or embarrassment, it would give greater pleasure still. It is wiser to disarm the ambivalent multitude by entering at once into friendly relations, by asking someone for information, guidance or help. You will then find a whole population at your service, smiling, talking, pointing out where you should go, what you should see, where stay, shoving and tugging at your car with cries of eager helpfulness, should it have become bogged in a sandy track. For the Spanish, and the Catalans almost first, are the most helpful, friendly and courteous people to strangers in a difficulty. In the matter of staring, history is probably too strong for them; they have been so often invaded, assaulted, plundered, occupied, by foreigners down the ages—Carthaginians, Romans, Goths, Moors, French (it is noticeable that 'Francés' is always the label applied to the visitor)—that excitement about what foreigners are up to may be in their blood. The Goths, they perhaps feel, are come again, to seize their lands and persons. The early invading Goths, who stood no nonsense, got indubitably the best of the encounters; we later Goths, much less tough than those whose lands we invade, come off worse. As to the Latin-Moorish attitude towards women, it is probably ineradicable. It is wise to ignore it, and go on our way unperturbed. The staring is, anyhow, a testimony to the rarity of foreign visitors. Summer visitors to the Costa Brava are (or were that summer, when the French frontier was closed) nearly all Spanish from the neighbouring inland towns. Calella, for instance, is a popular resort for the citizens of Palafrugell; on Sundays family parties invade it for picnics and bathing. But the Costa Brava has been, so far, preserved from cosmopolitan smartness; there are none of those beach amusements and entertainments, piers and pavilions, gramophones, casinos and smart hotels, that vulgarize the French riviera (of the British seaside I will not speak here; it is probably all that our silver sea deserves). The Costa Brava has, indeed, a few luxury hotels (as at S'Agaró), but they are rare, and the private villas down the coast have not yet spoilt the beaches as they have in France, where almost every jut of rock, almost every charming cove and beach and hill path, is fenced off as Défendu. On the Catalan and Spanish shores, the coast does, for the most part, belong to the people, though encroachment by private property has begun. There are little coves where solitude and peace are unbroken, except by an occasional fishing boat. Those who have known this coast for many years, like Señor Pla, lament its increasing popularity, and complain that such places, for instance, as Llafranc are not what they were, owing to the influx of visitors from Palafrugell and other towns. There was a time, some eleven centuries ago, when the population of the ancient Roman-founded sea town of Llafranc fled inland from the Norman pirates and settled in Palafrugell: later came the time for the return influx, and Palafrugell's citizens re-founded Llafranc. The original Llafranc is prodigiously old; probably a Phœnician port, and Greeks from Emporion came to it, dropping their coins about in the usual lavish manner of the ancients, to be picked up two thousand years later, when long out of currency. The Romans did the same. Llafranc is in a delightfully sheltered cove, guarded by the jutting rock of San Sebastiá, and was a charming resort; it became a prosperous Roman town; walls of Roman houses are still to be seen among the present buildings; Roman mosaic was found in a washing tank, Roman vases and pottery everywhere. Llafranc has been identified with the city of Cypsela, referred to by Avienus in the fourth century. The town was, apparently, burnt down by those disgusting Norsemen in one of their destructive raids; under its later mediæval surface (for it rose again after its destruction) there may lie the razed ruins of another Greco-Roman town, long since drifted over by sands and time. Unlike Ampurias, it will not be excavated, for now round that lovely moon of bay flourishes a seaside resort. Within living memory Llafranc still looked, with its old tower, mediæval: now it is a gay bay full of the houses of *veraneantes*. A place so favoured by nature is bound to prosper and increase.

Round the corner of its sheltering cape is San Sebastiá (the Celebandicum Promontorium of Avienus?) with its lighthouse, its fifteenth-century tower, and its charming eighteenth-century baroque church, much damaged by the destroyers of ten years ago, who also (I gather) destroyed what must have been a fascinating figure of Saint Sebastian in knight's dress, well breast-plated against arrows, and the votive offerings of ships that once filled the church (or possibly these were removed for safety during the war). Separated from the church by a patio is a great hostelry, once a hermitage. The Cape is protected by its presiding saint, who guards (if in the humour to do so, and if sufficiently bribed) ships through storms and sailors through plagues and rocks.

All these sea towns have bad roads running out to them from Palafrugell. Palafrugell is an ancient fort or palace (Palaz Frugell, Palace of Fruits); it has vestiges of Roman occupation (possibly it was Celebandica) and of eighth and ninth-century tombs. When the Llafrancians fled to it from the Norman pirates, it was a small walled city with a castle; it is now a largish town, and looks something like a star-fish, pale and clean, with a large central plaza and roads radiating out from it. The church has a carved baroque portal with a relief of a deliciously elegant equestrian saint. It was there, while I got petrol, with the usual interested crowd pressing round my car and the usual fifty children climbing on the running-boards, that I was offered many thousands of pesetas for the car. I said that I should not be permitted to arrive back in my native land without it; but, said they, I could say that it had met with an accident. Considering the rather battered and travel-worn look that my car had already begun to assume, I was flattered by the value put on it.

From Palafrugell there is a straight run of five miles down to Palamós, once a fortified town and the refuge of the unprotected dwellers along the coast and in the mountains round. It was a royal town—Port Royal of Palamós it was called— and was under the king's jurisdiction. It is finely placed, thrusting an arm out to sea round a jutting point that shelters the bay's inner curve; from the point you get, looking north and south, a tremendous view of coast. Palamós was, in the Middle Ages, and particularly after the closing of Torroella, a great port, quarrelling with San Felíu de Guixols for the right to serve Gerona with cargoes of wheat. Palamós won this fight, and in 1334 became the maritime district of Gerona and the busiest port of the coast. It was sacked and burned by Barbarossa and his Turkish fleet in 1543 (the catastrophic career of Spanish seaports is almost past belief), and fell into obscurity, fishing and selling earthen water pots, until, revived by the cork industry, it began to expand. It was badly battered from air and sea by the rebels and their allies during the civil war, four hundred houses being destroyed. To-day it lies pleasantly along its bay, a long white curved town, with its Calle Mayor running behind the playa, and full of small friendly shops and sea air, and what is said to be the best hotel in the province of Gerona (I did not stay in Palamós, so cannot say as to this). Out of the town runs a short road to the charming little beach of La Fosca, where you may sit on the terrace of the inn and drink coffee, looking down through pine trees at the sea.

From Palamós the lovely road runs skirting the coast, the great piney Gavarros mountains on the right, the sea below; one enchanted little cove and beach succeeds another; paths run down to them through (alas) forbidden woods, for this part of the Costa Brava is as privately owned as the French riviera, and every path to the sea is marked 'Prohibido el paso. Propriedad particular.' Only where there are villages is there access to the beaches. Looking down on them, one sees small bays and creeks, fishing boats drawn up on white sand or rocking in deep green pine-shadowed waters. On the lovely point of S'Agaró a large and beautiful hotel has been built, laid out with gardens, terraces, swimming pools, steps down to the beach, and every tasteful device; even a nice little white church has been built, for the benefit of devout visitors. It has become, of course, a very popular resort for those who can afford it, and the life there must be very comfortable, sociable and classy. I would not stay there myself, even had I the necessary pesetas, but for those who like that kind of thing, it is, I am sure, delightful. Should the Costa Brava ever become really rich and prosperous, one envisages a line of such fine hostelries all down it, alternating with private villas, and beautifying every cove with gardens and white arcaded terraces. That day, if it ever arrives, is still far, and the Costa Brava is still in the main a succession of little fishing ports and untenanted coves and rocks. Its natural beauty, like that of the Ligurian coast of Italy, nothing can defeat; but if it should ever become, as it would long since have become in Britain were such a coast conceivable in Britain, a continuous chain of luxury hotels and villas, I should not revisit it.

But such dangers are still remote. Skirting the bay of S'Agaró, one arrives at the very ancient port of San Felíu de Guixols, the mediæval rival of Palamós for the service of Gerona. In beauty, they cannot be rivals. San Felíu is of a pale grace and elegance that leaves the rather rectilinear Palamós at the post. San Felíu, which lives on cork and is surrounded by cork forests, lies round its nearly closed harbour with the blandest charm. From both ends of the town you come down to it from hills; on the north from the Gavarros mountains, on the south down the wriggling mountain road from Tossa, which leaves its steep pine and oak-shadowed zig-zagging high above the sea to slip down between cane groves and chirring crickets into the old town that clusters about the ancient Benedictine monastery and its church. San Felíu, though it has perhaps existed for ever, and was known to the Romans as Gesoria (hence Guixols), is, it seems, as a town of importance, of monastic origin; its great convent, originally Byzantine in style, was destroyed by Moorish pirates in the eighth or ninth century, was rebuilt in the eleventh, and was, after San Pere de Roda, the most important in Ampurdán. Its abbot was the feudal lord of San Felíu and the surrounding country; the town came into being as a result of a pact between the community of fishermen on the shore and the community of monks on the hill: in return for the protection given by the monastery's armed towers against the constant foes from land and sea, the monks enjoyed all tributary rights. Fostered by these powerful and fish-loving lords, the San Felíu fishing industry prospered greatly; the port exported wine and wheat, traded much with Italy and France, and became rich. It was in the fourteenth century the most important town of Ampurdán. Its *llotja* of merchants, the *navegantes,* were influential in Mediterranean maritime counsels; and it was in its seas that coral was first fished. Through the continual assaults, battles and piracies from which all Catalan ports suffered, San Felíu remained a living, prosperous and populous place. Throughout the Middle Ages its people fought their monastic overlords, and the abbey fought back with indomitable tenaciousness of its rights; like all the long struggles of the feudal lords, it was a losing battle, and San Felíu emerged free. In the eighteenth century the cork trade floated it buoyantly to further wealth. Now, above the pleasant, thriving town and port, the ruined monastery (burned and sacked, like so many others in this incendiary land, in the anti-clerical fit of 1835) stands, fortress-like and magnificent, a *fortaleza religiosa,* more, as has been said, like a castle than a religious house. It was once moated, and guarded by seven armed towers. With its great walls and gate, its fragments of cloister arches, and the fifteenth-century church at its foot, it presides like a brooding ghost over a city, a countryside, and an age which has long slipped from its once so formidable and tenacious hands. Round it the gay white town lies, still scarred by the bombs that assaulted it again and again during the civil war, destroying many houses and lives. But it has mended itself quickly, and still lies bland and serene, piled high about its church (which displays on its door the usual warning to women to wear in church such attire as will not provoke other worshippers by revealing elbows or legs) and dipping down to the

harbour, that shuts the bay like a smooth, curving shell. Along
the sea road boats are building; the harbour is full of ships
laden with cork, making ready to sail away, and is the loveliest sight. Swimming out into the smooth water, still and
sheltered and shimmering with the colour and sheen of pearls
in the early morning light, one looks across the harbour
through a forest of masts and sails; to the road that runs
behind the beach, gay with gardens, palms, casinos and
coloured umbrellas; and above town and harbour to the cork-
forested mountains that shut them round. San Felíu is an
engaging place, luminous, marinely urbane, rather Genoese,
looking up with cheerful worldly insouciance at its ruined
monastery, symbol of the paternal feudalism and the long
dark storm of the past from which it has emerged. It has been
through many storms, and the latest was only ten years ago.
But it seems to belong to a different world from the steep,
walled, narrow-streeted mediæval cities of its hinterland. Both
have the immense, effortless beauty of Catalonia, a beauty
only defeated by the miles of industrial suburban coast towns
on either side of Barcelona.

Coming up from San Felíu on to the road that zig-zags
fifteen miles through the mountains to Tossa, this beauty
leaps at you, tremendous, perilous, superb. Perilous because
the road's turns are so sharp and steep that, if you travel fast,
or meet another vehicle, the sudden end of your travelling
seems a good bet. You might easily twist over the edge into
one of the steep ravines of pine and cork-grown rocky mountain-side that hold the road high above the sea. But I met only
one mule cart, laden with pine boughs, and two very polite
*guardias civiles,* who wanted to see my papers. Every twist of
the road gave magnificent views of rocky coast and bays far
below, and always of the great blue half-circle that spread to
the horizon, winged with occasional sails. This San Felíu-
Tossa road (only made in the last few years) is a triumph of
engineering and of beauty, lovely in its beginning and in its
end. For it suddenly drops down into what is perhaps the

most interesting and beautiful of the Costa Brava towns—
Tossa de Mar. I own that I had, beforehand, a slight prejudice
against Tossa; it had been, before the civil war, a picturesque
resort of English artists and writers; worse, I had once read a
rather foolish book about it by someone who had built an hotel
there; the book was not really about Tossa; the writer did not
refer either to the Roman villa or to the mediæval *villa cluida*
with its Roman remains, and she believed the word 'natives' to
mean coloured people; I remembered that, to some inquiry
about the natives of Tossa, she boasted of having replied 'If
you mean coloured people, there are none here.' The hotel, a
white house now called Casa Blanca, still stands on a hill-side
(inaccessible by car), but its first owners have long since
departed, and also, it seems, most of the foreigners who used
to visit Tossa (though actually Tossa was one of the only two
places in Spain where I did meet any English travellers).

Tossa's popularity is not surprising. As the Spanish say,
'Tossa es una maravilla.' It has everything (except, fortunately,
those smart amenities believed to attract tourists). It was an
Iberian town; Celtic and Iberian pottery abounds. Greeks must
have traded here (probably from Emporion) for, as usual, they
had dropped their money about; but it first arrives in history
as a Roman station. In 1914 a Roman villa was discovered in
a garden above the town, and among the mediæval houses of
the Vila Vella are Roman walls and foundations; a Roman
fort apparently stood within the twelfth-century fortifications.

The Roman villa is romantically exciting. It lies on the slope
of a hill, among blackberry bushes and cypresses, and was
gradually excavated since its discovery, until the work was
stopped (one hopes only interrupted) by the civil war.

It has hardly [wrote Señor Castillo, the member of the Barcelona Archæological Museum who continued the work from
1933] begun to be excavated. There are a conjunction of buildings of importance. . . . On the slope of the mountain, above
the shore (the sea formerly came up farther into the land) some

five hundred metres from the Iberian-Roman town of Turissa, on the cape of Tossa and on the road to the port (which was in the present rocky cove of El Codolar) . . . its situation was magnificent.

The villa is on the Roman model of the first century A.D.; it was obviously the residence of the Roman lord of the manor, and by its side is the *villa rustica,* where his labourers lived and worked, and where stood the granaries and mill. The villa must have had every amenity, including three bathrooms, hot, tepid and cold, a fine hot-air heating system, and an excellently preserved piscina, either for swimming or for fish. The manorial gentry of Turissa lived an elegant and delightful life. How many more such villas lie about Tossa, as yet undiscovered, and may one day emerge? Alas, in the third century the barbarians who invaded and raided the coast, destroying Barcelona and getting as far south as Tarragona, knocked Turissa and its Roman villas to pieces. But a century later this villa, at least, was rebuilt. The bathing and heating system was not used; perhaps it was beyond repair and silted over with rubble; but the new Roman owner built himself a fine suite of rooms with mosaic floors. One of these mosaics has the portrait and the name of the owner—'Saliius Vital: Felix Turissa.' There are many other mosaic fragments in the little museum in the Vila Vella. But Saliius Vital and his successors could not for long keep their precarious tenure of this corner of the harassed coast. The fierce barbarian raids of the fifth century continually assaulted Tossa; it declined as a port and as a town, and was probably destroyed by the Moors in the eighth century, to build itself gradually up again under its feudal lords in the Middle Ages. But the Roman villa (named by the Catalans Els Anetelles) was by then long deserted and ruined; the feudal lords would, indeed, find little use for so elegant and urbane a dwelling; they preferred a fortified castle, and mosaics and bathrooms were quite out of their line.

Standing on the slope where the villa lies in the sunshine among the brambles, one imagines the Roman scene—the hills covered with olive gardens and vineyards, the busy little port exporting wine and oil, the ships coming in and out from Barcino, from Tarraco, from Emporiæ, from Gaul; above the port, on the top of the steep Tossa hill (Monte Gardí, but Ptolemy called it Promontorium Lunarium), the native Iberian population crowded together in their narrow streets and primitive houses behind the defence of Roman walls—the *indigines* who worked for Roman landlords and fished for their living in the bay. It was this native town that later became the mediæval Tossa, and it very likely looks much the same to-day as when Saliius Vital lived in his villa, except that of the Roman walls only foundations and fragments remain, some of the old houses being built on them, and (notable difference) the Vila Vella is now encircled by the superb twelfth-century walls that are Tossa's beauty and pride. Those walls, winding round the steep hill up which old Tossa climbs high above the sea, are, I think, the most attractive mediæval town walls left in Europe. Tarragona walls are tremendous and superb, but have not Tossa's lovely winding grace; even Avila and Ciudad Roderigo, perhaps owing to being terrestrial and not marine, rising above boulder-strewn plains and not above the Mediterranean, are less beautiful, though more forbidding. The Tossa walls, originally a strong double defence against which Barbary pirates battered in vain (the town was never captured after the early centuries), have suffered loss; many of their ancient towers have disappeared, one of them only thirty years ago, to make way for a lighthouse, an act of vandalism worthy of the Barbary pirates themselves. But several remain. Through one of them, the Torre de las Horas, one enters the Vila Vella, that mediæval twist of steep ancient streets and ruinous houses that climbs Monte Gardí to the summit where the ruined shell of a fourteenth-century Gothic church stands, framing with its empty broken arch the view of the little beach below, where the painted fishing boats lie at the sea's edge. From this height one gets a magnificent view of the coast, cape beyond cape, jutting, transparent indigo, into a peacock sea. Here the sentinels of Tossa watched, through the precarious centuries, for the sails of the savages of the sea, sounding the warnings that sent the men of Tossa to collect the arms from the towers, to herd the inhabitants within the walls, to draw up their fishing boats from the sea, and to shut and bar the double gates against assault.

Entering the Vila Vella to-day through its gate now open and unguarded, one comes, close under one of the towers, to the little museum—an admirable storehouse of mosaic fragments from the villa and round about, potteries, vases and paintings, and relics of local history.

In the tenth century Tossa was presented by the Count of Barcelona to the monastery of Ripoll; it was called the Castrum de Tursia, and was one of the strong points of coast defence. For many centuries the Tossenses have lived by fishing; in recent years, before the civil war, tourism too became a leading industry, especially cultivated foreign tourism, which discovered Tossa and found it a delight. Driven away by the discomforts and perils of war, by the inconveniences of bombing and starvation and the fear of anarchy, the foreign visitors have not yet returned in force, and Tossa wears to-day a more native air. Fortunately it was little damaged by the war, and the port and little town—the newer town outside the citadel, much of which, including the church, dates from the seventeenth and eighteenth centuries—are delightful. So are those who live there; beautiful, like most Catalans (who so happily mix a classical type with the indigenous), they seem also kind, charming, intelligent and good. They are strongly republican in sentiment (again like most Catalans), but appear to support the vicissitudes of fortune with cheerfulness and hope. In the cottage doors and windows of the Old Town there are displayed shells, and little horses of cane-leaf, which the women of the cottages make as they sit in the tiny plaza in the sun. The whole shape and colour of Tossa, its walled and towered citadel on the hill, its gay open town below, clustering round its white, tiled church, the little rocky port of Codolar lying at the foot of the walls, and the crescent of beach and boats lying round the present fishing harbour, make a picture of almost too pictorial charm.

There are several pleasant inns in the town. The Casa Blanca, on a steep hill above, looks attractive, but lacks access. Trying to drive up to it, I became involved in a vineyard, and stuck in a ditch, damaging a bush of tomatoes. A posse of strong young men, summoned by cries from women in adjacent cottages, heaved the car out with that effortless ease so enviable in strong young men and in oxen. I retreated to an agreeable inn in the town.

Next morning I saw the Vila Romana, being admitted through its wicket gate by a kind and handsome woman caretaker, who fed me with blackberries from the bramble bushes as she intelligently discoursed to me about the villa. Hearing that I was engaged in writing a book, she decided that I too must be intelligent, and subsequently informed all her neighbours of this—I fancy to account for the singularity of my travelling about alone.

If they go on excavating in and round Tossa, more Rome will turn up, and possibly, below Rome, Greece. It is interesting to read the account of Tossa in Pella y Forgas's sixty-years-old *Historia del Ampurdán,* and to note that he, of course, knew nothing about the Roman villa. What further discoveries lie buried beneath those vine-grown hills, I wondered, as my road climbed out of Tossa bay and took its twisting zig-zag way through the steep mountain gorge to Lloret. This road, like the San Felíu-Tossa road, runs high above the sea, between mountain flanks dark green with pines, cork, ilex and juniper, and smelling resinously in the hot sun. Far below, the sea runs up narrow inlets between red, pine-grown rocks. Footpaths twist down forested ravines to the sea; here and there white cottages cluster above a little beach. All along the road small vines grow, spreading tender green leaves and tendrils on the red earth. I passed above little playas well spoken of by the navigating Señor Pla, and I am sure they are most charming, but the road did not descend to them. This may account for their almost unviolated solitude and peace. To spend a summer in one of those lonely coves would be delicious. But sea and footpaths seem the only access.

The road dips down to the sea at Lloret, which the Romans called Loryma; a lively and flourishing place whose open streets are charmingly set with palms. Behind its well-off eighteenth-century prosperity (created largely, says Pla, by those who had made their fortunes in South America and returned to Lloret to build themselves elegant and commodious dwellings) Lloret history reaches back to antiquity. Prehistoric objects have been found in its fields, Greek coins from Emporion, a few Roman ruins. There is, too, a Roman sepulchral tower two kilometres east of the town, which the inhabitants call the *torre del Moros*. The history of Lloret, one infers, followed the usual course of Catalonian coast towns—Iberian, with Greek trading contacts, Carthaginian, Roman, then feudal; in mediæval times it belonged to the lords of Palafolls, who gave it up to the chapter of Gerona cathedral. It now looks pretty and prosperous, is much given to music, to dancing the sardana on the beach, and to festival processions, including a lovely annual procession of fishing boats sailing from Santa Cristina. It is the scene of Arietta and Camprodon's opera, *Marina*. It is said to have a charming climate, and to be beyond reach of the tramontana, which seldom gets south of Tossa. Its elegance and brightly coloured urbaneness and broad sheltered shore make it too much of a tourist resort for many people, who will hurry on to the more secluded little point and cove of Santa Cristina. To this charming little place a road runs down from the Lloret-Blanes highway, emerging on to a wooded plateau above the beach, with an attractive old hostelry built on, apparently, to the small white eighteenth-century church, a bijou little affair with red-tiled roof and apse, which used to contain models of seventeenth- and eighteenth-century ships, now moved to Barcelona to be out of harm's way during the civil war. Behind the church a gigantic pine spreads its shelter over an alfresco restaurant; down the wooded cliff a path leads to a little bathing beach and to more alfresco tables and benches; on the day I was there a bus from Blanes had brought a jolly crowd of picnickers to eat and bathe. I have no doubt they ate well: perhaps some of the succulent dishes of fish, lobsters and rice that are so delicious all down the Costa Brava.

If you have time and energy to scramble along the coast path that leads to Blanes, or to skirt it by boat, you should by all means do so, for so you will see the little calas of San Francisco and of La Forcenera. I am not sure if there is a right of passage, or if this path and these coves have been seized by private owners, those pests who prey on all desirable coasts, though less in Spain than elsewhere. At San Francisco there is a little half-ruined late seventeenth-century church. Blanes, indeed, is surrounded by little churches and convents, few to-day in working order.

Blanes, the end of the Costa Brava, is one of its most ancient towns, and one of its most modern. Sheltered by the point of Santa Ana, it faces west, and round the circle of the bay a sizable white town lies. Pla says that one must read the works of Joaquim Ruyra, who wrote of it, really to appreciate Blanes, its tranquil grace, its colour and light, its benignant calm, that obtains even in the busy streets where caulkers work and hammer and tools sound. I had not read Ruyra, so possibly my appreciation of Blanes fell short; I found it too modernized, too *turistica*. The ancient Blanes, or Blanda, probably an Iberian town, for excavations have uncovered pre-Greek coins and pottery, certainly a Roman town of importance, once full of aqueducts, statues, temples, is buried and obscured by thriving modernity, as in many towns of the same tradition it is not. The ancient town was destroyed in the ninth century by pirates; it resurrected two centuries later as Blanda, built up again by the feudal lords of Cabrera. It was they who later built the palace that once dominated the town, and in whose walls the Gothic church stood. In the palace stayed for three days in 1415, on his flight to the castle of Peñiscola, Papa Luna, that enterprising anti-pope Benedict XIII. Probably he and his cardinals would gladly have stayed there longer, had he felt safe, for Blanes was livelier, less utterly unlike Avignon, and several hundred miles nearer civilization, than the lonely sea-girt rock off the Valencian coast where he was to live for eight years and die. The magnificent Blanes palace is now a ruin; so is the Blanes church, which was burnt down by the *rojos* in '36. What *rojos,* I asked of the woman who told me this, as I turned away from the melancholy sight; were they of Blanes, or a visiting team? Alas! of Blanes, I was told. It seems that the masculine population of Blanes had cherished for the church and for the clergy a most violent and unfortunate distaste, which they had vented one dreadful night on their beautiful old Gothic *parroquial. 'Los hombres!'* my informant commented, with disapproving regret. (*Las mujeres,* one inferred, had taken no share in these excesses. Anyhow in Blanes.) 'What about the new church?' I asked; for a brand new church had already sprung up. 'God knows,' she replied. 'Perhaps Our Lady has now turned their hearts.' But she wore a dubious look, as of one who did not know what *los hombres* might next be up to.

It seems that Catalonian coast towns must always down the ages be destroyed, now by one set of Vandals, now by another; they resurrect, and in a few years, or a few centuries, look as well as ever. Certainly Blanes looks well and prosperous, as, indeed, it has increasingly been since, in the eighteenth century, Catalonia began to trade with America. It now hums with shipyards, lace-making and summer visitors.

And it is the end of the Costa Brava. That particular enchantment of sea, rocky coves, and pine-grown mountainsides is over. After Blanes one crosses the Tordera into a flatter, duller country. The coast road runs along the sea; one passes Malgrat, Pineda, where the church has an unusual chequer-board exterior, Canet, where there is a good castle, San Pol, a large, clean seaside town, with buildings tiled and white, in the style that the Franciscan friars of Mallorca and Catalonia took to California in the eighteenth century; the old Catalan church stands sombrely in the middle of this whiteness. At Arenys de Mar it would be better to leave the coast, which has become a line of dull industrial suburbs, and take the inland road to Barcelona, which goes through the mountains by Hostalrich and Granollers. Wishing to be early in Barcelona, I did not do this, but endured the long string of coast suburbs and the frightful tramway road, for the last five-and-twenty miles into the city. The entrance from this road is not an impressive approach to the capital of Catalonia; it arrives through the dingy suburb by the railway station, and along the long, ugly Calle Pedro IV. One would wish to descend on the magnificent city from the mountains that girdle it, or from the sea that has made it. In the days when it was Iberian Barcino, and later Colonia Julia Augusta Faventia Pia, the Roman capital of Laletania, and later still the royal residence of the first Visigoth kings, the important and favoured Moorish city, then the strong, walled capital of the Frankish counts of Barcelona who became also kings of Aragon, Barcelona must have been beautiful, with its great blue harbour full of ships, its maze of narrow streets, its tall, tawny, balconied houses, its climbing hills. One can see it century by century, in the plans of the city at different stages in the Barcelona History Museum, together with Roman excavations and walls and mosaic floors and remains of early basilicas. There is only a little Roman work still to be seen about Barcelona: three beautiful Corinthian columns of a temple (of Augustus or Hercules?) close to the cathedral; here and there a piece of wall; two towers, with mediæval additions, marking in the Plaza Nueva a fortified entrance to the Roman city which stood on the hill where the cathedral now stands. Barcino was one of the Romans' largest ports, and, after Tarragona, the most important town in Hispania Citerior. But its greatest centuries were later, when Catalonia, under the princes of the House of Barcelona, ruled not only Aragon but the land of Languedoc beyond the Pyrenees, southern France from Nice to the borders of Gascony (where they made friends with their neighbours the English occupiers of that province and their disreputable companies of mercenary knights and soldiers, fighting with them against France and Castile, as Froissart relates). Sicily, Sardinia, Naples and Malta were annexed by these enterprising princes; while those bold and formidable buccaneers, the Grand Catalan Company, careered about the Mediterranean world, domineering in Constantinople and Gallipoli, and seizing and holding Athens for eighty years of the fourteenth century; a strange and fantastic adventure which did not endear the Catalans to the Greeks, but which the former greatly enjoyed. They have left on record their appreciation of the Acropolis in an interesting document; the Parthenon they described as the most beautiful jewel in the world. Catalans have always been sensitive to foreign architecture. In Spain, meanwhile, Catalonia finished fairly soon its battles against the receding kingdom of the Moors, laid down the charter of the earliest parliamentary constitution in Europe, asserted a stable constitution based on the democratic rights for which Catalans have always so tenaciously fought, built the magnificent monasteries that for centuries shared feudal domination with counts and kings, established a maritime trade from the Levant to Britain that had no rival but Genoa, gave laws to regulate it, and at the same time was part of the great culture of Provence, a centre of poetry, troubadours (when arduous military activities allowed), painting, learning, science, mystical religion, and quarrels with the Pope. The golden age of Catalan literature, the thirteenth and fourteenth centuries, spread its renown over Castile, France and Italy. A magnificent ecclesiastical architecture flowered for centuries, deriving (for they were an assimilative people) from Byzantium, France, Lombardy, Rome, but developing characteristically Catalan forms. Proud, independent, threatened, as time went on, by the menacing shadow of the hated Castile, so different in temper and outlook, Catalonia turned to the Peninsula a wary and hostile back, to the Mediterranean world a welcoming face, reaching out across the Pyrenees hands of friendly, if acquisitive, kinship. While it has always been emphasized by the Catalans that they are members, with national characteristics of their own, of the *Hispaniæ,* in the Roman sense of a community of peoples, which survived in the federal organization of the Spanish Empire, they assert no less emphatically that Catalonia is not and never will be a part of a uniform Spain moulded on Castile. They believe that they are loyal to the best Hispanic tradition in remaining Catalans: the Spains, they say, 'are not a sun but a constellation.' They are another race from the Castilians—Iberian and largely Provençal, for the Frankish kings who liberated Catalonia from the Moors brought with them soldiers and civilians who settled on the land; they speak another language, that of Roussillon, have another literature, history, culture, political ideals, economic and industrial life, development and destiny. They are more European, more French, more of the Mediterranean culture, perhaps more Greek, by heritage, certainly greatly less African, than the rest of Spain. In short, they are Catalans; though beneath the Catalan is always the eternal Iberian, who has so fiercely resisted the invading foreigner down the ages.

Barcelona is the focus and centre of Catalanism, in all its proud, turbulent independence. More, perhaps, than any city in the world (Marseilles and Naples are near rivals) it gives an impression of tempestuous, surging, irrepressible life and *brio.* A Barcelona crowd roused to anger would be intimidating in a high degree. It is even a little intimidating when in its usual good humour. Drivers charge about the narrow streets and broad squares, sounding their horns loudly and continuously for sheer joy of noise; trams crash along, jangling shrill bells. After Barcelona, Madrid seems a genteel and almost soundless city. The Barcelonese seem to shout, scream, blow horns, laugh, stare, crowd, chatter, hang out flags, all day and all night. Up and down the ramblas they walk and talk, buy and sell, drink in the cafés, stare with unflagging interest at passers by (their preoccupation with people is as intense as elsewhere in Spain; never for a moment do they seem to neglect the proper study of mankind—only for 'man' one should substitute 'woman'). The famous ramblas are delightful; divided by a shady grove of plane trees, two narrow one-way streets run north and south, through the length of the Old Town, crowded with cafés, shops, kiosks, people, trams, motor vehicles, boot-blacks and sellers of lottery tickets. On the dividing promenade people stroll, among brilliant flower stalls, newspaper kiosks, *estanquillos,* and stalls crowded with birds in cages—parakeets, pigeons, blue, green and yellow tits, who fill the air with their liquid twitterings. Beside them swim goldfish, crabs and water tortoises; white mice, guinea-pigs, little dogs, and tiny chimpanzees run to and fro in their boxes, and all is animation. Secretive youths sidle up; insinuatingly they try to persuade you to buy a watch, or a fountain pen, or a ring, for three hundred pesetas; they come quickly down to thirty, twenty, ten; they end by seeming to beg you to take it as a gift, as if the police were (as perhaps they are) hot on their tracks. Buxom women and girls, with fine hatless heads of black hair, smart men with white suits and dark glasses and canes, nippy street urchins, assiduous persons offering lottery tickets—they might, no doubt, be met with in any Spanish town, but here they seem to wear a peculiar air of confidence and vivacity. I do not think they sleep, or even go to bed. My bedroom overlooked the rambla; when, soon after midnight, I went to bed, the population were always still strolling down there in a high state of animation. One morning I was awakened at four by loud conversation; going out on to my balcony and looking down, I perceived that the rambla was still full of people sitting at café tables or on seats beneath the trees, or strolling to and fro, talking, laughing and screaming with the greatest vivacity, the street lights that gleamed above the plane trees now paling a little in a faint dawn. I dare say the flower stalls and the bird and animal stalls and the little boot-shiners were all there too. It was a pretty and fantastic sight, this crowd bewitched into perpetual nocturnal animation.

The Barcelonese are, indeed, a vivid and a tireless people: one sees why they have always had so many revolutions, bombs, commotions, aspirations, political movements, industries and wealth. Their spirit and energy are tremendous. Directly General Franco began his revolution, the Barcelona incendiaries rushed jubilantly round their churches and set them on fire. Church-burning, which has been called the second national sport of Spain, has nearly always been part of Spanish revolutions; the hatred of church and priests has bitten so deep into a large proportion of this religious people that churches are burnt down and priests murdered; when the revolutionary side is pro-clerical, this gesture has to be made by the loyalists. The first attack on church and religious orders was in Queen Christina's days; the last Barcelona large-scale church-burnings had been in July 1909, when sixty-three religious buildings had been attacked. Those riots began as an expression of distaste (somewhat irrelevant) for the war in Morocco: the military authorities in Barcelona turned a blind eye on the incendiaries, whose religious activities were, perhaps, considered a convenient diversion from more important objectives. Between 1931 and 1939, the period of the Catalan autonomous government, no religious buildings in Catalonia were attacked, though in Madrid and elsewhere the anti-ecclesiastical flames periodically blazed. But in July, 1936, after the rising of the army, the Barcelona mobs got down to it in earnest, and nearly all the convents and churches were lit; only the modern Sagrada Familiar and the cathedral (which was later hit by nationalist bombs) escaped altogether. Fortunately Catalonian churches are solidly built; in most cases, even when the interiors were burnt out, the external structure proved less inflammable and, though the incendiaries did what they could during that reign of savagery and terror, when human lives and human art alike became a holocaust to mob passion and brutality, few buildings were destroyed past repair. Others have been well and quickly restored. On the whole Barcelona, ten years after the war, has not the appearance of a city badly scarred, either from fire or from bombs. The Republican government, though unable to stop the first mob outbreaks, succeeded, when it did take control, in salvaging works of art and guarding the buildings from further attack.

Barcelona is a city of magnificent buildings, secular and religious. Its civic buildings, Romanesque, Gothic, Renaissance, baroque, put up in the centuries of surging prosperity and commercial supremacy, decorate the Old Town with dignity and grace. There is the Episcopal Palace, with its great Gothic fourteenth-century window and its Romanesque patio; the exquisite group of buildings round the cathedral— the Gothic Canonry and the Pia Almoina, the Palacio Municipal, or Casa Consistorial, with its Gothic north façade, its beautiful portal topped by a lovely Archangel Raphæl, its fourteenth-century council hall and its graceful oblong patio. On the other side of the square is the Palacio de la Generalidad, the seat of the Catalan government from 1931 to 1939; it houses now the Diputación Provincial, with its fifteenth-century patio, its balustraded stairway, its upper court of oranges and gargoyles, and its chapel of St. George. Here the Institute of Catalan Studies used to be, before its abolition by the present government. Close to it is the Casa del Arcediano, the archdeaconry, with its fifteenth-century fountain, and patio wainscoted with charming modern azulejos; upstairs in this house are the municipal archives. In the Archivo de la Corona de Aragon, close by, a Renaissance building on the site of the old palace of the sovereigns of Catalonia and Aragon, with a particularly lovely gallery and stairway, there are four or five million documents of the mediæval State Chancellery. Opposite, still in the Plaza del Rey, is the old Royal Palace, with its tall fifteenth-century mirador, a charming object, with, on its right, the lovely thirteenth-century royal chapel of Santa Agueda, which houses a museum.

There are a number of attractive old private houses still undemolished in the streets and plazas, though modern vandalism has swept many away. Very lovely is the fifteenth-century Palacio de Centellas, its main façade quite unaltered, its patio and stairway unobtrusively restored; and the eighteenth-century baroque Casa de la Virreina on the Rambla de las Flores, once the home of a viceroy of Peru; its lower part has long been occupied by shops, which are now being removed. Among the few Barcelona baroque buildings, this house is particularly pretty and graceful, with its elegant roof balustrade, its balconies, its fine central window topped by the family arms. The Calle Monçada was once a street of fine houses; some, both Gothic and baroque, still remain, such as the palace of the Marqués de Llió, whose flowered and shrubbed balcony on two wide arches hangs gracefully over a delightful patio. In this street, too, is the eighteenth-century Casa Dalmases, probably Italian work, with a relief sculpture of the rape of Europa on its stairway balustrade; its first owner represented Catalonia in London during the war of the Spanish succession. There are some pretty devices in these baroque patios; some have faked truncated columns like those on the Renaissance stairway of the Generalitad; John Evelyn would have called them elegant cheats, and they have a charming ingenuous air. Another favourite eighteenth-century Barcelona trick was the covering of bricks and ashlars with plaster decorated with graffiti.

In the Old Town there are picturesque streets where Gothic houses still stand; and old arches and seventeenth-century porches and mediæval houses and shops with projecting upper stories and pillared arcades crowd one another in the barrio of Santa Maria del Mar (see, for instance, the ancient Calle del

Rech). This part of Barcelona is full of small isolated beauties, such as the two Gothic fountains of Santa Maria and San Justo. More self-conscious in its antiquity is the seventeenth-century señorial house which is now an inn, the Hostel de la Bona Sort, its patio got up to look like the courtyard of a mountain farm.

Of the fourteenth-century *llotja,* or exchange, only the great Gothic hall remains; a magnificent cathedral of trade, where Barcelona merchants have met daily for six hundred years. Most of the *llotja* was rebuilt in the 1770's, in handsome, rather dull baroque, with a fine fountain of Neptune in the courtyard and statues personifying the continents gesticulating nobly and continentally in four recesses; inside the hall there is an immense and masterly staircase. Much more attractive is the Gothic hospital of Santa Cruz (in Catalan, Santa Creu) which now makes a noble home for the Biblioteca de Catalunya. Its spacious patio and fifteenth-century gallery are delightful; its Casa de Convalecencia, a baroque seventeenth-century building, has a graceful well in its court; its vestibule and dining-room are gaily illustrated with tiles, and there are Viladomat paintings on the chapel roof. Santa Cruz is one of the most agreeable buildings in Barcelona.

But it is, of course, its churches that are the city's greatest architectural glory. Early Catalan Romanesque is beautifully represented by the little tenth-century cruciform Benedictine church of San Pablo del Campo, with its delightful twelfth-century cloister, on whose capitals the most charming animals beguile one—smiling lions, smug-looking snakes, and other agreeable creatures. San Pablo, said the Catalan republicans, after its partial burning, has been 'cleansed by fire of the presbytery which smothered its apse. The slum clearance has already begun, and it will soon allow the beauty of its proportions to be seen for the first time for centuries. Its cloister and immediate surroundings are to form a public garden.' Alas, the best-laid schemes of Spanish men go oft agley.

The other tenth-century Benedictine church, San Pedro de

las Puellas, also cruciform, has been badly spoilt by restoration and alteration; to a less extent the twelfth-century Santa Ana, which has fourteenth-century cloisters; this lovely church was badly damaged by the incendiarists, as was San Jaime. One can happily spend a whole day visiting the cloisters of the Barcelona churches; in them Catalan Gothic is seen at its most delightful. They have the tranquil charm, and often humour, that the sombre and impressive church interiors lack. The beautiful fourteenth and fifteenth-century cathedral cloisters, running round a court of orange trees, palms, aloes, flowers, fountains and Capitoline geese, have a most attractive rural air. The cathedral itself is a triumph of Catalan Gothic magnificence; its size, its colour (tawny golden), its position on its slight rise where once stood a Roman temple, then a mosque, in a quiet plaza in the centre of the tangled maze of streets that are the Old Town, make an overwhelming effect of dignity and majestic grace. The interior proportions are good; dense darkness fills it, a little light filtering in impressively through the stained-glass window slits. One would wish more light to see the wealth of beautiful detail, such, for instance, as the richly sculptured pulpit stairway with its exquisite elaborate door, and the reliefs on the coro. But if one explores it with a good guidebook, imagination gives an illusion of sight. 'The numerous side chapels are dark, and it is often difficult to find the keys,' says my guidebook rather wearily.

But it is outside my scope and power to emulate the guidebooks in their persevering, detailed and admirable accounts of church interiors. Quitting (to use Baedeker's favourite phrase) the cathedral, we emerge into its peaceful surrounding plazas, set about with their beautiful groups of collegiate-looking buildings, and make our way to Santa Maria del Pino, to deplore the fire damage and to admire the great aisle-less nave. Indeed, these Catalan naves are very noble, in their effect of space and unbroken stretch, an effect too often spoilt, however, by the placing of the heavy choir in the middle. Even more beautiful than the Pino is the grand fourteenth-century Santa Maria de Mar, wide naved, with narrow aisles. It was a good deal damaged inside by the incendiaries, but, since much of the interior seems to have been regarded by experts as uncommonly disagreeable and incongruous baroque, this seems to have been for the best. Outside, it is infinitely lovely. Indeed, the exterior beauty of Catalan churches greatly and nearly always exceeds the interior.

The baroque church of Belén, on the rambla, with Viladomat paintings, was badly burnt. The Republican Council of Culture intended, it seems, to turn it into a flower market, but this scheme was naturally foiled by the victory of the side which prefers churches to remain churches. The secular uses to which ecclesiastical buildings were destined would, no doubt, have added greatly to the innocent pleasures of the Barcelonian citizenry.

It is, by serious and cultured persons, considered a pity that both fire and bombs have (so far) spared the great modern architectural high-spot of Barcelona, the pride of its simpler citizens, the jest of the more cultivated, Gaudi's unfinished church of the Sagrada Familia. This remarkable expression of neo-Catalan architecture, begun by public subscription in 1882, has the amiable and fantastic air of a group of fun-fair towers —twisted mosaic pinnacles, scrolled round with cries of devotion and praise, a south façade dripping with sugar-icing stalactites, a fragment of cloister, a crypt. A detailed and vivid description of this extravaganza can be found in Mr. Evelyn Waugh's *Labels*; he saw it in 1929; it was then badly cracked and its poise seemed (and seems still) precarious. It is said Mr. Waugh, unlikely to be finished; he suggests that its completion might well be undertaken by some millionaire a little wrong in the head. Gaudi planned that it should be the work of several generations, each continuing it in their own style; if this should ever be done, the final product will be indeed worth a visit. That this rather unbalanced Templo Expiatorio survived the heavy Italian bombs that battered Barcelona during the civil war is regarded by some Barcelonese as a testimony to its divine protection; that the population omitted to burn it is certainly a testimony to their pride in it. What sins the church was built to expiate, I do not know; but no doubt Barcelona, like other cities, has committed plenty. Days of expiation are now solemnized in its precincts. Such an occasion (for expiation of blasphemy) was placarded on the wall that encircles it, exhorting all Barcelona to come and assist, in the pious tradition of their fathers. This expiatory occasion had occurred in June; it probably had something to do with the church-burnings. The Sagrada Familia, and other ebullitions of Gaudi and his school, such as the Guell pleasure-park houses that look like the sugar-plum dwellings of elves, are greatly prized by the Barcelonese. 'What do you think of the Sagrada Familia?' a little boy asked me, through the window of my car, as I was driving away. I told him it was beautiful; he smirked possessively. There is a naïve, endearing quality in these magnificent extravaganzas of bad taste, as in the tawdry décor, the simpering painted plaster figures of saints and choir boys with alms-plates who posture like pious puppets within the sombre magnificence of Spanish churches. Latin bad taste does nothing by halves; it has the courage of its convictions. In the cemetery of the Italian town where I lived as a child, the defunct little girls who stood poised in marmoreal bliss upon their graves wore marble drawers exquisitely embroidered; they were greatly and generally admired; I should have admired them myself had they not been coldly regarded by our parents.

It is not easy in Barcelona to find all the things that one wants to see, for they move about. The churches and other buildings are more or less stationary, though in fact ancient houses (such as the tenth-century Casa Padellas) are sometimes removed to another street. More often the buildings have been, at one time or another, restored out of their original semblance, keeping their old names. But the many museums that house pictures, sculpture, archæological finds, historical

77

exhibits, and so on, seem to be moved in Barcelona, as else-where in Spain, from one habitation to another every few years, or else their names are changed; no one (except the Turismo office) can give you their latest address. There is so far no complete modern guidebook to Spain obtainable, though there is one in progress, coming out in parts. But Spanish guidebooks would need new editions every two years or so if they tried to keep pace with the restless flitting about of places of interest. They would have to work hard, too, to keep up with the street name changes. As we all know, when-ever a Spanish government falls and a new one takes its place, and more particularly when the change is effected, in the good old Spanish way, by violence or force of arms, the main streets in every town have to be re-named. In Barcelona the affair is complicated further by the purge of Catalan patriotism; about two hundred streets and squares have been purified of names connected with Catalan history, and given instead names of which Castilians are proud; and at least two well-known monuments to prominent and learned Catalans have been demolished. But in every Spanish town of any size now there seems to be one street named Generalissimo Franco, another José Antonio, and often a third called Calvo Sotelo, and so on; so that the guidebook street plans are outmoded. This naturally adds to the difficulties of finding one's way. On the other hand, there are no people more helpful in direct-ing the stranger. But it took me several days to run to earth the excavations from Ampurias. One of my guidebooks was compiled before they were excavated; another placed them in the Provincial Archæological Museum in the church of Santa Agueda; the porter at this museum told me they were, he be-lieved, in the Parque de la Ciudadela, in a museum which shut at one so I was too late; this museum next morning in-formed me I should find them in the Palacio Nacional at Montjuich. This huge palace, which was built for the exhibi-tion of 1929, houses many collections of objects—Catalan art down the ages, wall paintings from churches in the Pyrenees, potteries and ceramics, and an interesting collection of pictures, from the fourteenth century to Picasso. Its staff, however, denied any knowledge of the Ampurias things; so did the charmingly helpful Catalan Arts and Crafts Department in another section of the palace. At last, however, I met a municipal architect, all kindness and information, who not only directed me to the Ampurias collection, which was shut, but got the porter to admit me. There were some beautiful things: amphoræ, vases, statues, sculptures, mosaic floors.

I had some difficulty, too, in tracking down the Museo de Historia de Barcelona in the Casa Padellas; it turned out to be in the Plaza del Rey, and had an admirable collection of Roman excavations, remains of Christian basilicas, Arab baths (almost the only remains in Barcelona of the eighty years of Moorish occupation), and plans and reconstructions of old Barcelona, showing its growth through the centuries.

One could, of course, spend a long time in the Barcelona museums. But, when one leaves museums, churches, galleries, houses, one comes out, with a shock of pleasure, into Barcelona itself, sweeping ebulliently and grandly down from the mountains to the sea, many-coloured, shouting, alive. Down to the docks and the great harbour full of ships run the thronged streets crowded with exuberant Catalans, the green public parks, the fine new rondas that sweep round the old city, taking the place, alas! of the ancient town walls, demolished in the 1860's. Gautier said they laced the city in too stiffly and tightly; but how noble they must have looked. My guidebook told me that one of these rondas, the Marques del Duero, was 'usually crowded with a throng of pleasure-seekers,' so I went down it several times seeking pleasure, and explored the harbour group of avenues and plazas named after marquises, palaces and queens, with Christopher Columbus presiding on his column in the centre. But for my part I found more pleasure in the ramblas, which are certainly the gayest and most animated part of the town. 'You should go up to Tibidabo in the funicular,' said the newsvendor at the kiosk where I bought papers. 'One sees from there the whole of Barcelona, one eats well, and there are many diversions.' I took his advice on Sunday afternoon. The funicular carries you up a steep mountain-side to the highest peak of the hills that back Barcelona, and lands you in a fun-fair, as full of diversions as Olympia or Blackpool. There is a fine large restaurant and a magnificent view of the great sea city queening it above its thronged harbour of ships, and of the Mediterranean, spread like a peacock's tail, ruffling and deepening and shading under the broad wind to north and east and south: faintly and transparently looming, you may just see Mallorca. Behind climb the mountains, forested, vineyarded, strewn on their lower slopes with white farms and villas, intimidatingly backed and topped by the fierce jagged line of Montserrat. If it were not for the funicular, the restaurants, the fun-fair, the scenic railway, the bijou white church on the summit, Tibidabo would be deliciously and romantically beautiful.

The church, though bijou, is also grandiose: it is called El Templo del Sagrado Corazon de Jesus, and subtitled El Templo Nacional y Expiatorio de España. More expiation. In this case the expiation, like so many, is for that fatal day in July, 1936, when 'the Satanic fury of the enemies of God and of the country' sacked the crypt and destroyed the still unfinished church. It has been almost rebuilt, but still needs a great deal of money and begs for alms. Inside it is gay and pretty, outside very clean and white. The first church was built by the Italian saint, Juan Bosco, who visited Barcelona in 1886. During his journey, an inner voice kept saying to him 'Tibi dabo.' 'The saint could translate this Latin phrase, but without penetrating the mystery that the Lord wished to indicate by it.' He had a terrific reception in Barcelona, performed miracles, and blessed the crowd from a balcony, and the gentleman who owned the mountain called Tibidabo presented it to him that he might build a hermitage there. The saint exclaimed, 'Not a hermitage but a grandiose temple we will erect, with God's help, on this hill.' The temple was built, only to be destroyed fifty years later by the busy and incendiary enemies of religion, who must have spent a very enjoyable evening ascending in the funicular, riding on the scenic railway, turning dizzily round the great wheel, eating and drinking uproariously in the restaurant, looting and setting fire to the church, and desecrating the smiling image of its saint. But the church has triumphed; it has been almost rebuilt, and San Juan presides over it and smiles once more. He entreats your alms for the completion of the good work. To further it, you can purchase all kinds of holy relics, ornaments, and hagiologies in the vestibule.

A quite different kind of expedition is the drive up into the hills to Tarrasa and San Cugat del Vallés. It was restful to get out of Barcelona (which was *en fête* for July 18th, the anniversary of the Glorious Revolution) and to drive out among hills, olive gardens and vineyards, villages, and dust-pale, winding roads. For the Barcelona country is very lovely. San Cugat (Benedictine abbey and church) is ten or twelve miles out, and lies in a charming village. The church was, of course, shut; I knocked up the sacristan, who took me in and showed me round. The twelfth-century cloister is one of the most beautiful of the beautiful Romanesque cloisters of Catalonia; two rows of arcaded pillars, their capitals delightfully carved with different scenes, figures, animals mythical and real, foliage and fruit; particularly engaging are the scenes from Noah's ark. The little garden is green with lemon trees, cypresses and sweet-smelling shrubs; in the middle is a stone well; it was most peaceful and lovely in the hot afternoon sunshine. There are Roman fragments from some earlier building set in the cloister walls. In a room off the cloister there is a bright mosaic retablo. The church has a fine west rose window. The sacristan, a bright, ugly little Catalan, full of information and eagerness, showed me everything in detail.

He was still full of the civil war; the English radio and papers, said he, had not understood it, had got the facts wrong. Actually there had been many Russians fighting for the Republicans, and very few—but *pocos, pocos*—Germans and Italians on the nationalist side, and such few Italians as there were had run away; he indicated rapid flight with gesture and sound. I cannot remember if he said that San Cugat had been damaged by the *rojos* or not. It was used during the war as a store-house, but apparently had been treated with care.

I left this lovely place to go on to Tarrasa, ten miles north-west. Tarrasa, the ancient Egara, is an industrial town and makes cloth; but it has three beautiful and interesting Romanesque churches, San Pedro, Santa Maria and the baptistery of San Miguel. All have been classed in the past as substantially Visigothic work; experts now differ as to this. They were, anyhow, restored and partly reconstructed as late as the twelfth century. There seems a good case for all three having been built on Visigoth sites, and probably bases, after the Moslem destruction of Egara and its churches, and at the same time as San Pablo del Campo in Barcelona. The original building of San Miguel seems to have been the baptistery of the completely vanished Egara basilica, of which only a mosaic pavement remains in Santa Maria. When archæologists differ about dates, the layman obviously cannot rush in. Fortunately ignorance does not hinder enthusiasm; these Romanesque buildings, with their tiled, domed and clustered apses (San Pedro's is trefoil), horseshoe arches, rough exterior masonry, and setting of tall cypresses, have extraordinary interest and charm.

Barcelona, when I drove back into it through the hill country steeped in evening light, was making merry over its revolutionary anniversary; coloured paper and flags decorated the rambla, and every one was very gay. Even those who grumble, who hate the régime, the poverty, the lack of liberty, the fettering of Catalonia to Castile, the sense of defeat, as it is obvious very many of them do, will on a day of merry-making make merry. Lest they should make merry at my expense, as they were apt to do when I walked the streets in a hat of any kind (from the attention it excited, my ordinary and inconspicuous hat might have been a Red Indian's feathers), I usually left it off in Barcelona; it was restful not to be stared at, but rather hot and dazzling. Another female traveller in Spain, fifteen years back, wrote that she continued to wear her shady hat and defied the jeering, as she did not care to be 'cowed by savages.' She was made of sterner stuff than I, who am easily cowed. Some people say that the derision of hats dates from the civil war, when only fascist (i.e. well-off) women wore them; but it must from all accounts go back further than this; a French visitor in the mid-nineteenth century wrote that the ladies of his party had, in self-defence, to take to mantillas, and Marie Bashkirtseff was hooted about Seville. However this may be, walking about Barcelona bare-headed after sunset, mixing with the cheerful crowd that thronged the ramblas, with only a finger pointed now and then, and an occasional cry of 'Francés', was very pleasant.

I could have stayed much longer in Barcelona; there were a hundred things still to see, or to see again—Pedralbes, many churches, the museums, the ancient streets and houses, the lovely civic buildings. I should have liked, too, to read in the library of the Casa del Arcediano, among the archives of the former Institute of Catalan Studies, looking out on the arcaded gallery and the tiled and fountained patio. To touch only the fringes of this magnificent historic centre of Catalan culture, round which so much mediæval European history swirled, which reached out so adventurously into far lands and seas, gathering and absorbing artistic and literary treasures for planting afresh in Catalonian soil so that they grew up there with vigorous and characteristic life—to visit Barcelona, in short, for so brief a time, was tantalizing. One can have no sympathy with those who complain that Barcelona is ugly,

industrial, aggressively commercial, and rail against its inhabitants in the manner of the outrageous Ford—

> Catalonia is no place for the man of pleasure, taste or litera-
> ture . . . here cotton is spun, vice and discontent bred, revolu-
> tions concocted . . . Catalans are the curse and weakness of
> Spain . . . neither courteous nor hospitable to strangers, whom
> they fear and hate . . . the Berber-like inhabitants . . . the lower
> orders are brutal . . .

and so on. Ford was a traveller of great culture and knowledge, who seemed continually to fall into fits of ill-tempered
prejudice; what occurred in Catalonia, and, indeed, all over
Spain, to enrage him, we do not know, but the insults ex-
purgated from the first edition of Murray's Handbook can
scarcely be worse than those left in it.

What is really ugly about this exciting city is its suburbs,
which stretch drearily beyond its encircling rondas for miles.
Avoiding the road that went down to join the coast at Sitges,
which I knew for a dull industrial stretch, I left Barcelona by
the San Cugat road, visited these beautiful cloisters again, and
joined the Llobregat valley road at Martorell, going on north
from there to Montserrat (a magnificent expedition, at once
too familiar and too far inland to be dwelt on here; I had last
made it by train, twenty years ago). I came down the Llobregat again to the steep Roman bridge of Martorell, the Pont del
Diable, and its triumphal arch that appears Roman but has
been without evidence ascribed to Hannibal; beneath the
bridge the Llobregat swirls down its ravine. Turning west
here, I drove through the mountains down the Noya valley,
twisting between castled heights and ravines, with the jagged
saw of Montserrat high against the sky to the right. It was a
wild red mountain land, to which farms and little towns clung
steeply. I passed Gelida, with its church built on a Roman
castle, San Sadurní d'Anoia (whose wines, I read, sparkle like
champagne, and the Romans greatly enjoyed them, but I had
no time to stop and try them), Villafranca del Panadés, which
has mansions and palaces, and from which I turned aside to

drive seven miles to the beautiful little church of San Martí Sarroca; its arcaded apse and its capitals are exquisite French Catalan Romanesque of the twelfth century. I came down from the hills to the sea at Villanueva y Geltrú; I had missed Sitges, where the Romans loved to stay, where the malvoisie is good, the women beautiful and the bathing excellent; but on this part of the coast the mountain hinterland and its towns are far better than the sea road, which is flat and not interesting.

That night I slept at the tiny fishing beach of Calafell. Entering it, my car got stuck in a sandy shore track, and it took the whole population of Calafell playa to dig it out. The Miramar inn, where I put up, was on the shore; its great roofed open-air restaurant ran down almost to the sea, which, when I bathed after dark, was very warm, with a lap of small waves. It was a lovely sight—a crescent moon, the arc of lights round Calafell bay, and the lit fishing boats out on the dark sea. I went to sleep to the soft sound and stir of waves; delicious after the shrieking of the rambla. Next morning it took my landlord till eleven to grapple with the complications of my triptica, a document new and unfamiliar to him, but the police had told him it must be filled in. They had not, it seemed, had foreign visitors before at Calafell playa.

The town of Calafell is above the playa, old and ruinous, with Gothic church and ruined castle; its streets, and the road running down to the playa, are broken and pot-holed and strewn with boulders; indeed, all the roads except the main roads are thus. A film of pale dust lay over the olive-grey and terraced country; pink and ochre stone gate posts opened on to olive gardens and vineyards, as in Italy; to the south spread the blue and misty sea.

The road bent inland to Vendrell, a pleasant, palmy town, with plazas and cafés and dust; the church has a tall tower and a baroque (or is it a late Renaissance?) door. These quiet pale towns set back from the sea have an elegance, a tranquil grace, a dignity and pleasantness, a casual Mediterranean *savoir vivre,* that perhaps descends from the days when Roman gentlemen had their villas all along this coast. For this is the Via Maxima, and took Roman gentlemen down from the Rhône to Tarraco, the Greeks' beautiful Callipolis, where Romans so loved to be.

The road joined the coast again, and suddenly there was the Arco de Bará, tawny and high, bestriding the Via Maxima in memory of some forgotten Roman triumph of eighteen centuries ago, reminding us who pass under it of the legions marching through Hispania Citerior along this road, of Augustus driving into Tarraco to the plaudits of worshipping multitudes, of consuls and prætors and poets wintering on this charming coast and riding about it to hunt stags and boars; of the continuous bustle, the incessant lively comings and goings of imperial Rome in Spain. This is indeed Roman country, the Campo de Tarragona, and we shall soon be in Tarraco, the earliest Spanish city to be romanized, and this is Tarraconensis, and it seems as full of Roman ghosts (cheerful and enjoying colonists and visitors as well as marching troops and governing prefects) as Ampurias is of the whispering shades of Greeks bartering and strolling in their stoa above the sea, watched by dark, suspicious Iberians from beyond their wall. Iberians, naturally, are everywhere down their own coast, and Tarragona too was an Iberian city before it was visited by Phœnicians, Carthaginians, Greeks, Romans, Goths, Moors or Franks. It is perhaps because the Iberians remain, while the visitors have come and gone, that it is the visitors who haunt and whisper down the Mediterranean shores and in the sun-baked vine and olive-grown hinterland.

The road to Tarragona is delightful. There are Roman or mediæval stone gates and arches set in the garden walls; there is a mediæval or Renaissance or baroque church (or a mixture of the three) in every village; ruined castles tower on hills and capes; little aloe-grown playas and coves lie below the narrow broken tracks that lead through cultivated *huertas* to the sea. Altafulla has three castles; one of them seems likely to precipitate itself some day from its cliff into the sea. Tamarit has a lonely, pebbly little beach beneath the splendid castle on its rock; it was there that I for the first time bathed with my wrist watch on and stopped it.

Eight kilometres out from Tarragona there is Clot del Medol, where a great Roman quarry, Cantera del Medol, lies on the hill among cypresses and stones. Beyond this is the Torre de los Escipiones, a square, broken, three-staged tower, standing on the hill-side above the road, a sepulchral monument of the end of the first century A.D., unconnected with the Scipio family. It stands brown and solid among cypresses, pines, ilex, juniper and aloes on the baked hill-side; from it one has a superb view of Tarragona and its coast, the blue and green and peacock sea stretching beyond the grey shimmer of the twisted olives round the deep bay, Tarragona at its far end, magnificently piled on its rocky hill sheer above the sea.

Tarragona is possibly the most grandly poised city in Europe. The shape formed by the steep walls that encircle it, and the climbing mass of the ancient town crowned by the cathedral on its summit, is theatrically superb. The imagination, long haunted, is at first glance captured and possessed for ever by this Roman-mediæval city—Callipolis, Tarraco Togata, Colonia Julia Victrix Triumphans, where Scipio wintered with the army that was to beat Carthage out of Spain, where Roman consuls and prefects administered the province of Hispania Tarraconensis, where armies and civilians landed from Italy in the harbour which the Romans later built, and from which the influence of Rome spread up the Ebro valley into Celtibera. Strabo said, probably wrongly, for he was never in Spain, that Tarraco had in his day no harbour—

but it is situated on a bay, and is adequately supplied with all other advantages, and at present it is not less populous than New Carthage. Indeed, it is naturally suited for the residence of the prefects, and is a metropolis not only of Hispania this side of the Iberus, but also of the greater part of the country beyond it.

And the Gymnesian Islands, which lie near by off the coast, and Ebusus, all noteworthy islands, suggest that the position of the city is a happy one.

As to the governor, 'he passes his winters administering justice in the regions by the sea, and especially in New Carthage and Tarraco, while in the summer-time he goes the rounds of his province.' Happy governor! *Urbs opulentissima,* gay colony of cultured Roman sophisticates, poets and emperors, sun-warmed refuge of dwellers in the black mountain country inland. *'Hibernans in Tarraconis maritimis'*—wintering on the coast of Tarraco—how often we read this in the accounts of Roman leaders operating in Spain.

> At cum December canus et bruma impotens
> Aquilone rauco mugiet,
> Aprica repetes Tarraconis litora. . . .

So Martial wrote to a friend. Martial liked Tarraco. Apart from its sunny shores, and apart from the stags and boars he told his friend he could chase there, and apart from its excellent wines, he liked it much better than living on his country estate in Bilbilis, where he had retired to escape the corruptions and fatigues of life in Rome. He enjoyed country life very much for a time, but soon found that his neighbours were stupid and provincial; they were, no doubt, brutish Celtiberians, and seldom wore togas. They knew nothing of literature or drama, and had no intelligent social life. Tarraco, on the other hand, was always full of society and goings on —a Rome from Rome, with its forum and its theatres, its chariot races and its games and its pleasant social intercourse. Augustus had long since made it a pet resort; he stood in relation to it rather as George IV to Brighton, but was more of a god there (as indeed elsewhere), and had a fine altar, palace and temple dedicated to him by an enthusiastically devout citizenry. Hadrian also frequented this elegant city, and the historian Florus settled there in his reign to teach rhetoric, and praised its temperate climate, its scenery, and its social amenities with enthusiasm—'*civitas nobis ipsa blanditur . . .*' and, 'of all cities which are chosen for a rest, if you will believe me, who know many, it is the most delightful; socially it is high class, for Cæsar's prætor resides there and foreign nobility frequent it', and so on; (it is worth while reading the whole passage in Florus's *Fragmentum de Vergilio oratore an Poeta*). What Florus, or Martial, or the Cæsars, or their prætors and governors, would have thought of the later, mediæval Tarragona which is the city we now see, is doubtful; they might well have preferred the new part of the town, the fine broad Paseo sweeping round outside the mighty walls, with its Balcon from which to gaze at the sea and the ships in the port, the smart modern ramblas with their cafés, restaurants, theatres and hotels, ramblas re-named every few years for some new political or military leader, which the Romans would have felt to be quite in order.

The city is divided sharply into old and new, so that the old remains unspoiled. Coming in by the Paseo San Antonio, one can go round the cyclopean and Roman walls, of which on the west side the foundations alone remain, to the north side, where they are highest and sheerest and most complete, and from which the view of the steeply piled city is most imposing. I entered the town through the Puerta del Rosario, leaving my car in the little Plaza Pallol, where once there stood the Roman Forum. From here one walks through a maze of narrow and fascinating streets, which have something of interest and beauty at every corner, some house façade or doorway or fragment of sculpture, to the Calle Mayor, the Roman Via Triumphalis, and here a magnificent flight of steps flies up to the cathedral. The cathedral is glorious; twelfth and thirteenth-century Romanesque-Gothic, golden brown, with tiled apses clustering round the central tower, begun (or rebuilt) after the expulsion of the Moors, on the site of a mosque, and incorporating some admirable Moorish work. It is, no doubt, partly its grand position, crowning the walled citadel at the top of its flight of steps, that gives this cathedral its unique splendour among Catalan Romanesque churches; for Romanesque is the main effect of the solid, fortress-like, apsed exterior; the Spanish were late in assimilating Gothic. The west portal, however, richly sculptured, is pure Gothic. Inside there are pointed arches, tiny windows, and a suite of interesting side chapels, veiled in thick Catalan ecclesiastical darkness, but can be explored if someone will switch on the lights, and will be found to be crowded with objects of varying attraction and beauty, from rich Renaissance and baroque monuments and Gothic retablos to the bones of archbishops.

A beautiful round-arched Byzantine portal opens on to the cloisters, some of the loveliest of their kind, on the model of the French Cistercian cloisters at Fontfroide near Narbonne. Whether its architects and builders were Narbonnese is uncertain, as with so much Catalan Cistercian of this date. The capitals are sumptuously and exquisitely carved with different aspects of human, animal and vegetable life; the round windows over them have delicate Moorish traceries; there is a Moorish arched prayer niche in the west wall, dated 958. It may be supposed that there was always a temple of some kind here, Iberian, Roman (a temple of Jupiter), Visigothic, Moorish, each using some of the materials of its predecessors for its building, and that this twelfth-century church that was built on the mosque's site when the ancient see of Tarragona was recovered for Christendom is largely made of stones that the Romans found assembled in the Iberian fort when, the first labours of conquest completed, they proceeded, most lavishly and opulently, to adornment and building. It is probable that there was an Arab cloister where the Christian one now stands. It can scarcely have been more lovely than these, with their delicate shafts and rich capitals and arcading, and the garden of oranges, palms, roses and sweet shrubs that crowds round the central fountain.

Close to the cathedral is the tiny twelfth-century church of

Santa Tecla la Vieja, the tutelary saint of Tarragona; it is thought to have served as parish church while the cathedral was building. Near it is the chapel of San Pablo, built where St. Paul preached, with his customary enterprise and success, to the citizens of Tarragona, which became a very religious city, supplied several martyrs, became a bishopric in the third century, an archbishopric in the fifth, and again, after the Moorish interlude, in the eleventh. That it was a flourishing ecclesiastical centre under the Visigoths is shown by the holding there of a church council in 516.

The Visigoths, as usual, have left few traces of their three centuries of occupation. We know that they ruled in Tarragona, valued it, made it a bishopric, and the seat of the Duke who governed the province and resided in the Roman prætor's house. There is no record of their having destroyed it, as some historians say. Nor, as more say, that the Moors destroyed it, massacred all its inhabitants, and left it an unpopulated desert for four centuries, though, when the Catalan reconquerors took it, it had a desolate untended air after some years of being a centre of war. 'Historians,' wrote a Spanish chronicler of last century, 'have ruined Tarragona every little while, no doubt to have the pleasure of restoring her again in as short a time.' Anyhow, the Moors must have lived in Tarragona; they had arsenals and dockyards there, built ships, and had at least one mosque. Nor would it have been characteristic of the Moors to waste so fine a city. Also, more importance was attached by the Pope and by the Counts of Barcelona to its reconquest than would have been given to the forested and unpeopled wilderness that it has been sometimes represented. One may safely believe that Tarragona had a continuous, though often assaulted and disturbed, life, from the days when the Scipios captured it and its people became the first *gens togata* in Spain, through the six and a half centuries of Roman glory, culture, luxury and civilization that perished in misrule, the three centuries of Gothic turbulence, the nearly four of Moorish militant defence and battle. But the Moors, like the Visigoths, have left little trace of themselves; or, if they did, the Frankish conquerors destroyed most of it. The Cessetani Iberians left some coins, and the foundations of their tremendous walls; the Romans have left the walls they built on these, traces of a harbour, fragments of an Augustan temple, a wealth of statues, baths, columns, sarcophagi, a prætorium, a prætor's house, tablets with inscriptions built into the walls of mediæval houses, the haunting ghosts of a forum, a theatre, an amphitheatre, a circus, a Christian necropolis. Tarragona is a Roman and mediæval city; from its successive sackings and near-destructions down the centuries (including the British in 1705 and the French in 1811), it has emerged in its Roman and mediæval grandeur and solidity, and still stands to-day like a sentinel on its Mediterranean rock, looking southward over the sea, northward to the fertile mountain lands where the sun-baked imperial aqueduct on its double tiered arches strides across country.

A walk through the Tarragona streets is full of exciting discoveries—Roman reliefs, carvings and inscriptions, Renaissance doors on mediæval houses. One comes on what is left of the Circus Maximus, where charioteers competed and died before enthusiastic thousands; on the south-eastern slope between city and sea lie remains of the amphitheatre where Bishop Fructuosus and his deacons were burnt in 258, before spectators doubtless equally numerous and enthusiastic. There are slight traces of a semi-circular theatre; here dramas were performed, and the spectators were possibly fewer and certainly more critical. Of the temple to Divus Augustus only fragments remain—an altar, some friezes and the great bell; of the other shrines, little. The archæological museum has an admirable collection of sculptures, statues, columns, sarcophagi and coins. There is now another museum, in the tobacco factory, of tombs and monuments discovered in the lately excavated Christian necropolis. Below this lies the present harbour (begun by Ferdinand the Catholic in 1491); it is beautiful and delightful, a great blue basin full of ships and boats, with a bathing beach and a fisherman's quarter.

There seems a duality, almost a conflict, haunting Tarragona behind its magnificent external scene; as if the ghost of the Augustan imperial city were pulling against its long mediæval history; the pride and sophistication of the *urbs opulentissima,* the pagan prosperity of Callipolis before it, that Callipolis which the Massiliot sailor recorded in his periplus as he navigated the long coast home from the far western ocean—all this ancient past dragging like an undertow against the turbulent feudal darkness and splendour of the *edad media* centuries, and the smart modern prosperity of the new town south and west of the Rambla San Juan (now temporarily the Avenida Generalissimo Franco). And strangely from time to time the modern age and its town dissolve away; and the Middle Age and Christianity; and the Cæsars and Rome; and one is left with the great cyclopean walls beneath the Roman, and a few Iberian inscriptions cut into the stones. The descendants of those who cut them still live in these steep and narrow streets, talking a dialect of their Latin conquerors' speech, watching darkly, with aloof yet derisive interest, while civilizations come and go.

It was some time before I could discover how to reach Centcellas, of which I had read in Lampérez's *Arquitectura Cristiana Española,* but nowhere else; it seems to be in no guidebook, and no one in Tarragona knew where it was, until, in the Turismo office, I met a gentleman who told me it was near the village of Constantí, five or six kilometres from Tarragona along the road that ran up the river Francoli. He had not himself seen it, but told me it had been for about a hundred and fifty years a farm-house, and now belonged to a Señor Sole, who, with his family, lived there. He wrote it down for me in my note-book, in large English characters, for he had learned this tongue. 'CENTCELLES Not far from CONSTANTÍ only 5 kilometres from TARRAGONA belongs to Srs SOLE who are lieving there.' He was a very kind, cultivated man. So I drove off to Constantí, along a charming, dusty road between cane groves, and made inquiries in that attractive little town. They knew all about Centcellas there, and a well-informed ox-cart driver indicated to me a group of buildings in the distance beyond fields; he said a road went there. Having failed to discover this road, I asked a group of citizens in the church plaza; one of them kindly proposed to show me the way. It was a bad road, he said, but possible. It was certainly a bad road, more of a donkey track, along which I had to steer between precipitously deep ruts and huge boulders. In muddy weather it must be impassable. After two kilometres or so I gave it up (my front bumper had been jolted off again); we left the car on the edge of the track, and walked the last quarter of a mile, through cane groves and vineyards, till suddenly these opened out, and there before us was Centcellas, the group of farm buildings and ruins pictured in Lampérez's book, with the pond in front. The buildings are, it seems, a still unsolved archæological riddle. They were once thought to be the ruins of a Byzantine basilica founded by the first Greek monks who came here from the east; then they were supposed to be the baths of a Roman villa of the time of Hadrian; coins of this time have been found round about, and it would be a likely place enough for a Roman gentleman in Tarragona to have a country villa. But some archæologists declare Centcellas to have been the first basilica of Tarragona diocese, with a Byzantine baptistery, and possibly a convent. The chief building of the group, however, seems certainly to have been once a villa of Hadrian's time. The group consists of a cubic-shaped building, with another block attached to it, and others further off. The main building has on the ground floor a large room, now a living-room and kitchen, and upstairs another large room, circular, roofed with a hemispherical vault, which is adorned with fine mosaics of hunting scenes, figures, buildings, and Greek linear designs. It was getting dark when I saw it; the woman of the house kindly showed it to me by the light of a hand lamp. It was very impressive. Could it happen anywhere but in Spain that such a treasure from the antique past would be allowed to fall into ruin in the hands of farmer owners, instead of being acquired and preserved by the State or by some ancient building preservation society, and thoroughly explored?

Expert opinion seems divided as to whether this villa became later a Constantine basilica; some think that the mosaics were covered over for this purpose, and recesses built in the sides for baptistery and sacristy. Señor Lampérez doubts this; he guesses that the only religious buildings were the more distant ruins. Are they, he speculates, the remains of the early basilica? Or of an abbey founded after the expulsion of the Moors? All the buildings but the central one are too much ruined for their purpose to be identified; there appear to be remains of ovens; most of the walls are wholly destroyed.

Centcellas is a riddle. Until the ruins are properly explored, and their plan reconstructed, it must remain so. Meanwhile, it lies, neglected and mouldering down the centuries, in this remote farm at the end of a rutted path.

Leaving Tarragona, I had to choose between two historic mountain monasteries, Santas Creus and Poblet. I chose Poblet. The best road there from Tarragona goes through Valls and Montblanch, up the Francoli valley—a fine mountain drive between ranges of magnificent peaks. Valls and Montblanch are both attractive mediæval towns; Valls has walls and a fine sixteenth-century church; Montblanch has walls and a fine Romanesque one. The views all the way up are of mountains, rust-brown and deep green, with purple-grey shadows in the clefts. At Espluga, thirty miles or so from Tarragona, a road turns south-west, climbing along the side of the Sierra de San José, and, after a couple of miles, you see Poblet, lying in a hollow of the hills. The huge town of a place, once the first monastery in Catalonia, perhaps in Spain, sprawls over a great expanse of ground, white and magnificent, still largely ruinous, but restored, and now inhabited again (after a century first of desolation and abandonment, then of national protection), by the Cistercian order which founded it. A daughter foundation of Fontfroide, it was founded in the twelfth century by Count Ramón Berenguer IV of Catalonia and Aragon, and was lived in by the Cistercians from 1153, while building after building was added during the next two centuries. It became, as it grew, a magnificent fortified manorial village, girt by its great wall—monastery, church and chapels, cloister, chapter house, orchards and gardens, huge wine cellars, granaries, store-houses, stables, hostels, domestic offices for servants, all the dependencies of a great feudal monastery. The church was the burial-place of the Aragon kings, and is full of their splendid tombs. The French invaders, as usual, smashed, plundered and desecrated monastery, church and tombs in 1812. But, until 1835, when furious anti-clerical mobs stormed, smashed and looted it, it must have been the most magnificent of sights, with its battle-mented walls and towered gateway, its great Romanesque and Gothic cloister, with clustered columns and pierced arches, its large stone-basined fountain beneath a vaulted hexagonal roof, the lovely walk running round the rose garden (the cloister, like Tarragona's, is on the Fontfroide model), the huge library, refectory, kitchens, chapter house, and great nine-bayed dormitory, the abbots' palace, the beautiful unfinished royal palace of the fourteenth and seventeenth centuries, and the church full of the tombs of the Aragon kings. The fury of 1835, when the local peasantry, who loathed and dreaded the monastery and its monks and their feudal powers (which, besides the possession of estates coveted by the peasants, were reputed popularly to include kidnapping, torture and extortion, and even the rights to the bridal night, though the tribute to which this, if it ever existed, had been long since commuted had lapsed some years before), stormed and wrecked and sacked, and left the monastery in the state thus described thirty-six years later by Augustus Hare.

It is the very abomination of desolation . . . the most utterly ruined ruin that can exist. Violence and vengeance are written on every stone. The vast walls, the mighty courts, the endless cloisters, look as if the shock of a terrible earthquake had passed over them. There is no soothing vegetation, no ivy, no flowers, and the very intense beauty and delicacy of the fragments of sculpture which remain in the riven and rifted walls, where they were too high up for the spoiler's hand to reach them, only make stronger contrast with the coarse gaps where the outer coverings of the walls have been violently torn away, and where the marble pillars and beautiful tracery lie dashed to atoms upon the ground. . . .

He describes chapels windowless and grass-grown, the hospital a mere shell, the church, with donkeys stalled in the ante-chapel round the tombs of kings, fragments of royal monuments piled one upon another, mutilated marble sculptures and shattered retablo reliefs, the tombs hammered and battered to bits.

Caryatides without arms or faces, floating angels wingless and headless, flowers without stems, and leaves without branches, all dust-laden, cracked and crumbling. . . . Above one side of the great cloister, in the delicate tracery of its still remaining windows, rises the shell of the palace. . . . Space would not suffice to describe in detail each court through which the visitor is led, in increasing wonder and distress, to the terrible torture-chamber. . . . Surely no picture that the world can offer of the sudden destruction of human power can be more appalling than fallen Poblet, beautiful still, but most awful in the agony of its destruction.

Since Hare's description, Poblet has been taken over by the State, cleaned up and largely restored; it is no longer in this dilapidated condition. The late republican government did much for it, and the present government continued the work, and now the monks are back in their monastery. From the point of view of sightseers, this is a drawback; one is no longer allowed to go over the whole monastery: the Tarragona Turismo staff complain that the Church, as usual, is determined to keep its property for its own exclusive use. It is perhaps hard to blame the monks for not wanting visitors and architecture students tramping all about their dwelling. One may still see much of it, and its feudal monastic splendour, largely restored though it is, but still partly ruinous, is staggering. The great gate-house, the delicately-rich church portal, the exquisite cloisters and fountain, the chapter house and hall of archives, the palaces, and the great sprawl of manorial buildings round the convent, lying palely within their towered walls, remain magnificent. Imagination, haunted by the past, looks to see the sixty-six nobly born grandee monks riding through the ancient gateway on their snow-white mules, the kings of Aragon riding into the royal palace to make their souls, the weary pilgrims seeking rest and healing in the hospital, our own Jacobite Duke of Wharton, erstwhile president of the Hell Fire Club, and patron of Freemasonry, coming in destitute to die, and the slow, creaking ox-carts bringing in grapes from the great mountain vineyards to the monastic wine presses and vats. But one sees no white mules, no riding monks, no penitent monarchs or stone-broke Jacobite Freemason dukes, though pilgrims still come, and, no doubt, wine. Poblet will not, presumably, ever enjoy again its old dominion; but its grandeur survives all change.

I drove down again to the coast by Alcover and Reus, and the sea road ran along the Playa de Cambrils. It wound, or rather zigzagged, beyond all reason, dashing down into precipitous ravines and up again, with sharp turns every few yards; it went through hot, dust-filmed olive country, with small vines and terraced hills and red earth. On my right a magnificent line of mountains swept, dark and clear and castled, against the orange-gold western sky. The country grew barer, less cultivated, more heath-like, dotted with low palms; the fertile Campo de Tarragona was left behind. Then came the Gulf of San Jorge, with its blue, lagoon-like harbour, and at Puerto del Fangal, the little port in its deep bay, the road turned from the sea towards Tortosa on the Ebro, the

Roman Dertosa Julia Augusta, guardian of the navigable Ebro where it is crossed by the Via Maxima from Tarragona, a few miles from the two great natural harbours of Fangal and Alfaques. Between Tortosa and the sea spreads the marshy, lagoon-strewn delta of the Ebro, and the strange encircling hook, like a parrot's beak, of the Punta del Calacho curls protectingly round the almost enclosed harbour basin that for centuries was fought for by Romans, Carthaginians, Saracens, French and Spaniards. It is indeed a harbour, as Tortosa is a city and the Ebro a river, worth fighting for.

Wishing to get nearer the tremendous Ebro, I crossed it at Amposta, an ancient town piled steeply, house on house, above the greatest river of Spain. Amposta was always, it seems, as hard to capture as it looks. Richard Ford, with his usual arrogance, called it a century ago 'a miserable, aguish, mosquito-plagued port on the Ebro, with some thousand sallow souls . . . miserable Amposta.' He made no reference to its past, to the days when it was Ibera, described by Livy as *urbem a propinquo flumine Iberam apellatam opulentissima regionis ejus,* the richest town of the Ebro region. The ally of Carthage, it was besieged for long in vain by the Scipios, and was not taken until Hasdrubal himself was beaten. It remained Ibera till, in the twelfth century, Count Ramón Berenguer III built a castle there as a base fortress from which to attack the still Moorish Tortosa up the river. Amposta remained one of the strongest towns of Catalonia; so far as appears, it still is.

Crossing its bridge, I went on by a very bad road to Santa Barbara, turned north up the Ebro, re-crossed it at Roquetas, and so into Tortosa, by a peculiarly vile pot-holed approach. What ails a city of Tortosa's standing and prosperity that it should leave its main approaches in such a condition of pits and crevasses as almost to upset a car that tackles them; the condition, no doubt in which they were found by the Scipios, who presumably repaired them? Kept in good order for six and a half centuries, they must have lapsed badly under the activities of Euric the Goth and his successors; nor is there reason to suppose that they were greatly improved by the Walis who ruled in Tortosa after 713 or so. Any slight finish their surface may have acquired under these Arabs must have been completely ruined by the repeated onslaughts of Charlemagne and his Franks, who coveted Tortosa so much, after they had taken Barcelona from the infidels, that a Frankish army arrived four times to besiege it in vain, battering its walls for weeks with every kind of engine, but each time driven ignominiously away by the determined Arabs of the Ebro, who kept Tortosa for three centuries more. When, in 1148, the impregnable stronghold was at last captured after a six months' siege by Ramón Berenguer V and an army of Genoese, Pisan, and Knights Templar allies, the roads all round it were, no doubt, reduced to the abominable state in which, just eight centuries later, I found them. It cannot be thought that they were improved during these eight centuries by the repeated and violent exploits on them of French invaders, Carlists, and quarrelling Spaniards, who have all had a go at Tortosa several times. But it is, of course, much the same with the approaches to other Spanish cities; after all, few of them have not, at one time or another, suffered siege, and some of them many times. Anyhow, and for whatever reasons, when the tree-planted avenue that heralds a town begins, the road disintegrates into pits that shake car springs to bits, ruin tyres, and jerk off essential portions of the fabric. Are the roads left thus because there is so little motoring in Spain, or is it the other way round? (I hasten to add that the main roads all about the country, apart from these town approaches, are admirable.)

Tortosa, when you get there, is worth many jolts. It is a very beautiful walled old city; its cathedral fourteenth-century French-Catalan Gothic, with baroque façade. It was built on the site of the twelfth-century church put up by the liberators, which had itself been on the site of the tenth-century mosque.

The guidebooks have always complained about the overloaded classical-baroque façade, out of harmony with the castle-like Gothic structure and the interior; 'the demon of churriguerismo,' says Murray, 'has been at work.' I liked it. After all, why should a façade be in harmony with the interior? One does not see them both at once; and the effect of these baroque portals so often added in Spain to Gothic and Romanesque buildings is often delightful in itself, besides suggesting the live and continuous development of architecture. The Tortosa façade has beauty, dignity and grace, and goes piquantly with the flying buttresses and russet-tiled roofs of the battlemented building. But the best thing about the cathedral is its cloister, with its lovely lancet arches and its richly carved capitals. I inspected these, stalked silently and at a distance by a mob of boys who had spied a stranger, and, in the usual Spanish way, deserted all other pursuits and enjoyments in order to track her. Spanish children will eagerly pursue this entrancing sport all day; it takes precedence over any games with which they might otherwise be busy; they are not great games players, and foreigners are to them big game, to be stalked with immense excitement and unwearied pertinacity. Followed, then, by these hunters lurking behind pillars and fleeing if I looked round, I examined the charming and various capitals, carved with donkeys drawing castles, knights chain-mailed to the teeth, supporting tabernacles, and other agreeable and improbable scenes. Round the cloister walls are set mural tables, effigies and reliefs, alabaster houses and knights, some mediæval, some seventeenth century. The flowered and cedared garden has a carved well. After these exquisite cloisters, the interior of the cathedral seems uninteresting, in spite of some rich carving, some fine coloured marbles in the chapel of the miracle-working Holy Girdle, the tombs of four early bishops, and the portal leading to the cloister.

Coming out, and still tracked by my stalkers, who grew in number as we processed along the mediæval streets (were these young tortosinos partly descended from those Genoese soldiers to whom Ramón Berenguer presented a third of the liberated city?), I saw the Bishop's Palace and the Lonja (both fourteenth century), and the Colegio, mostly Renaissance of the sixteenth, with a classical patio and cloisters.

I left Tortosa by the left-bank road this time, crossing the Ebro again at Amposta and running down to the great Puerto de los Alfaques at the little fishing village of San Carlos de la Rápita, down a dusty, broken lane from the road. It was getting dark, and I had meant to sleep in this little port. Had Charles III, from whom it was named, finished his plan of building in the village of Rápita (where there were in 1770 only a church, a convent and a few fishermen's houses) an important mercantile port, there would, presumably, have been some kind of inn for me to sleep at. But Charles died too soon, and San Carlos was never proceeded with; it stayed a sandy village and beach, with no road, a group of fishermen's houses, a crowd of shouting children, some large unfinished buildings, and its new grandiose name. There was, they told me, no inn in the village; I was sent on to the neighbouring tiny hamlet of Las Casas (perhaps some of the houses that Charles III had built for his new port). Here I arrived, in the almost dark, on to a fishing beach full of boats and innumerable children, who ran to surround me and my car. The little inn was full; they took me to a near house, where a very amiable old woman showed me a bed in an alcove behind a reed curtain; there was no light, no window and no water (either running or stationary); but they let me wash in the kitchen sink; the bed was comfortable and, like nearly all the beds I slept in in Spain, immaculately clean. I supped at the inn, and conversed with its kind and charming host, hostess and pretty daughter, and with a pleasant guest who was staying there for fishing and spoke English. My car was stabled in a huge barn, among bleating sheep, poultry, waggons and hay. No one thought of wanting my passport or triptica. The village was gay and decorated for a fiesta next day, and no one of any age can have gone to bed before midnight. I had mislaid my suit-case keys; the fishing guest and the landlord's son removed the padlock for me with great efficiency and helpfulness. There is an obliging kindness and courtesy about the Spanish, when they see occasion for it, that exceeds, I think, any other.

I got up early next morning, and bathed from a steeply shelving beach in a smooth and tepid sea, among fishermen, nets, boats, and a crowd of donkeys, poultry and children that made the beach look like a market-day fair. I got a wonderful view of the half-circle of the great harbour of Alfaques, and of the Punta del Calacho that swept round it from north to south guarding it from winds and waves. After coffee at the inn, I went to the barn and groomed and watered the car, helped by a large family of niños and niñas, who brought me a great pot of water, flicked the pall of white dust from car and windows with my feather broom, (after a day on the roads the car was always shrouded like a ghost so that children wrote their names on it with their fingers) and climbed about the inside to examine all they saw. I drove off finally with a cargo of them, eager to show me the way up to the main road. The village was gay for the fiesta with flags, coloured paper and bells. I dropped my guides beyond it, and drove away along the dusty road through olives and small vines. At a fork near Alcanar I turned off up a road that climbed over the Sierra de Montsiá, to see Ulldecona, which is the last town of Catalonia, and has a church with an octagonal tower and a cluster of russet-tiled roofs grouped round it, a sculptured door, gargoyles, a carved drinking-trough in the wall. All these towns are lovely and graceful with their painted houses, tiled ornaments, green blinds, narrow streets, and balconies piled high with golden cucumbers. Rather ambitiously, considering how many miles it is from the sea and that it possesses neither watch-tower nor harbour, Ulldecona has in the past been one of the several improbable claimants for the position of the old Greek Hemeroskopeion.

The last town of Catalonia. The 'ancient green kingdom of Valencia' is just across the dry rambla of the Cenia, and already the towns (Ulldecona for example) wear a Valencian look, the landscape a Valencian air. So farewell to Catalonia, till I pass this way again.

## CHAPTER TWO

## VALENCIAN SHORE

ONE enters the kingdom of Valencia with thoughts of oranges, *huertas* of fruit and grain, animated and dancing Valencians in gay costumes. But Valencia is much better than this boring paradise for tourists. One had not known—that is, I had not known—about the blue-tiled church domes and graceful towers, the wealth of baroque, the azulejos, the lovely towns, the great pine-forested sierras, unspoiled by cultivation and *huertas*. Nor had I realized that 'Valenciano' was a dialect of Catalan, introduced by Jaime I when he won Valencia, and that the Valencians were no easier to understand, except when they condescended to Castilian, than the Catalonians; this was disappointing. Nor had I known how deep and how pervasive was the Moorish strain. Unlike Catalonia, Valencia was in Moorish hands (except for a few years at the end of the eleventh century) from 712 to 1238, and at the reconquest was a land of Saracens and Mozarabes, who were not expelled until 1610, by the foolish Philip III. To-day many of them have the dark, classic beauty so often the outcome of the happy fusion of Moor, Iberian and Roman, and growing commoner as one travels south down the coast. It is difficult to compare the different parts of this glorious coast; but on the whole I found more charm in the kingdom of Valencia than in any of the other ancient divisions. One feels, as the Moors felt, that *cœlum hic cecidisse putes*. Everywhere are Moorish towns and villages, place-names, mosques, minarets, irrigation channels and water-mills. The language has Arab words, much of the music and song is African by descent; the ancient civilization, that, together with its climate, fertility and propinquity, so excited the cupidity of the Christian reconquerors of Catalonia and Aragon that they could not rest until they won it, still lingers in those towns and in those lovely gardened shores.

> No part of the Peninsula [says a Spanish chronicler] has been so coveted as Valencia; the frequent passage of foreign conquerors, destroying one after another the footprints already there, has destroyed successively the works of past generations. The Carthaginian destroyed Iberian relics, the Roman completed the destruction, raising in their place other impressive monuments, which the Goths transformed, the Arabs demolished, and the Christian conquerors replaced in part with works of another character, under the double inspiration of religion and of feudalism.

But nothing could replace the Arab learning and arts that flourished in the Valencian towns during the pre-conquest centuries.

Valencian cities and small towns have often a peculiar loveliness. The first you come to from Catalonia is Vinaroz, at the mouth of the river Carbol. It is a delicious town, full of elegant houses and palacios, with gardens, *azoteas* and *miradores*; there are pretty plazas, and at least one street is bordered with barrel palms set in beds tiled with blue azulejos— a lovely Valencian conceit, like the dark blue lustre-tiled church domes that gleam all about the province. The church, standing in a small plaza, has great walls like a castle and a baroque west façade, ochre-coloured, richly decorated with emblems and adornments, with four twisted salamonic black columns beside the high portal; the effect is very beautiful; it was designed between 1698 and 1702 by two Valencians, one of whom designed also the tower of Santa Catalina in Valencia. The church was begun in 1596; the interior, broadnaved, with a balustrade of gilded iron running above it, was constructed through the seventeenth century; there is a charming chapel of the Sacrament, built in 1658. The church is full of altars. When I went into it, a high mass was being sung, for some festival; the chanting and music surged above the quiet sea. I came out into a sunlit plaza; against a wall stood a small donkey with panniers full of melons; on its back a tiny boy sat, munching. All that my guidebook had to say of this delightful town was that its bay was noted for sturgeons and lampreys, that the Duc de Vendôme died there in 1742 from a surfeit of the local fish and that his body was taken to the Escorial. As if it mattered what he died of, or where his body was taken.

Two or three miles down the coast is Benicarló, an attractive, still partly walled little town (it used to have four gates) whose Arab origin is shown by its name. Its church (San Bartolomé) is baroque of 1724-43; it has a fine façade, rather like Vinaroz, with the same type of twisted columns, but not black; the image of the patron saint is in the middle. The tall, beautiful octagonal bell tower is detached; the cupolas are tiled, one in purple lustre, the others in russet. Like Vinaroz, Benicarló was assaulted by the Carlists of 1837; both towns were then strongly walled. A century later, Dr. Manuel Azaña here composed his melancholy philosophic conversation about a later civil war. Down by the sea there is a government-run parador, with a large tiled swimming-pool in the garden. I spent an afternoon and a night at this delightful inn; one eats on the circular terrace and bathes in the pool, where the sea flows in and out perpetually through pipes, lapping limpidly against green tiles warm in the burning sun. From behind the hotel a little coast road runs to Peñiscola, that tremendous castle poised on its high rock that juts out to sea at the end of a narrow stalk of causeway. On each side of the isthmus a little fishing harbour lies sheltered, green beneath the shadow of the great pile of walled rock that climbs steeply up, by winding, narrow alleys, to the two ancient churches and the citadel at the top. Whoever first built this fort (considered *casi inexpugnable*) it has many times suffered siege. The Moors held it for some time against Jaime the Conquistador, but surrendered it in 1233, on condition that its inhabitants might live according to their own laws and religion; I dare say they still do. Jaime gave Peñiscola to the Templars, it passed to the

Knights of St. John, then to another Order, whose master presented it to the Avignon anti-pope, Benedict XIII, Papa Luna, when in 1415 he retreated there with his little suite of cardinals and other prelates, to keep his remote seat in the castle for the last eight years of his earthly life. At the end of these, legend tells us, he did not die, but vanished mysteriously into the sea, where he still resides, blowing up foam, like a spouting whale, through a hole in the rocks called *el bufador de Papa Luna*. Peñiscola can have changed but little since his sojourn. He too saw from his castle those steep climbing streets and tall blue houses that almost meet across them, their balconies growing shrubs and aloes and bright flowers, and piled with ripening melons and hung with washing. He too paced those high ramparts, and stared across the Mediterranean towards Rome, surrounded by his bored, Rome-sick, Avignon-sick cardinals, while he caused a stretch of wall to be added to the ramparts, and a little triangular fort at the end, the Torreta de Papa Luna, which was knocked about nearly four centuries later by the French. Besides adding to the fortifications, he composed and declaimed angry bulls, that should cause the future to change, the Council of Constance to reverse its declaration of schism and summon him from his so tedious way of life. Did the young Moors of Peñiscola stare and jeer and throw stones from the ramparts as the fallen anti-pope and his cardinals swept in and out of the ancient church, or up and down those steep streets to the little beach and back (but not to bathe, for they condemned that as an infidel and unchristian practice)? Did poor Papa Luna look a proud pope, or merely a lonely, weary, schismatic, disgruntled elderly man? And what was the attitude towards him of the Peñiscola parish priest? The position was delicate. Presumably he had to read the bulls aloud in church. One would have liked to visit Peñiscola during those years; and also, and still more, sixteen centuries or so earlier, to have seen Hamilcar arriving in it with elephants and munitions, the elephants pacing heavily over the narrow causeway and up the steep streets, cheered and pelted by the residents from the ramparts and balconies.

Tyrian, pre-Carthaginian origin is claimed for this place; how old are the various towers and batteries I do not know, nor the age of the present houses; there was much destruction by the French during the War of Independence, which damaged also the ancient *parroquial*; this church is half mediæval, half eighteenth century. An extraordinary town; it must be unique.

The road from Benicarló south runs between two hill ranges, back from the sea. Its beauty lies rather in its towns than in its landscape—the lovely sequence of small Valencian towns, so different in style from the small mediæval Catalan towns, and from those, so white and African, further south. Grace and elegance is the note. Not that Africa is not already here; all the way there are minaret-like, lustre-tiled deep blue church domes gleaming among palms, with russet-tiled buff and brown houses clustering about them. And in the fields stand the white, pointed-roofed, thatched Valencian barraccas among the orange groves, rice and grain fields, carobs, donkey-wells and channels of running water that the African cultivators left as a heritage.

Alcalá de Chisvert, fourteen miles from Benicarló, is a most elegant town, with its group of buildings round its plaza, its ochre and blue houses with balconies and tiled roofs, and behind them the high late eighteenth-century octagonal belfry of the baroque church, balustraded and spired, with tiers of arcaded windows; the cupolas have the glossy slate-blue lustre tiles. These tiles (usually early nineteenth century) may not be everyone's taste, and I prefer myself the much older, often mediæval, russet type; but they add a distinctive note to Valencian and Andalucian churches, and have great charm; they go very well with palms.

Was it Oropesa or Benicasím that had a baroque church with two ochre towers, one dated 1736, the other 1783–1805? The town was in fiesta, and the children danced in the plaza.

I think it was Benicasím; Oropesa, I read, a town of great antiquity, was named Tenebrio by Ptolemy, and even Ptolemy, with his peculiar views on the universe, must have perceived that such a name was unsuitable to the town that I saw dancing in the sunshine on that August morning. Near Benicasím a path turned off the road up a steep hill to the monastery of the Desierto de las Palmas, that stands nearly three thousand feet up in the mountains. I wanted to see it; its mountain surround was said to be extremely strange and convulsed, and in a state of permanent disintegration and collapse, so that the huge convent walls are most precariously poised. There had lived there bare-foot Carmelite friars, celebrated for their great virtues and the rigour of their observances, among which was walking bare-foot about the rugged boulders that surrounded their convent. They were such excellent friars that, in 1835, the municipality of Castellón de la Plana begged that they might not be secularized, and they were allowed to remain, provided that they renounced their habit and dressed as secular priests. My out-of-date guidebook maintained that they were still there, providing simple but clean quarters and food for visitors (donation expected; ladies accommodated in separate wing). But I never saw them, nor the magnificent view of the Mediterranean which was thrown in. That donkey of which the guidebooks are so full would get there, it seems, in one and a half to two hours; you apply to the station master at Benicasím for this animal. I felt no confidence that the station master would have a donkey for me; so attracted by the monastery in its palmy desert, the separate ladies' wing, and the Mediterranean view, I tackled the path in my car, and got about a mile up it before it disintegrated into an impossible track; then, lacking both energy to walk it (it was very hot) and space to turn the car, I backed and zigzagged precariously down to the road again, leaving the convent lying in its mountain desert of palms for ever (I fear) unseen. But I was too greatly relieved at having slid down the mountain intact to grieve much over this.

Next time I shall inquire for the donkey of the station master.

The road ran on through fertile fruit groves to Castellón de la Plana. Castellón is the capital of a province, makes azulejos, and exports oranges. What else it does, I am not sure. It does not wear an interesting look, and I dare say it looked better on the mountain a mile and a half away where it stood once, until Jaime the Conqueror, having taken it from the Moors, and thinking it would get on better down in the *huerta* among the vegetation than up on the barren mountain-top, translated it in 1251. Its Gothic church, which had two pictures by Ribalta, was admired; I missed it by just eleven years, as it was destroyed in 1936 by those who did not care for churches; I did not discover whether the Ribaltas were destroyed too. Nor whether the ruins of the ancient Castellón are still to be seen on their mountain, as they were some years ago. I lunched at Castellón, in a broad open plaza, and took the road without exploring further.

The country was now one great orange garden. In the orange season it must be delicious, with the golden fruit shining among the dark glossy leaves. The next town, Villar-real, royal town, built by Jaime for his children, was burnt and half destroyed in the War of Succession at the beginning of the eighteenth century, so was rebuilt in baroque, and has a very pleasant look, standing at cross-roads close to the large river Mijares, which waters the orange groves for miles about it. The town has grape-coloured domes among palms, attractive houses, pleasant plazas and fountain troughs; the church has a fine octagonal tower. I should like to visit this country, 'la fertil vega de Burriana,' during the orange harvest, to see the gathering and the loading of the great baskets on to the ox carts that take them into the market towns and down to the shipping port of Burriana. Oranges, even in high summer, are piled on every market stall in the towns, and in the panniers of the small donkeys that smaller boys ride about streets and roads; one can eat as many as one has a mind for, thanking the Moors for their intelligent irrigation. Moorish engineering, Moorish castles, Moorish-looking minarets and domes, Moorish faces and songs, memories of Moorish battles against the armies of Jaime the Conqueror, who fought them all down this coast and hinterland and finally beat them and took their kingdom, but still they stayed on the land, and their Moorish-Iberian descendants now darkly and beautifully ride their donkeys about the roads, and walk gracefully from the water troughs with their tall Moorish pitchers on their heads.

There are Roman memories down this road, too—ruins of temples, aqueducts and arches. We are nearing Sagunto; the road, as usual, disintegrates into pot-holes and pits. A bend brings into view Sagunto, that splendid, breath-taking, castled Roman-Iberian-Moorish pile of walls and houses on its steep rocky hill above the river Palencia, now two miles back from the sea, once a port. Muri veteres, Murviedro, old walls; it was aptly so named after Rome's decline abandoned it to ruin. The walls are original Iberian; Sagunto, through all changes, has remained, and appears now, an Iberian city, beneath its Roman ruins, its relics of the Moorish centuries, and its mediæval superstructure. It was the Iberians who held the citadel against the fierce nine months' assault of the Carthaginians, and rather than surrender, immolated themselves, with their families and goods, in flames (but, as Herodotus kept remarking, I do not myself wholly credit this legend); it was the Romans who failed to come to their help until too late. The well-known story now raises bitter modern echoes: Rome allying herself with the independent city of Saguntum, guaranteeing her against attack by the common foe, the Carthaginian aggressor, in order to stay the aggressor's course; Carthage, not to be stayed, attacking this key to Roman Spain; the Saguntines trusting in the arrival of succour from their great ally, holding on desperately while that succour failed to come—*dum Romæ consultitur, Saguntum expugnatur*—and finally battered to pieces and taken by storm. Rome, too late to save Saguntum, accepted the aggressor's challenge to their dominion in Europe, and thus began the second Punic War; which, as we know, they won, and Carthage in Spain fell for always.

The young Saguntines of to-day, darkly peering at strangers, stalking them through the streets in mobs, have perhaps a hereditary xenophobia; in the depths of ancestral memory lurk those hated invaders, the Carthaginians. Some years ago, I was told, a French diplomat and his wife who were visiting Sagunto were mobbed and mocked, until the French gentleman, losing patience, turned on one of the young natives and cuffed him; an unfortunate incident, for the boy fell and cut his head open on a stone. This may account for the way the barbarian children ducked and scuttled when I turned round. '*Muy mal educados*,' said a disapproving woman watching from her doorway; it was she who told me of the incident of the French diplomat. 'But what,' she added, 'can one expect in times like these? It is the new Spain.' But it is the Spain that is older than Moors or Goths or Romans, as ancient as its own mountains. Did the Romans, when they rebuilt and occupied the smashed city, ever civilize its tribes? Did they ever become *togati*, or did they remain the surly barbarian tribes referred to so often by Roman writers? Did they attend performances and declamations in the Roman theatre? More probably they only saw the games and races in the circus on the river bank below the town.

It would be pleasant to explore Sagunto alone with the ghosts of the past. But not even the young Saguntines can spoil Sagunto. The semi-circular theatre is stupendous. One reaches it by streets winding steeply up the hill crowned by the Moorish castillo, the hill where stood the ancient Iberian city. It is extraordinarily well preserved (though Suchet's for-ever-damned soldiers did their worst against it, as against all monuments of the past); the auditorium is one hundred and sixty-five feet across, the circling tiers of seats, hewn out of the rock, must have held nine hundred spectators. It is not so

fine a Roman theatre as those at Merida or Italica, but, lying
on that steep acropolis in the blazing Spanish sun, the heart
of the ancient Saguntum above the mediæval town, it is even
more dramatic in effect than these. From it one climbs a steep
winding lane up the rocky slope to the castle, and the jumble
of ancient walls and fragments, Iberian, Roman, Moorish, that
lie round it. The walls, towers and gates are mostly Moorish
and mediæval, with Roman or Iberian foundations; there are
remains of a Roman temple, sculptures, fragments, capitals,
inscriptions, tessellated pavement; an Arab cistern, a mediæval
mill. A fascinating jumble of ages; and from its rocky heights
a tremendous view, looking east over the Mediterranean,
north down the hill at whose base the mediæval town clusters,
and beyond it over the huerta to Castellón and the Desierto
de las Palmas, west to the pine-grown mountains among
which Porta Coeli lies, south down a sheer precipice of cactus-
grown rock, and beyond it across the plains to the faint
shimmer, eighteen miles away, of the domes of Valencia
city.

Coming down from the acropolis to the mediæval town, we
still find the jumble of ages, for Gothic churches are built out
of Moorish mosques, and adorned with Roman stones and inscriptions without and baroque and Renaissance decorations
within; Roman columns support the arcades in the plaza,
there are Moorish gates and remains of Iberian walls, a statue
of an Iberian guerrillero shot by the French in 1812, a plaza
near the railway station named after a modern novelist, and
the remains of a Roman circus lying in vegetable gardens by
the river. Ancient and modern civilizations, ancient and
modern savageries, always so closely intertwined in Spain.

The road to Valencia runs smoothly through a plain of
orange gardens and rice fields and other vegetable lands. It all
looks smiling and fruity and very well watered by trenches
and wells. The soil is red; the white houses are set in gardens
of palms, cypresses, oranges, lemons, olives, carobs and figs.
All pretty enough, but tamer, more docile, more utilitarian,

than most of Spain. An odd contrast to the wild cactus heights of Sagunto, precipitously rearing against the blue sky to the north. Yet on this smiling road too there are reminders of desperate battles; we pass El Puig, where Jaime I beat the Moors in 1237 and won the kingdom of Valencia, and down all this coast Christian and Saracen battled, while the huerta smiled greenly about them and the September sun ripened the grapes.

About the capital of this ancient kingdom, the opinions of visitors have always differed. The Romans, said Livy, founded it in 138 B.C., but it is impossible not to believe that, in such a fine and prosperous situation on sea and river, and in such fertile land, the Iberians had not built a city for themselves. Anyhow, under the Romans Valencia prospered greatly, was sacked by Pompey, revived again, prospered more, was occupied by Visigoths for three centuries, by Moors for five, except for a short interval of five years at the end of the eleventh century when it was seized by that enterprising, ferocious and perfidious mercenary, the Cid. Then the conquering James of Aragon annexed it from the Moors, and presently the Catholic Kings annexed it for Castile. Everyone, in short, coveted this city in turn. It must, before it was de-walled and badly modernized, have been one of the most beautiful cities in Spain. It is still full of beauties, but as a whole its effect is uncertain and confused, as if it hesitated between a lovely past and a smart cosmopolitan future. Many visitors have found it disappointing. Augustus Hare called it 'a very concentration of dullness, stagnation, and ugliness'; he was justly indignant at the 'warfare against antiquities' which had been hard at work (he was there in 1872) modernizing streets and houses, pulling down the grand mediæval city walls in order to give employment to the poor (indeed, the de-walling of Spanish cities in the nineteenth century was an æsthetic tragedy hard to forgive), and removing 'the most interesting historical fragment in the town,' the Albufat tower, with the cross placed there when the Cid took Valencia after his long siege, and the Puerta de Cid by which he entered the city. Hare was also bothered by the waterless condition of the bed of the Turia. He was right that Valencia would look much finer girt by its ancient walls and a fine flowing river, as it is shown in old engravings (but when did the river flow?), instead of by a dull boulevard and a dry rambla.

Gautier (in 1840, when the walls and the gate of the Cid still stood, but the Turia was equally dry) found the city flat, sprawling, confused in plan, without the advantage of standing on hilly ground. The tall houses had an aspect *'assez maussade'*; some had escutcheons, and damaged fragments of sculpture, and here and there he saw a Renaissance window in a modern wall, but Valencia on the whole wore to him an air *tout modern*. The cathedral had little to detain his attention; the other churches were decorated in strange taste; one could not but regret such waste of talent. He admired the Gothic Lonja, and the cloister garden of the Mercéd convent; for the rest, he was only interested in the population, the Moorish-looking men and the beautiful women; and what he really wanted was a *bateau à vapeur* to take him back to Paris and *la vie civilisée*.

Ford, five years later, got and gave quite another impression. Valencians he viewed with his usual disdainful suspicion.

They are perfidious, vindictive, sullen, fickle and treacherous. Theirs is a sort of *tigre singe* character, of cruelty allied with frivolity so blithe, so smooth, so gay, yet empty of all good; nor can their pleasantry be trusted; at the least rub they pass, like the laughing hyena, into a snarl and bite, and murder while they smile. . . . The Ponteiff Alexander VI and his children Lucrezia and Cæsar Borgia were Valencians. . . . The narrow streets of Valencia seem contrived for murder and intrigue, which once they were. . . . The physiognomy of the Valencians is African: they are dusky Moors, and have the peculiar look in their eyes of half cunning, half ferocity, of the Berbers. The burning sun not only tans their complexions but excites their nervous systems; hence they are highly irritable, imaginative, superstitious and mariolatrous.

After this indictment (one never knows how much of poor Ford's ill temper with foreigners was constitutional, how much due to some rudeness received and unduly resented) he advises us to walk round the walls and observe the eight gates with their towers (alas, only two remain) and calls the city 'very Moorish and closely packed,' with narrow, tortuous streets and lofty, gloomy houses; he describes the view from the Miguelete, of crowded flat roofs, blue and white tiled domes, a forest of spires. The cathedral he found unremarkable, and its principal door (baroque of 1760) abominable; he was always bothered by baroque and Churriguerresque, which he found fussy, vulgar and deplorable, and in Valencia his eyes were continually affronted by it ('in no place has churriguerresque done more mischief . . . A fondness for stucco ornament is another peculiarity of this unsubstantial city'). So he could only be happy there within limits; all the same, his account is excellent, learned and detailed, and more particularly of the paintings, both in galleries and churches.

Here he differs greatly from that sentimental and uninformed tourist, Hans Christian Andersen, who visited Valencia in 1864, and felt the heat as only Scandinavians do. He was there in mid-September, I in August, so I dare say I was hotter. When I was there, the Valencians were fanning themselves and remarking 'Mucho calor.' I too bought a fan: it was useful not only for fanning, but for shading one's eyes against the glare when, out of cowardice, one walked hatless. Hans Andersen was, like so many travellers of his period, tiresomely occupied with the appearance of the women, the costumes of the men, and the legends of the Cid, but finds time also to mention a few gardens and squares and to promenade by the river: of buildings he says nothing. But he was not architecturally minded (what most interested him in the beautiful city of Murcia was 'the gipsy tribes that are settled there').

It seemed to me, when I saw Valencia, that strangely little enthusiasm had been shown for it in recent years (except by

such baroque enthusiasts as Mr. Sacheverell Sitwell). It is not
a magnificent homogeneous shapely city like Tarragona,
whose beauty of structure hits you between the eyes; it has
not the shrieking zest and exuberance of Barcelona, the
Moorish exquisiteness of Seville, the white African strange-
ness of Algeciras and Tarifa, the grace of Lorca, the sherry-
coloured charm of Jerez, the maritime beauty of the ports,
the mediæval grandeur of the walled cities on their hills; it
is, with its ill-assorted medley of old and new, its often taste-
less modernization surrounding (and too often engulfing)
elegant seventeenth- and eighteenth-century houses, its
tendency to disintegrate into dusty squares that have the air
of building lots, an untidy town; as Gautier complained, confused and without plan. But, once one has made one's way
into the right parts, the unspoiled parts, one enters an in-
describable atmosphere of grace, of decayed and dusty
elegance, of an aristocracy once prosperous, rich, fashionable,
living behind those graceful façades, those *ajimez* windows
and escutcheoned doors, now declined into slippered languor,
the flirted fans laid by, dust gathering in saloons and patios,
the parties over but for echoes and dreams. Perhaps Valencians, inhabiting their great prosperous city, would find this
absurd; perhaps it is that all cities are rather like this in
August; but to me the streets and plazas and tall houses
(though too many of them are rebuilt), with their ironwork
balconies and green blinds, seemed of another age, and strayed
revellers from a ghostly past seemed to whisper about them.
An atmosphere wholly different from the featureless, cosmopolitan modernity of Madrid, or the devotional-cum-Arab
smartness of Seville, with its black-clad ladies in lace mantillas
(who seem always to be tripping to or from church) and its
air of being a show-place of the world. Valencia seems an
eighteenth-century gentleman, unpretentious, a little down at
heel, happy and at ease, though brooding a little wistfully
over his past.

I stayed in the only hotel that should be stayed at, because

it is in the Plaza Dos Aguas (once the Plaza Villarrasa), a
pretty little plaza with acacia trees and ochre houses, and the
hotel is next door to the Palacio del Marqués de Dos Aguas,
whose famous rococo portal, by Ignacio Vergera, is one of the
loveliest things in Valencia. For a charming description of
the exquisite and softly graded colours of this alabaster portal,
changing in different lights from tawny to silver, lilac to
maroon, green to pale russet, I commend Sacheverell Sitwell's
*Spanish Baroque*. For chilly unperceptiveness, see Ford's 'a
grotesque portal, a fricassée of palm trees, Indians, serpents
and absurd forms.' Why absurd? The sculptured luxuriance
of the twined and wreathed fruit, foliage and serpents, the
crouching Atlantean figures supporting the lintel, the benefi-
cent females offering fruit and fish to the mother and child
enshrined in a richly decorated recess above, is very exquisite
and agreeable. The mother and child, and the two little naked
*putti* clinging to her draperies, are all charming to look at;
the child has longish, curling hair, his mother a delightful
face, kind, a little amused, faintly ironic, beautiful; she is the
only madonna I should care to know, except Botticelli's, and
possibly the Sistine (who might, however, be a little heavy in
her calm and noble benignity). Most of them look dull, or
simpering, or merely null. The great portal is set in a lovely
façade with richly carved windows, stone-balconied and
elaborately shuttered. The stone balustrades have taken the
place of a long iron balcony that used to run unbroken across
the façade, concealing part of the carving. The whole effect is
so beautiful that one is tempted to sit outside the Hotel Inglés
and gaze at it for hours. The palace has for three years been
closed and empty, and no visitors are allowed to see the inside;
the owner, who came into possession by marriage, prefers to
live in Barcelona; I was told that negotiations were on foot to
buy it for the State, as a national monument. I dare say the
inside would be disappointing.

One would like to spend several days in Valencia looking at
its seventeenth- and eighteenth-century houses. Many have

been destroyed or rebuilt, and the Calle de Caballeros is not what it was; but there are still some noble houses, with fine colonnaded patios, *ajimez* windows and good iron balconies, which have so far escaped the alarming municipal lust for destruction, street widening and rebuilding. It is presumably because of its prosperity that Valencia has suffered, and is suffering, from this maniacal lust, a lust that ruined nearly all English cities long since. Most Spanish towns, fortunately, have not been able to indulge this whim; even Barcelona has added new districts without greatly destroying the old, though it unfortunately shared in the general de-walling passion that swept Spain like a plague last century. Granada is a bad case of modernization; the damage there is mostly already done, and it is now, on the whole, a modern town, in which the Arab glories blossom like a rich rose garden in a cabbage bed; it has not Valencia's precarious air (I hope illusory) of being about to be destroyed street by street, building by building. One sees ominous ladders against ancient walls; the Renaissance Audiencia, for instance, already restored, was, when I saw it, fraught with workmen.

Meanwhile, Valencia is still full of exquisite and exciting things. The Lonja, for instance, the late fifteenth-century silk exchange, with its Gothic door and windows, gargoyles, coats-of-arms held up by angels, crowned battlements and arcaded gallery, is perhaps the most beautiful building in the city. Inside is the great exchange hall, where tall spiral columns hold up a vaulted roof. The Lonja stands in the Plaza del Mercado, the great historic market square, once the stage for tournaments, festivals, tortures, executions, buryings alive, now mainly for market stalls; it is all a hum of a morning with buying and selling. There are miniature markets in the streets near it, where Valencian pottery ware is sold—azulejos, elegant blue and white and yellow china baskets piled high with clusters of china oranges, figs, apples, melons, grapes and slices of pomegranate—charming and delicious cheats. Near by are several delightful churches; one, Los Santos

Juanes, is opposite the Lonja—fourteenth-century Gothic with charming Churriguerresque façade in pale stone, and a cupola painted by Palomino. Among the rich baroque interior decoration stood life-size modern painted plaster figures of rosy-cheeked choir-boys in red cassocks, smiling sweetly and holding out plates for alms. Under elaborate canopies, gauze-veiled madonnas simper. The whole effect is of an entrancing puppetry. San Martín also is Gothic with baroque façade; inside there is a Ribalta entombment and a Goya portrait. San Andrés has a rich and lovely baroque door, with twisted pillars, shells, scrolls, and, above, a richly sculptured recess for the saint; all the colour of pale dust. San Andrés was built out of a mosque; it has some attractive azulejos and a Ribalta Pieta.

Baroque and azulejos and Ribaltas are to be seen all about Valencia, which had a happy craze for dressing up its old churches thus. A tour round all these agreeable minor churches with their rococo fanfare provides an education in seventeenth- and eighteenth-century Valencian painting. So, indeed, does the cathedral. The Gothic cathedral (on the site of a temple of Diana, a Christian basilica, and a mosque) was, like most other Valencian churches, done over in baroque when baroque came in: the west door, golden ochre in colour, with statues by Vergera, has that worldly, elaborate Neapolitan appearance which is so delightful to some, so repugnant to others, who deplore both its *décor* and its concave shape. The other doors remain Gothic and Romanesque; the Puerta del Palau is particularly rich and beautiful. The octagonal cimborio is very light and graceful. One can seldom get inside the cathedral, as it seems rarely open; but when one hits on one of these rare moments one finds oneself in a low, long, dusky space, among Corinthian marble columns, rich alabaster trascoro, a mass of baroque ornament, and rows of dark side chapels full of a wealth of paintings and sculpture —Ribalta, Goya, all the Valencian school. The high altar, badly damaged and plundered by the French, is restored and modernized; there are painted panels after Leonardo, but they were not on view.

The Miguelete tower was shut when I was there; I felt at the time that this was as well, as the day was extremely hot and there are two hundred and seven steps. The Cid made his wife and daughters ascend the Moorish tower which the Miguelete replaced, and showed them the wonderful view of the city and province which he had just conquered; I do not know if the weather was hot, but probably anyhow the ladies had to do as the Cid bade them. They were rewarded by the sight of Valencia with its domes and roofs, and the country stretching from Sagunto to Alicante, with the Mediterranean before it. I am sorry I missed this famous view. I returned next morning, hoping to climb the two hundred and seven steps before the heat of the day, but of course it was shut then too; perhaps in August it always is.

Having visited the chapel of Nuestra Señora de los Desamperados, and admired its egg-like shape, the Palomino frescoes on the vault, and the sumptuously jewelled image of Nuestra Señora (carved for a lunatic asylum in 1410, by order of anti-pope Luna) and having crossed the bridge to the eighteenth-century Archbishop's Palace, I went to look for the Musco Provincial, which had, of course, like all other Spanish museums, moved its position since the last guide-books were published, and is now (or was last summer) on the north bank of the river, across the Puente de la Trinidad, in what used to be the Colegio of Pius V. (But I do not know where it is now, or will be any other year.) It is a fine collection of pictures (the second best in Spain), largely of the Valencian school (many taken from the suppressed convents), including a number of charming primitives, and many Ribaltas and Espinosas and others; but there are also a Pinturicchio, an Andrea del Sarto, a Murillo, a number of Goyas and a Velasquez portrait of an unknown (or self-portrait). There is a good selection from the Italian schools, introduced by the Borgias into their native Valencia; one of them, Rodrigo

GERONA                    *Plate 1*

*Plate 2*                    TOSSA DE MAR

UNFINISHED CHURCH OF THE     *Plate 3*
SAGRADA FAMILIA, BARCELONA

ESCALERA DE SANTO DOMINGO, GERONA

*Plate 4*

*Plate 5*

SAGUNTO, CASTLE AND AMPHITHEATRE

Plate 6

MOJACAR

PALACIO DEL MARQUÉS DE DOS
AGUAS, VALENCIA

Plate 7

*Plate 8*

TOCADOR DE LA REINA, ALHAMBRA, GRANADA

Borgia, appears as donor in Pinturicchio's Virgin and Child. Besides paintings, there are some beautiful examples of Valencian retablos and reliefs, and some delightful marble sarcophagi, white and coloured, resting on little lions, with the figure of the corpse in relief outside.

Coming out of this museum, one finds oneself close to the Alameda, that famous tree-shaded promenade on the river's north bank, where fashionable Valencia walks of an afternoon, and which was the delight of nineteenth-century tourists. I thought it dull; these new northern boulevards only make one reflect sadly on how beautiful Valencia must have looked a century ago, lifting her spires and blue and white domes above her battlemented and gated walls. The spires, the domes, the hundred belfries, still rear against the sky, but the raw encircling boulevards rob them of half their effect.

Leaving the Alameda, I re-entered the city by the fourteenth-century Torres de Serranos, one of the only two old town gates left (the other is the Torres de Cuarte, in the southwest) and walked down the Calle de Roteros to Santa Cruz—very admirable with its galleried bell tower, its tiled dome, and its pillared, sainted, rectilinear classical-baroque façade against a severe wall. Then down to the Audiencia, to look again at the lovely Sala Dorada, with its ceiling panelled in coloured and gilded wood, and at the azulejos and paintings and Renaissance gallery of the Salón de las Cortes. The Audiencia is in the heart of eighteenth-century fashionable Valencia; from it one strolls down streets and plazas once full of seigniorial houses, escutcheoned and balconied, past churches all rebuilt in baroque (usually late seventeenth, sometimes eighteenth, century), San Bartolomé, prettily towered, San Nicolas, originally built on a mosque, San Miguel, twin-towered, with richly populated and pillared façade between the towers, Santa Catalina, one of the highest and most charming bell towers, hexagonal, with graceful gallery, twisted black and white columns, and domed, arcaded belvedere. The same architects designed the lovely church at Vinaroz. Rising up from the shadow of narrow streets, a small plaza, and high balconied houses, Santa Catalina has an exquisite lightness and grace. Crossing the Plaza de la Reina and down the Calle de la Paz, one comes to the Colegio del Patriarca, a Herrera-like Renaissance building into which female visitors may not trespass; and round the corner is the Plaza Dos Aguas again, with the marquis's palace door gleaming like oranges and lemons in the hot afternoon light.

Of walking about Valencia I think one would never tire (mentally, that is, for physically it is, in hot weather, exhausting). There are a thousand enchanting things to see in this gay, baroque, aristocratic city—façades, street corners, old houses, balconies, market stalls. Its people too are, on the whole, gay and handsome and charming. Its live oranges are delicious to eat, its pottery ones delicious to see. I came away with baskets of both kinds. I started about six in the evening, along a horrible jolting tram-lined road that ran north through dusty and dilapidated suburbs, for I wanted to visit the Cartuja of Porta Coeli, twenty-one miles north-west in the mountains. The horrid road ran through Betera, and later became a woodland track that wound through mountains with scarcely a habitation. I came at last to two cottages, and, about a kilometre on, standing just beyond a bridge, there was the Cartuja, a great blanched pile in the dusk, surrounded by a few disused monastic farm buildings—I suppose they had been granaries and the like—alone in the magnificent and sombre solitude of the pine-grown mountains. At its foot were walled fruit gardens, carefully cultivated. Porta Coeli, founded in 1272, the third in age of the twenty-one Cartujas of Spain and for centuries the most powerful monastery in the Valencia hinterland, was suppressed in 1835, and stood empty and abandoned for over a century; three years ago a few monks returned to it; these now carry on their Carthusian rule, and each morning their great bell rings for mass.

My guidebook said there was an inn here ('Hotel; good');

probably one of the adjacent farm buildings was so used before the monastery came to life again; there is no inn now for many miles. It was already dusk. The wind whispered and sighed among the pines; a distant storm, I thought, for faint lightning flashed far off. I drove back to the cottages; they told me that the nearest inn was at Serra, ten kilometres away along a cart track through the forest. They advised me to return to Betera and sleep there. But I did not want to leave Porta Coeli, so I drove the car off the road into a clearing by a pool, half a mile from the convent, and prepared to spend the night there. A young man with a horn slung from his shoulder and wearing a badge that proclaimed him a Guardia de las Montanas passed by, and stopped to speak to me; he said I had better not sleep in the forest, a storm was approaching. I told him I should be all right in the car. When he had gone I spread my lilo and rug under a huge pine and lay there; the dim vault of pine roofed over me like a groined apse in the strange moonlight, making a dark pattern against the pale sky; its great boughs swept about me in a wide circle, their dark plumes almost on the ground. The distant storm still flashed. All night the wind sang in the pines, frogs in the pool, mosquitoes round my bed. The air was warm, and smelt of pine. At about three the moon set, and I could no longer see the line of mountains against the sky, until, two hours later, a pale dawn began. An early donkey cart creaked by, with a great load of grass and a driver asleep on the top of it.

At half-past six I went to the Cartuja; its bell was ringing for some office. I could see it more clearly this morning, the clustering group of great pale walls and tiled roofs, with the church tower topping them, standing among the rocky, pine-green mountains. Some of the surrounding buildings were dilapidated. The walled gardens were full of orange and lemon trees, olives, vines, vegetables, and among them one palm. In the distance is a fifteenth-century aqueduct. The door of the church is rectangular, pillared eighteenth-century baroque; a statue of San Bruno, the Carthusian founder, stands above it. I pulled the bell of the Porteria; after a while the porter came; he was small and friendly, and said there would be a mass to which the public were admitted at eight. He took me into the church and cloisters; the church is frescoed and baroqued; it was once, it seems, a treasury of pictures and sculptures, but these have been mostly removed to the Valencia museum. The Romanesque cloisters round their garden are solid and plain. Everywhere there are azulejos, in gay, pretty colours; those in the entrance court have eighteenth-century gentlemen shooting deer; those in the church are less sporting, but attractive. The Chapel of the Counts has beautiful painted bosses; there are pictures all round the church. How many monks were in residence, I asked? 'Tan pocos,' the porter replied.

I stayed for mass; and the porter and his wife were the congregation; there were two priests at the altar, and they used, I believe, the Carthusian rite.

After mass I went back across the bridge, and took the vile cart track through the woods to Serra; it was not a road, but two deep ruts. After a mile or two it improved, and presently opened out into a lovely road, which climbed up to the steep mountain village of Serra. Here there was a pretty fonda, called Luisa, on whose terrace I had coffee, sitting among blue-tiled pillars beneath a vine trellis in front of an enormous mountain view. With my coffee I ate ripe black figs, which I had purchased in the road for two pesetas (sevenpence) a kilo. The woman of the fonda was charming, and lamented that she had no bread for me.

From Serra a newly made and beautiful road zigzagged through the mountains to join the Segorbe–Sagunto road at Torres-Torres (which has a Moorish castle and wall). From here I turned south-east towards the coast, passing through one charming old coloured town or village after another. At Gilet there was a Renaissance-looking stone washing fountain and tank in the plaza, with dolphins, and a pretty ochre

church. Everywhere the houses had gay, tiled patios and interiors, looking cool and charming; it is an azulejos country.
All down the road there were terraces of olives and almonds.
We are again in the garden of Spain; a term which cannot be
applied to the mountains, pines and rocks twenty kilometres
back of Valencia.

Joining the coast road, I turned south, through the fertile,
smiling country that I had been through before between
Sagunto and Valencia. This time I only skirted Valencia,
going past some crowded bathing playas, rather like Blackpool, and the Grao, the dull-looking commercial harbour.
The road south was excellently paved. It passed the curious
great lagoon of Albufera, almost enclosed from the sea by a
long narrow pine-grown arm, the Pinada de la Dehesa; the
huge blue water is full of wild fowl and reeds, and people
bathe and fish and boat about its islands and sandy beaches.
It is surrounded by a plain of rice and canes, orange groves,
maize, alfalfa, carobs and palms; the line of mountains is far
back.

We are now unmistakably in southern Spain. The people,
and the buildings, grow more Moorish. The little towns are
charming. To this coast the Phocæan Greeks came in the sixth
century B.C., before they founded Emporion in the Gulf of
Rosas beneath the Pyrenees. They formed their trading settlements, built their temples, scattered their money and their
vases, before Carthage and Rome took possession. This part
of Greek colonial history is still veiled; excavations and finds
have revealed a little of it, piece by piece; further excavations
will reveal more. We do not even know for certain where
Hemeroskopeion, the first Phocæan town in Spain, was. All
we know of this lovely olive-grown coast strip between Valencia and Alicante is that on it first the Phocæan then the
Massiliot Greeks traded and left their towns. There is even,
it may be fancied by the romantic, a Greek look about the
olive-gardened, vineyarded hills and the small dusty roads
that wind through them, in spite of the Saracen and Gothic

and Spanish castles on their summits, and the Saracen men and women and children riding their asses about them.

As so often, one was torn between a wish to travel by two roads, for the inland road went by Alcira, Jativa (family home of the Borgias), Alcóy and a number of other interesting hill towns. I was faithful, however, to the coast road, and was richly rewarded by its pale olive and vine landscape and its ancient towns—Cullera with its castle, in the deep mouth of the Jucar, Gandia, very lovely behind its walls, the river Serpis running by, with its rich sixteenth- and eighteenth-century palace of the Borgias, who were also dukes of Gandia, its fine fifteenth-century *iglesia colegial,* built in the time of the Borgia pope Calixtus III, its Escuelas Pias, once a Jesuit college, founded by St. Francis Borgia, when he was superior of the order. The whole effect of this fine, considerable town is very noble. From it a bumpy road runs down to its picturesque port and beach. A few miles further along this admirable road is Oliva, a pale, ancient, dusty little town of great grace; it too has its palace, and is full of olives, mulberries, muscatels and raisins. For we are now in the raisin country, of which Denia used to be the great exporting centre. We pass into the province of Alicante, and through Vergel, its first town, then Ondara, where we turn off the paved road and take the jolting dusty one that runs to Denia, four miles off by the sea.

Of all the lovely places down the Iberian seaboard, I believe Denia (the Roman Dianium) to be the most attractive, and the one in which I would most gladly spend my days. Was it Hemeroskopeion, the Greek Watch Tower, as Strabo said, and as tradition has usually accepted? Other places on this coast have been suggested for this rôle; the most recent and the likeliest is the tall rock of Ifach, round the other side of Cape Nao. In support of this theory, Professor Rhys Carpenter has mustered a fascinating and impressive weight of evidence. As he points out, there is near Denia no such great rock as is described by Strabo and others as being visible far off to sailors and a stronghold for pirates. Nor is there any trace of the lagoon or marsh described by Avienus in the fourth century as being on Hemeroskopeion's by then desolate site. Nor, it seems, are there any remains of the famed temple of Diana which tradition has assigned to Dianium, but only a temple of Venus. And no Greek potteries have been so far discovered among the Roman antiquities, though there have been some Greek coins. And Denia was never called Hemeroskopeion by contemporary writers; Pliny, Cicero and others call it Dianium (the Roman rendering of the Greek Artemision). Strabo identified the two; but Strabo was often inaccurate, and had never been in Spain. It has been suggested by the Spanish historian Dr. Bosch Gimpera that Hemeroskopeion was destroyed by the Carthaginians about 237 B.C., and that its inhabitants fled to Artemision, which caused Strabo to confuse the two places. If Dianium was not Hemeroskopeion, it was not founded by the Phocæan Greeks at the beginning of the sixth century, but by the Greeks from Massalia nearly a century later. It had been before that an Iberian town, Diniu. It became an important Roman port; possibly Sertorius used it, as Strabo says, for the headquarters of his rebel pirate fleet, while he sent messages to Mithradates of Pontus for armed help against Rome, and received from this king a galley of Roman deserters which sailed down the coast to raze the Spanish towns. Or possibly this rebel fleet sheltered under the rock of Ifach. Whether or not Sertorius operated from Dianium, it was a town and harbour of great Roman fame and importance, until ruined by the barbarian raids of the reign of Gallienus in the third century. But under the Moors, Denia became again immensely prosperous, rich and populated; it tenaciously held out against the Christian re-conquerors, till taken at last in a bloody street battle which ended in the houses of resisters being burnt down. But it remained prosperous under its new rulers, until the blow dealt it by the expulsion of the Moors and Moriscos in 1609.

From the walls of the ancient town the sea has receded; the

fishing port lies on the beach below it. The town lies at the foot of the little hill of San Nicolas, on the top of which first the Moor then the Aragon conqueror kept the castle that, now ruinous, dominates Denia to-day. From this vine-grown, rocky height one looks up the exquisite curve of coast to Valencia, and west to the mountain ranges that guard it; to the south-east, the Cape of San Antonio juts out and shuts the bay. To see down the coast to Alicante bay, one must climb Mongó, the mountain a mile south, Mons Arijum, described by Avienus, which some have said was Hemeroskopeion itself.

The little town is delightful, with its remains of old walls and ramparts, its sleepy Plaza Mayor with, along one side, the Casa Consistorial, along another the baroque, azulejo-domed church, built on to an old convent now ruined, with figs and brambles and golden flowers growing tall in the sun among the broken arches. Afternoon peace and solitude, broken only by the sleepy churring of crickets, lay warmly in those brambled, roofless cells and little cloisters. The church was shut; but the caretaker, who lived in ancient rooms over the convent, up two flights of stone stairs, let me in; it has charming azulejos. When I came out of it into the sun-steeped plaza, I saw a largish, rather decayed building in one corner, marked, in faded capitals, 'Wholesale Co-operative Society'. 'Yes,' said the caretaker, in answer to my comment, 'there were many English in Denia for business once, until the civil war ruined trade and they left. It was the raisin trade; many London firms had agents here. They are nearly all gone. A few French and Germans remain, but the English are gone. They had houses all round Denia; there were many at Las Rotas, and all up the coast.'

Were I connected with the raisin trade, I would return to Denia. The British Co-operative, which used to export raisins, now only keeps, I gathered, a few stores, and is in foreign hands. Standing there in the little sunny plaza, it strikes a strange British note; yet not strange really, in our ubiquitous merchant race.

It was very hot. I went down a shady road called the Plaza, which was set all along with market stalls, where I bought fruit. I saw the site of the supposed temple of Diana, really, it seems, of Venus, beneath the hill; there is also the remains of a mosque. I determined to pass the night in Denia, and went down to the harbour and playa to look for a marine inn. I was told that this was two kilometres along the beach; two friendly men were going there to spend the evening, and came in my car to show me the way, which was along a track through the sands, well marked by the wheels of the coach that plies twice a day between Denia and Ondara. The inn, Las Arenas, was tiny and blue, with a large verandah on the shore; it had fourteen rooms, but none for me. The proprietor, a very amiable and delightful man, said I could put my car in the little open vine-trellised patio by the inn, and sleep in one of the bathing huts that stand round it. I bathed very exquisitely, in a level, limpid, shot-silk sea, rather warmer than the air, beneath a red sunset sky and half a moon. Round the palm-fringed curve of beach lights began to twinkle out; behind and above them, the lights of Denia town, and in front of them those of the fishing boats putting out for the night's catch. The sea was shallow near the beach; to swim I had to go out some way, and all the smooth evening bay was spread round me.

After supper at the inn, which we ate on the verandah on the shore (the Señora cooks deliciously), I sat and talked with friendly Denia people, then spread my lilo on the patio beside my car and blew it up, a process which greatly interested the other visitors at the inn; summoning one another to look, they crowded round me with interested commentary until the thing was inflated; they then hoped I should pass a comfortable night and left me to it. Denia people have a most pleasant way of making strangers feel at home among them.

The night was beautiful. At half-past seven I got up and bathed, in a translucent morning sea. It was Sunday, and very hot. I spent the day exploring Denia and its neighbourhood, lunching on biscuits and fruit on the Cabo San Antonio, the Roman Promontorium Dianium, about five miles down the coast (view). Some people have said that Hemeroskopeion was on this cape. Close to it is Javea, a fascinating walled town on the river Jalón, surrounded by castled mountains, with a beautiful domed and tiled church. Some people have said that Hemeroskopeion was in the bay of Javea; perhaps it was. Others guess Javea to have been the Greek Alonæ. Whatever its past, one might stay a long time there; it is even more beautiful and picturesque than Denia, and the valleys and mountains behind it offer more beautiful walks. It is about a mile back from the sea, but has its modern marine town and bathing resort. The bay of Javea is magnificent, backed by steep mountains, and with islands and reefs offshore; one island is fifty feet out, and of some size. Among these islands, and in the cove of San Martín, the Algerian pirates used to shelter; it was against them that the castles were built on the capes and hills.

I returned to Denia, and bathed again; a little wind had got up, and made tiny waves; it was like a warm, rippling bath. Everyone at the inn was lying down for their siesta, either inside the inn or on the beach in the shade of tents; except for a few children. A little naked boy of three ran all the afternoon about the shore and terrace and patio, talking and shouting—as pretty as a Cupid off a ceiling. At about eight o'clock the coach came over the sands, full of people coming to spend Sunday evening at the inn. They all danced in the patio, three men playing a flageolet, a guitar and a drum, the most charming music and tunes, none of our vulgar swing and jazz dance music. It was a lovely sight and sound, those dancing Valencians, men, women and children, footing it in the lit, trellised court above the glimmering sands and darkening sea. A regular Sunday amusement, the landlord told me. There were a great many small children with their parents; supper was not till after ten, so they made a night of it, as, indeed, the children of Spain always do. They were all dancing. I watched two pretty little girls of nine or ten dancing gravely together, round and round the patio; a little boy, quite alone, was dancing on the sands; toddlers danced on the tables, together or alone; they needed no encouragement from their elders; dancing is in their blood, and their little feet and bodies moved in time to the music as if they would never tire. At any time between ten and eleven the children, however tiny, sat down with their parents to a large dinner, tucking into it with the business-like zest with which they had danced. 'Isn't he tired? Doesn't he want to sleep?' I asked a mother with a two-year-old on her knee, as we watched the dancing. 'Oh, no,' she replied, surprised. 'He doesn't sleep till *much* later.' It was explained to me that, in Spain, parents liked to have their children with them in their amusements; in England, we agreed, it was perhaps different, and children led a separate life, going to bed early, eating different food, and so on. Spanish children seem to thrive and to enjoy themselves on their large and late adult meals, and so do English children, in spite of the unwholesome draughts of milk which they are made to imbibe in the middle of the morning (which lay the foundation of the exclusively British adult practice of thinking they need a meal between breakfast and lunch; perhaps also of British drunkenness). Spanish children are not over-fed; Spaniards seldom are this, and at present many of them are pretty hungry; but they get the meals their parents get, and enjoy the same nocturnal revels. In any town or village you may see them playing in the streets at midnight—or rather, you may see the little boys, for little Spanish girls in cities seem to lead rather immured lives, in the old Arab tradition.

But to-night, on the sands of Denia, niños and niñas alike shared in the revels of their elders. The Valencians, like the Catalans, are a very gay race. Where, indeed, are the grave and reserved Spaniards of whom one has always heard? I suppose in Castile; perhaps in Aragon, Estremadura, Navarre, Leon. Certainly not down the Ora Maritima of the south-east.

Another thing about the Spanish—they never seem to get drunk. The only intoxicated people I saw in Spain were one or two Britons. Drunkenness and gluttony are, of course, traditional old British vices; both Saxons and Celts have always hugely drunk and hugely eaten. Possibly in the more Celtic parts of Spain they get more drunk; it is certain that the invading Goths, Visigoths and Franks did so; on the other hand the Iberians are not natural drunkards, nor, of course, are the Moors who left their stamp so deeply printed down the Iberian Ora Maritima (though it must be added that these Saracen teetotallers seem to have been early and zealous converts to the cultivation of the vineyards, which they greatly and scientifically improved). Nor, in spite of the luxurious Romans who drank themselves under their supper tables, is drunkenness a Latin, as it is a Nordic, vice. Anyhow, I never saw a Spaniard drunk.

Next morning I drove into Denia at eight o'clock, taking Señor Pepe, my charming host; he took me to the garage of a man I had met at the dancing last night, a very friendly man, who had offered to show me some of the places round Denia. There I got the car oiled and greased, while I shopped in the plaza market for postcards and cheese and fruit and a tin of butter, the first butter I had seen on sale in Spain. At the garage they also opened my locked suitcase and made me a new key, for I had last night lost my purse with keys and money. Probably it had been picked up when I left it on the bar counter by one of the visitors who had come in on the bus; not, I felt sure, by a native of Denia. They do not steal much in Spain; far less than we now do in Britain; I was only robbed twice during the whole time I was there; though children scrambled all over my car, peering through the windows and examining everything with goggle-eyed interest, they never took anything. One does not have the feeling that one now has in England that it is not safe to leave any possessions unlocked for a moment.

My garage friend came out with me, and we drove along

the rugged coast track to Las Rotas, a pretty little cove and jut of rocks at the other end of Denia bay, where green water lapped among rocks, and where the hill-sides above the sea were dotted with white villas and chalets; many of these had belonged to English raisin merchants, I was told, until the civil war had spoilt the raisin trade. Now there were no English, only a few Germans and French. We drank iced coffee on a little terrace above the rocks. My companion had fought against Franco, and had spent some time in prison. He said that most Spaniards wanted Franco to go; he himself (polite man) would prefer a democracy on the English plan. He was a great reader of English books and admired English films— Shaw, Daphne du Maurier, Laurence Olivier, etc. He took me to the English cemetery, a white-walled cypress garden above the sea, a century old, where raisin merchants and English sailors lie; the merchants have monuments and inscriptions, the sailors sleep nameless, beneath piles of stones. We were admitted to the cemetery by a hospitable Anglo-Spanish brother and sister who owned a delightful finca in the hills and grew vines; their father, now in the cemetery, had been English, but a silent man, so that they had, they said, picked up little of their paternal tongue from him, and they spoke always Spanish, their mother having been more loquacious. They were charming people, like everyone else in or near Denia.

We returned to Denia, my companion to his garage and I to drive about dusty lanes till I regained the main Alicante road at Ondara. It is a wonderful road, winding round the great Cabo de la Nao, four or five miles from the sea, through strange ash-pale country, very dry, with little vines and olives, and huge, odd-shaped rocks and mountains, through which the road sometimes tunnels; the rock tunnels made beautiful frames for the very blue glimpses of sea at their further end. Cape after cape jutted out, bay after bay curved in, round this great prow-shaped promontory. Then the road neared the sea, and on the left was the ancient town of Calpe, and that startling thousand-foot tower of sheer rock, the Point of Ifach, that stands out to sea like a huge pillar of Hercules, with the tiled brown town clustered under it. Calpe is on the site of a Roman town, and perhaps a Greek settlement. Mosaics and other Roman things have been found there. The present town looks mediæval, but must be largely later, for it was destroyed in some later century and rebuilt. It is a closely built, narrow-streeted, russet-coloured town, like many Alicante towns in its general look; it lies above the deep bay and beach, and close to a little river, and, shutting the bay on the east, stands the huge rock watch-tower that may have marked Hemero-skopeion, the first Greek settlement in Spain.

> On its slopes [says Professor Rhys Carpenter in *The Greeks in Spain*] there are traces of Cyclopean walls and great quantities of broken potsherds lying from two to six feet below the sur-face of the soil and belonging to Hellenistic, Iberian and late red-figure Attic ware (second to fifth centuries B.C.). Until the site has been excavated, this is all that can be said of Hemero-skopeion.

But he says some more of it, comparing the lie of the land below the rock with Avienus's description, finding the *languidum stagnum*, the stagnant marsh, in the heart of the site of the ancient town, as Avienus, writing long after the town's destruction, described it—'a town once populated; now the soil, emptied of inhabitants, is covered with the sleeping waters of a marsh.' Above all, the shape and size of the rock fit it for the watch-tower, Strabo's 'stronghold for pirates, visible from far to those who sail towards it,' as no other rock down this coast is fitted. A German archæological expedition in 1927 confirmed Rhys Carpenter's opinion that there had been a temple there, Greek or Roman.

It would be fascinating to stay at Ifach and pursue the matter further, with Rhys Carpenter's careful plans in hand. There is a delightful bathing bay; there is also *alpinismo*, for one can climb about the rock, and from its summit view the sea as far as the Balearics and Alicante. The rock-guarded water is smooth and sheltered, and has some good reefs. You may search the bay for the remains of ancient monuments, but probably in vain; still abounding in the late eighteenth century, they had mostly disappeared by the middle of the nineteenth. Ifach, like Denia, is a place to which I shall return.

This is a haunted shore: ghosts crowd each bay, each little town, each castled rock, whispering in the lap of waves and in the low rumour of the sea wind in the palms. I drove round Calpe bay; then, after driving through a mountain in a most surprising manner, I emerged at the turning off of the road that runs up the mountains to Alcoy. I should have liked to take it; but I lacked the time. I ran on instead down the coast, closely hugging the bay of Altea, where Scipio's fleet, having beaten Carthage in the Ebro's mouth and sailed south, landed and sacked the ancient Greek colony of Honosca, where now (perhaps) stands La Nucia on the Guadalest. Offshore, lying like a moored ship, is the Isla de Altea; the sea was so still that it scarcely foamed as it lapped the island's base. The little port of Altea, raised above the sea in an inlet, at the mouth of the clear stream of the Algar, is delightful and strange.

The Moorish air increases as we drive south towards Alicante. Palms fringe the beaches and white towns. Benidorm (the sixth-century B.C. Massiliot colony of Alonæ?), whose sandy bay is like a crescent moon, stands crowded very beautifully round its domed and tiled church on a rocky peninsula. The mountains, the Sierra Helada, come down close behind it, and have, it seems, in some past hour of excitement thrown off an island into the bay, the Islote de Benidorm. The land round Benidorm is barren and poor; in recompense, the sea is rich in fish. Benidorm is said to be an open door for smugglers. A few miles further is Villajoyosa, on the sea and on the river Sella, with Puigcampana towering behind it. It was probably a Greek colony; it contains a Roman sepulchral tower called the Torre de San José. It is a long town, built along the walled road above the sea; when I was there it was having its annual fiesta for the defeat of the Moors seven centuries ago. Painted scaffolding, with tiers of seats, adorned both sides of the main street, and Moors and Christians, turbaned or armoured, rode caparisoned horses or donkeys, wearing on their trappings the crescent or the cross. Both sects were very gay; it was interesting to see the handsome brown Moors of Villajoyosa making so merry over the defeat of their relations long ago. I was told that the same fiesta was celebrated at this time in Seville. Presently there would be a tournament, which the Christians would win; early next morning there would be a naval battle in the harbour, and the Christians would win that too. I should like to have stayed to see this, but wanted to get to Alicante, ten miles on, so I left Christians and infidels to fight it out, and drove on along the hot and shadeless road, where no tree offered (at noon) a patch of shadow in which to stop and cool my car and eat my lunch. Or rather, there was one patch, beneath a group of carob trees, but it was already occupied by a donkey cart, its driver stretched in siesta beside it.

The fertile *vega,* with its red-brown earth, green tasselled rice, canes, vines, orange groves, tomato vines, irrigation trenches intersecting them, became a narrow strip, surrounded by dry, torridly African country. The strip of luxuriant vegetation cut across the Cabo de las Huertas; it was sprinkled with white farms, country houses and fruitful gardens, with vineyards bearing the famous Alicante grapes. The road passed through picturesque towns—Muchamel, with Campello by the sea on the left, San Juan. A small road turned off seaward; according to my map, it led to Lucentum, or Tossal de Manises, the site of the supposed ancient town, destroyed or abandoned before Alicante was built. It was no road for a car; I went down it on foot, and came to the small acropolis over the sea where stand fragments of Iberian-Carthaginian and Iberian-Roman walls, Roman cisterns, and remains of buildings. They were excavated here last century, together with coins, mosaic fragments, washing vessels, fragments of columns, a broken Roman statue, an inscription indicating a temple. Many of these things were taken to the Alicante museum. Here, it has been thought, was the original Greek Massiliot Leuke Akra (one of Strabo's 'three small Massiliot cities' between the Sucro river and New Carthage), or, if there was no Greek city, anyhow the Iberian town, then the Carthaginian, then the Roman Lucentum, destroyed and abandoned before the Moors built Al-Lekant three kilometres west down the bay. But other archæologists have believed the Tossal ruins to have been but an outlying stronghold of Alicante, which stood always where it now stands, Iberian, Greek, Carthaginian, Roman, Visigothic, Moorish, and now Iberian again. The temple, the baths, the statue, they say, would naturally accompany such an outpost fort. More time, more digging, more research, may one day throw more light on Lucentum's history; or it may remain one of the many un-solved Spanish Mediterranean riddles.

I left it, and went on to the present Alicante, now in sight beneath its hill (once, it seems, shining white, now more pale dun colour) that towers, castle-crowned, above the wide bay. Curved whitely round its great ship-crowded harbour and beach, with the luxuriant fringe of palms along its waterfront, and its tiers of white, flat-roofed eastern houses climbing be-hind, Alicante is a handsome, luminous, oriental city and port. Under the palms winds a fine modern alameda, set all along with cafés and hotels. Behind the smart modern frontage is the older town, a maze of steep narrow streets climbing up towards the mediæval Castillo of Santa Barbara, said to be practically untakable. The French failed before it when they took most of the other Spanish Mediterranean ports (though they did blow it up, English garrison and all, in 1707). I did not even try to take it, it was so hot a day, and I believe a permit is needed. Nor did I attempt the assault of San Fernando, the other and later castle, on the hill to the north. Instead, I looked at the Colegiata of San Nicolas, a fine Herrera church with a good cloister, and Santa Maria, the fourteenth-century *parroquial,* built on a mosque, standing in a white plaza near the sea, with a most beautiful Churriguerresque portal, very richly carved, with twisted columns; the church has a charming balustrade and a deep blue dome, and an interior only open during services, so I did not see it; this excessive cageyness of Spanish churches is discouraging. I found the baroque Casa Consistorial in a plaza newly named 18 de Julio, after the Glorious Revolution. You will also find in Alicante, to atone for its having backed the wrong side, plazas, avenidas and streets named for José Antonio, Calva Sotelo, General Mola, and other revolutionary leaders. The house where José Antonio, the Founder of the Falange, used to reside has been consecrated into a chapel, which I did not visit, though it is listed as a *lugar historico.*

In the evening I went on down the coast to Santa Pola. This ancient little Roman port, lying under the arm of the cape of its name, is, in the summer season, a lively bathing place. On the harbour quay is a fish market, where a noisy fish auction proceeds. There are hotels, and the restaurant Miramar built out on stakes over the harbour water, so that while you eat, and drink Alicante wine, you can watch the ships at close quarters and smell the port mud. But for this drainy smell it would be a perfect eating place, jutting out over the smooth and shining sea full of fishing boats. The beach is not very good; you have to wade out some way before you can swim.

The people sitting in the loggia outside my inn told me next morning that Elche, which lies ten miles inland, was extremely hot; whenever they mentioned it they fanned themselves and puffed; I began to feel such apprehensions as must have disturbed Shadrach, Meshach and Abednego when they approached the seven times heated furnace. Like them, however, I did not flinch. It was a straight, flat road to Elche, at first through salt marshes (no doubt useful, but smelly), but

presently palms appeared, thickening as I approached Elche.
A miracle must have been wrought for me, as for the three
Children of Israel in the furnace, for I did not find Elche,
lying breathless in its baked plains, so much hotter than Santa
Pola by the sea.

Where the ancient Roman and Iberian Ilici precisely stood
no one seems to be certain; whether close to the present Elche
or down by the sea near Santa Pola; Iberian and Greco-
Iberian and Roman pottery and sculpture have been dug up
at both places; in fact, they abound all round Elche. It was
on the site called Ilici, just outside Elche, that they found the
famous Greek-Iberian bust of the fifth century B.C., the Lady
of Elche. I saw it later in the Prado, that richly caparisoned
head, that calm Greek face of half ironic, sensuous, intellec-
tual beauty, only slightly marred by one eye being smaller
than the other. It is for its bust, its Assumption mystery play,
its Iberian pottery, its palm forest, its African aspect, and its
frying-pan heat, that Elche is celebrated. The mystery play
would not occur for a day or two, the bust was in Madrid, the
heat, the African air and the palm forest were all about me.
The ancient Iberian pottery was in museums; Iberian pots of
to-day were sold in the streets. Elche is a fascinating town;
low, white, flat-roofed Arab houses crowd together like a box
of bricks, topped by blue-tiled domes, cleft by deep shadowed
trenches of streets; palms wave about them; the palm forest
stretches round, with its undergrowth of red pomegranates,
beneath a glare of hot sky. The town stands on both sides of
the dry, cactus-grown rambla of the Vinalapó; from the further
side one looks across at the strange, dusty, ash-coloured African
town, with its terraced roofs, a domed and palm-surrounded
town in a desert. I drove back into it across the old bridge,
and saw the seventeenth-century church of Santa Maria, with
its fine façade and portal, dome and tower, and the attractive
San Juan. Energetic visitors climb the tower and get a remarkable view of the palm forest, which must be very delightful, but hard work. Instead, I strolled about the charming

town, and sat in the tree-shaded Plaza Mercéd, which has a raised terrace set round with tiled benches and palm-tubs, and a fountain in the middle. A young gentleman wanted to conduct me on a tour of the palm forest, but I have seen plenty of palms in my life and declined, much as I love palms, and in spite of the famous and peculiar shapes, habits and sex lives of those in the Elche forest, where Augustus Hare wandered enchanted for three days in February, 1872, where countless tourists have nearly swooned in the ecstasy caused by beholding such a great number of date palms all together. I dare say I should have swooned too, had I entered the forest. But I wanted instead to see the Visigothic basilica foundations discovered on the small hill of Alcadia in 1905. When I got into my car to look at the map, I was mobbed by an interested crowd of all ages; pleasant, friendly people, who had not, it seemed, seen a woman driving a car before; and anyhow, as one of them amiably explained, 'We always stare at strangers; it is not to be discourteous, but because we are interested.' The puzzling thing is that all the inhabitants of Spanish towns seem to have so much time on their hands. They kindly told me how I should go to Ilici, and to the hill Alcadia, and showed the most animated and sympathetic interest in my journey and aims, though a little disappointed that I did not intend a date-palm tour.

There is not much of the basilica; only an oblong nave with an apse, paved with mosaic, and some nearly illegible inscriptions in Greek lettering. Both mosaic and building are thought to be fifth or sixth century A.D., and part of a Visigothic basilica of Byzantine type; it is one of the few examples of Visigothic architecture in Spain, though too fragmentary to throw much light on that obscure subject.

I had then to choose between returning to Santa Pola and taking the coast road to Cartagena, by the Albufera de Elche, Torrevieja and the Mar Menor, and going inland by Orihuela and Murcia. I chose the cities, and set out on the mountain-surrounded road to Orihuela. To the west the Sierra de

Crevillente, bare and gaunt, hazily indigo in its shadowed clefts, coppery on its high slopes, sawed the hot sky. By the road there were cactuses and vineyards and maize fields and pomegranates and figs; round the reed-thatched farms and villages palms grew. Each village had its little domed and minareted church. The landscape, the buildings, the climate, seemed of Africa: so did the dark, turbaned people riding their asses along the dusty road. Dust lay thickly on the vines and olives and cactuses by the wayside; it formed a grey film on my car, drifting in through windows and doors. To follow in the wake of another vehicle—usually an ox or donkey cart, for motor traffic was rare—was to move in a pillar of dust. After some fifteen miles the little African town of Callosa de Segura lay at the foot of castle-crowned mountains, in a kind of gorge; it had houses built into the rocks, and a Charles V church, with cupola and belfry. The gorge opened out into a fertile valley, a great garden of corn, fig-trees, oranges and pomegranates, mulberries and vines; palms waved about them, and prickly pears and aloes scrambled over the rocks by the roadside and grew in tall thickets about the steep-roofed, reed-thatched cottages. Tall palms bordered the roads, lovely against the clear mountains. This was the Orihuela *huerta*, watered by the Segura; out of this luxuriant garden rises, backed by mountains, the ancient city of Orihuela, the Roman Aurariola, the Moorish Auriwelah, the Gothic Orcelis. Through the town runs the Segura, feeding the rich *huerta* for miles around. It is a charming town, long and rather narrow, full of church towers and palms, dominated by the usual ruined castle; the houses have tiled roofs, and orange-trees crowd behind the white garden walls. The cathedral is Gothic, but was damaged by earthquake in 1829 and ill restored. The Episcopal Palace (1733) stands on the left bank of the river that bisects the town and washes its foundations dangerously. Its façade and portal are lordly; its cloister has good galleries; its stairway of rose-coloured jasper is beautiful. There are a number of fine aristocratic houses, though the flood of 1834 destroyed many. The Colegio of Santo Domingo is a fine baroque building, inside which I failed to penetrate, so did not see its double cloisters, its refectory, or Velasquez's *Temptation of St. Thomas Aquinas*. (I am ashamed to confess that I do not even know what this temptation was, or whether Aquinas fell.) The church of Santiago has a fine Renaissance sculptured portal; I got no further into this handsome church than that.

But these details, good though they are, do not convey Orihuela, the way it stands under the mountains on its quiet river, the old Moorish towers and domes and flat-roofed houses among their palms, rising sheer above the shining water which holds their rippling images, the vine trellises and tall earthen pots on the terraces, the brooding heat of the ancient oriental town in its afternoon sleep. They make pots in Orihuela; but when I was there no one seemed to be making anything; the Orihuelans sat at their doors in the shade of the deep streets and stared in amazement at the foreigner and her car.

I left Orihuela in the late afternoon, and drove south-west along the dusty road, through the huerta of Murcia, the low sun like a blinding fire in my eyes. Around the road a great garden land lay, rich with grain and fruit trees, tomatoes, carobs, pumpkins, great melons, rustling canes, with palms spreading delicate fingers above them and little vines crawling on the ground. It was fifteen miles to Murcia city; the old kingdom of Murcia I entered a few miles beyond Orihuela, the last town of Valencia.

## CHAPTER THREE

## MURCIAN SHORE

CROSSING from the kingdom of Valencia into that of Murcia, I remembered the learned, prejudiced and passionate Richard Ford's description of the Murcians of a century ago; how he had condemned this region, 'lying in an out of the way corner,' as 'the Boetia of the south,' where

> Murtia, the pagan goddess of apathy and ignorance, rules undisturbed and undisputed. Dullness o'er all usurps her ancient reign. The better classes vegetate in a monotonous unsocial existence; their pursuits are the cigar and the siesta. Few men in any wise illustrious have ever been produced by this Dunciad province. The lower classes are alternately sluggish and industrious. Their physiognomy is African, and many have emigrated latterly to Algeria. They are superstitious, litigious and revengeful.

Up in the mountains, 'the side ways are studded with crosses, erected over sites where wine and women have led to murder.'

I do not know how Ford knew all his scandal, but he had a great appetite for it. So it was with some apprehension that I drove into and through that golden and westering land, the setting sun in my eyes, the spires and towers of the capital rising against an orange sky. Murcia lies in the fertile basin of the Segura, that oasis in a desert, transformed into a garden by Moorish irrigation; round it spreads a parched, tawny wilderness of sun-scorched plain and wild, barren mountains.

Murcia is a large town; larger than Cartagena, Granada or Cadiz, though not so large as Seville or Valencia. But, though no longer walled, it has a compact look, owing to being of a circular shape and lying in a plain girdled and guarded by mountains. Though there are plenty of modern streets and buildings, particularly round the Arenal, with its smart paseos, gardens and hotels, and on the south side of the river, which has unattractive alamedas, public gardens and plazas named after royalty and Floridablanca, in spite of all this, Murcia has, by not destroying too many of its old buildings, avoided an air of aggressive modernity; and it still looks partly African (beneath its baroque), as befits a city that first rose to importance at the beginning of the Moorish occupation. Some of its patriots say that it became important under the Visigoths, from being a small and obscure Roman town (there are Roman remains in it), others that the Visigoths let it down, if they did not actually destroy it. Anyhow, Murcia took kindly to the Moors, who made it an independent kingdom, and its capital a town of importance. It rebelled against the Christian conquest, though now there are, it is said, no more devout and ritualistic Christians in Spain.

Murcia is deliciously full of baroque; no wonder Ford found it dull. All he can say of Francisco Zarcillo, who did much of the sculpture, is that had he lived in a better age he might have done good work. But there are really few dull moments in Murcia. When I entered it the golden evening lay on it ripely, as on a garden of bright fruit; for many of the houses are painted gay, trees and gardens grow about them, blue grape domes bloom above them, and the river runs between. The Gothic cathedral's Churriguerresque façade in golden stone, by Jaime Bort, is very rich and pleasing, and has an animated figure in every Corinthian-columned and fluted recess; bishops, saints and angels stand with elegant firmness in niches and on pediments, or balance with charming precariousness on curved whorls, all pyramiding up to the arched summit, where, above the Assumption in an apse, voluminously garbed angels support a shield. The evening sunshine blazing on this ornately beautiful scene made it appear the golden gate of some urbane and cheerful paradise. There was a service proceeding inside, which floated out with the utmost sweetness and accomplishment. The tall, domed belfry tower is very elegant, though built in several different styles. The richly carved Renaissance octagonal chapel of the Marqués de los Vélez, sculptured with armorial shields and manueline-like chains, projects from the south-east corner. All the cathedral portals are rich and good. Inside, darkness and benediction combined to hinder complete observation, and I did not explore the many chapels, not even the plateresque Vélez, or the Sacristía Mayor, which has a lovely door.

Across the plaza is the Palacio Episcopal, one of the most attractive of baroque palaces, with its fine doors and tiled dome like a pigeon's breast; from its south front one looks across a tree-shaded paseo to the river and beyond it. I walked about the town. There are about a dozen churches in it and several colegios and disused convents. Many have charming façades, towers, azulejos and domes. More attractive still are many of the details—carved doors and windows and wrought-iron balconies, and armorial shields that decorate the hidalgos' houses and small palaces scattered about the streets between the baroque churches with their dove's-breast tiled domes. In the Calle del Principe Alfonso (the old Calle de la Traperia) among the shops and cafés are Renaissance windows and doors, with sculptured pillars and lintels, their iron balconies making delicate shadows on the white or coloured walls. In another street Doric columns twist up on either side of a door to a carved lintel which supports the all slim pillars of a narrow window; on the corner of this house heraldic creatures hold a shield. There is the Casa Huerta de la Bombas, where beneath the balustrade that runs along the terraced roof, a rich escutcheon bearing a royal crown is guarded by two rampant beasts and two shaggy wild men standing above twisted pillars. The palace of the Marqués de Almodovar has, to guard its tall carved window, two naked warriors with clubs; between them a little balcony is bright with flowers in pots. These hidalgo façades, of all periods, late Gothic, Renaissance, baroque, are everywhere among the more modern houses with their awnings down against the sun. In

a quiet, pretty plaza, near the church of Santa Catalina, is
the solid seventeenth-century house of the Contraste, carved
with coats-of-arms and wreaths, with a fine square door;
round it are old balconied houses and market stalls. There are
charming patios, and plazas planted with oranges and palms,
and no street in the older part of the town is dull. Its inhabitants may be so; I did not see enough of them to find out,
though they seemed cheerful and sociable enough. Certainly
the portraits of the Murcian worthies in the *Cronica de Murcia*
have not a very lively air—San Fulgencio, for example, looks
a bishop rather earnest than animated; the Count of Floridablanca, who expelled the Jesuits under Charles III and, as a
citizen of Murcia, had a public garden named after him, wears
a worried look (but this may be the result of expelling Jesuits;
even Pombal in his later life had a touch of it); Don Diego
Saavedra Fajardo, a seventeenth-century representative of this
noble Murcian family, looks, though plump, also apprehen-
sive; the Marqués de Corvera (mid-nineteenth century)
frowns, his mind on railways and public works. It is true that
few Murcians have been great creative artists; true also that
the province suffered intellectually, as well as financially and
agriculturally, from the expulsion of the Moriscos in 1609,
and has never, so they say, been the same since.

All the same, when I went out into the town next morning,
after a night somewhat broken by bells, Murcia seemed sufficiently animated, and the market by the river quays was a
lively scene. I visited the cathedral again, which was, for
some reason, open, and saw the fine riot of plateresque ornament, and the chapels and carved sacristy, and the urn con-
taining portions of Alfonso el Sabio, and other vessels with
ashes of saints. The French, as usual, looted the cathedral and
city of everything of value on which they could lay hands;
until one day, when General Soult was feasting in the Bishop's
Palace, the Murcians turned on their oppressors, and Soult
'rose panic-stricken from the table and fled, committing
atrocities which cannot be related,' for the French army in

the Peninsula, as reported by their foes, committed atrocities even at the least likely moments. Fortunately the French army did not care for the pretty little coloured wooden statue of St. Anthony in Capuchin habit carved by Alonso Cano, which is, therefore, still on the altar of the church of San Nicolas.

It was very hot on the morning I left Murcia. The dust-filmed landscape shimmered and danced, the distant hills were colourless. My road ran whitely through the plain, crossed a mountain ridge, then the plain again; thirty miles of dullish country, animated by fantastic, airy Murcian windmills, and then there was Cartagena and the sea.

No one, since it was the pride, glory, wealth and commercial capital first of the Massian Iberians, then of Carthaginian, then of Roman Spain, has seemed to care much for Cartagena. I did not care much for it myself; it is too large, too noisy, too modernized and industrialized. Yet it is magnificently set on its steep hill above the finest harbour in Spain; the mountains just round it to east and west, as Polybius describes; the island of Hercules (now Escombrera) lies at the harbour's mouth and so shuts it in that the gulf is always smooth except when the wind beats it into foam. It would hold a large fleet; and, indeed, often has. The town has long since lost its walls and gates, those walls first built by the Iberians with huge cyclopean stones, rebuilt by the Carthaginians when they turned the Massian stronghold into Carthago Nova, kept up by the Roman and all successive conquerors, until the nineteenth-century devallation mania pulled them down at the beginning of this century. The city, however, is still guarded by castles and forts. Its streets climb steeply up the hill behind it. But it is not what it was two thousand years ago, when Strabo wrote:

New Carthage is by far the most powerful of all the cities in this country, for it is adorned by secure fortifications, by walls handsomely built, by harbours, by a lake, and by the silver mines of which I have spoken. And the fish-salting industry is large. Furthermore, New Carthage is a rather important emporium, of imports from the sea for the inhabitants of the interior, and exports from the interior for all the outside world.

Yes, New Carthage was a place then. And two centuries before that, when Scipio so cleverly captured it from the Carthaginians. It is not easy to follow closely Polybius's account of this exploit, for the landscape has changed, and the ebbing lagoon that Scipio's army ran across has now ebbed quite away, and New Carthage is no longer on an isthmus. But the clash and echo of the siege, of the scaling of the walls, the shouting and the slaughter and the Carthaginian rout, still tremble on the hot air, and the great harbour seems full of Roman galleys. Carthago Nova, the great Punic stronghold, so proudly later to become Colonia Victrix Julia Nova Kartago, is dwindled from her one-time grandeur, but is still a large and busy arsenal and port. A melancholy place many visitors have found it; Gautier complained that it was mournful, shut in by barren rocks, the houses having a prison-like air, reminiscent of Castile, the windows all grilled. Henry Swinburne, in 1775, complained of cruelty to the galley slaves who worked in the docks till they dropped dead with exhaustion. I myself noticed none of these disadvantages. I admired the harbour and the ships; I thought of the elephants of Carthage trumpeting up and down the steep streets, of the silver mines, which have dazzled and enriched the cupidinous world down the ringing, clinking centuries, the mines where kings and merchants have looted wealth to build cities, navies, palaces and empires, where slaves have toiled and died. I thought of the barbarians (Vandals in the fifth century, Goths in the seventh), who had sacked and burnt this wealthy city, but it was always rebuilt. I remembered how the Roman governors had liked to winter here, alternating with Tarraco, a far better place. I looked in vain for a bathing beach, thought it would be very pleasant to take a boat out to Escombrera, did not really explore the town or look for the remains of the Temple of Asclepius or of the

palace of Hasdrubal, or visit the one-time cathedral (said to be
no good) or climb Castle Hill to get a view of Scipio's ford
across the lagoon, or journey out to see the silver mines. I felt
depressed by the noisy streets; probably when the Romans
wintered there they were noisier still. I found my way, with
some difficulty, to the Vice-Consulate of my country, and
called there for letters. The Vice-Consul, who knew all about
Cartagena and all about the road round it, told me it was
practically impossible to go by the coast road to Almeria, it
was too bad, and that between Almeria and Motril it was
blocked by road works; the best way to Granada was by Lorca
and the inland mountain road. As I wanted to see Lorca, this
seemed a good plan. I was sorry not to see also the gulf of
Almeria, but I remembered how Avienus had said of this gulf
*in illis oris ignobilia sunt oppida,*' and that between the Cabo
de Gata and Malaga there had been once many towns and a
multitude of Phœnicians living there, but that now, in his
time, it was uncultivated desert sand. It might have revived a
little since Avienus wrote, but Murray said that the houses
were small and the women and climate African (he does not
say if the men were more European), and I knew Lorca and
Guadix and the Granada mountains to be good.

There is no bathing in Cartagena, said the British Vice-
Consul. Once, yes; in the last century it was a bathing resort
of its hated rival Murcia (hated because Murcia was given by
Pope Nicholas IV Cartagena's ancient episcopal see), and
families migrated there in the summer from the interior. But
now, in all that beautiful almost enclosed gulf, there is no
bathing. Murcia has constructed for itself swimming pools,
and goes for week-ends to the shores of the Mar Menor,
which must be a wonderful bathing lake, almost land-locked
behind the two long mountain arms that encircle it, and
strewn with enchanting islands, but, it is said, shallow and
warm.

The Vice-Consul said that in Lorca one stayed at the
Comercio, a seventeenth-century inn, and that in the moun-

tains between Guadix and Granada it was wiser not to drive
after dark, as they were infested by a predatory maquis, who
held up travellers and cars by night, to show their disapproval
of the present government. He sent his chauffeur out with me
to show me the Lorca road; the chauffeur and I drank *café
helado* outside a plaza café, and I started for Lorca, along a
road that ran through a blasted heath, smothering in dust all
vehicles that disturbed it. I drove for some way behind a
Lorca–Cartagena diligence, which was veiled in a white,
whirling cloud. Dust flung itself through my windows,
through every interstice in the car's frame, lying whitely on
seats and cushions and luggage, drifting into the boot and
seeping into my picnic basket. Each day the car became so
coated with this deposit of the roads of Spain that, whenever I
paused in a town, little boys wrote their names on it. But the
cross-country road that ran by Fuente Alamo to the main
Murcia–Lorca road was, I think, the dustiest that I met in
Spain. After thirty-five miles it reached the main road, that
ran south-west to Lorca, a line of mountains on its right. In
sight of these mountains I stopped and lunched; I had bread,
cheese, and a melon inside which I had put figs, grapes and
peaches, to keep them cool. The water in my water-pot was
deliciously cold.

Lorca, pale and dusty, burned luminously on its hill in the
August afternoon sun. It is an infinitely agreeable town.
Though it is Roman and Moorish, and has a Moorish name
and a partly Moorish castle, it has the air of belonging almost
wholly to the sixteenth, seventeenth and eighteenth centuries;
nothing in it, anyhow, looks new. Almost every street has
charming baroque or Renaissance doorways, coats-of-arms,
terraced houses. I got a room in the Comercio, the seventeenth-century inn. Opposite it was the richly-carved two-
storied Churriguerresque doorway of a seigniorial house, with
pale, twisted, foliated columns, sportive figures and dignified
birds, and, above, a richly sculptured coat-of-arms. On either
side of the door iron window-balconies festooned with flower-

ing shrubs cast light shadows on the terra-cotta walls. It was
a very beautiful house-front. Round the corner was the church
of Rosario. In front of my bedroom window was an old house
with a flat terrace; on it aloes grew, in deep blue pots, and
vines trellised above it.

The Comercio is cool and open, built in a circle round a
stone stairway—very pleasant. The proprietor too was
pleasant. He was interested in my car; he said he had heard
that women in England drove cars, and did many other things
that, in Spain, were done exclusively by men. He knew about
English doings, for he had listened to the B.B.C. during the
war. But I must not be surprised, he told me, if Spaniards,
who saw few foreigners, were astonished at seeing me at the
wheel. I had, I told him, long ceased to be surprised at that:
their astonishment, whether I was at the wheel or on foot,
had pursued me all down Spain.

I wandered about the enchanting town after dusk. In the
hot, steep narrow streets people strolled and sat, children
played, lights gleamed out of open windows and from the
stalls on the pavements that sold fruits and combs and pots.
Lorca was very gay in the night. Ford called it a dull, unsocial
place, and Henry Swinburne 'saw nothing in it to make a
note of but the dress of a gypsy, the daughter of the inn-
keeper.' How sartorially minded, what costumiers, tourists
used to be! To spare a glance for the dress of a gypsy (or,
indeed, of anyone else) when surrounded by the seventeenth-
century loveliness and elegance of Lorca, argues an interest in
clothes and human creatures almost morbid; perhaps they
caught it from the Spanish. For Lorca is truly lovely, with
the rare, blanched pastel beauty of a Wedgwood vase. I was
out in it early next morning, before it grew hot, when the pale
early sunshine bathed the Plaza de España (for so it seemed to
be called, though all the books call it the Plaza Mayor; perhaps the new name is part of the nationalist movement; it was
a relief to find no Plaza Generalissimo Franco). High above
this lovely plaza, which has white stone benches round it, and

trees, and in the middle a flower garden with a fountain, stands the Colegiata de San Patricio, at the top of a steep flight of steps; it has two baroque doors, and in the arms of the statues of saints and bishops on the parapet live pigeons nestle and coo. Along one side of the plaza are Renaissance and baroque houses, with balconies and sculptured porches and windows, about which the pigeons rustle and coo and drop; across the other side is the baroque Ayuntamiento.

Walking back to the Comercio down the steep pale streets, past carved gateways and balconies heaped with cucumbers, I came to the market, in a circle of arcades round a flowering garden; it had possibly once been the cloister of a convent. Vegetables and fruit and cheese, bread and meat, rope shoes, *esparto* baskets and brooms, dates and raisins, were being sold in a babel of chatter and chaffering. I do not know if Richard Ford had been to the mercado when he called Lorca a dull unsocial place.

The streets were alive with little donkeys slung with panniers; some were collecting the dust, which seemed a good plan; others had their panniers full of water pots, and were ridden by pretty little boys (never little girls).

I returned to the Comercio for coffee, and went out again to see more Churriguerresque churches. Lorca was once full of convents; I do not know how many are left of these.

I drove out of seventeenth-century Spain into the Spain of the Moors—a menacing landscape, a heave of burnt hills, quite dry and bare. If the maquis were lurking about these mountains, there seemed little cover for them. Nothing, once the green vale of Lorca with its fruity *huerta* was past, except cactus, aloes, prickly pears, tawny rocks, and pale, clay-coloured villages built, one house on another, into the sides of the hills. There was an occasional peasant's house, surrounded by a few olives and figs and beehive-shaped ricks of straw. The desolate road was shadowless and treeless, choked with dust, scorched with sun; the shade temperature was 102. Nothing travelled on the road but flocks of little brown goats and an occasional donkey, its cart or panniers piled high with branches or grass, ridden or driven by a beautiful brown child, or by a turbaned, classically featured brown Moor. These are a very handsome people. Murcia, which I was about to leave, is a most delightful province.

## CHAPTER FOUR

## ANDALUCIAN SHORE

THE milestone, which said 'Provincia de Almeria' on its thither side and 'Provincia de Murcia' on its hither, was exciting, for Almeria is the first province in the great realm of Andalucia, which stretches from Murcia down the Mediterranean, past the Straits, and down the Atlantic to Portugal: Andaluz, 'the land of the west,' the land of Tartessos, of the Hesperides, of the exploits of the Homeric heroes, of the Phœnician settlements, of the first Greek colonies, of the great Arab culture, of the last stronghold of the Moors in Spain. One does not enter Andalucia without a leaping of the blood.

The frontier is within a few miles of Velez Rubio, a town on a gentle hill, on which most guidebooks are silent because the railway does not run that way, and guidebook writers find it troublesome to leave trains. It is a steep-streeted town, climbing up to a castle and surrounded by hills; it has some charming plazas, a Casa Consistorial, three fountains round the walls, a number of one-time convents, a good baroque *parroquial* of 1753 (the old one having been destroyed by earthquake in 1751). The stone portal is very nice, with columns and statues and cornices and a gilded cross supported by angels, and above the door the arms of the house of Velez. It has two high towers, with beautiful capitals, surrounded by galleries from which, were one up in them, one would see a superb view. I neither went inside the church (which was, of course, shut) nor up the towers. Velez Rubio is a very attractive place, which gains in romance, no doubt, from being the first Andalucian town one comes to from Murcia. From it the road ran desolately on through the burnt, cactus-sharp, breathless sprawl of hills. Noon blazed down on road and moorland; not an olive tree gave shade for rest and lunch. Ochre villages burrowed into hill-sides, hovel piled on hovel, backed by steep rock. The road entered the province of Granada. In a steep ravine straggled Cullar de Baza; a few miles on was Baza, a primitive Iberian town, later the Roman Basti, an early bishopric, then an important stronghold of the Moors, from whom it was won at last by Isabella of Castile after a long siege. The town and its surrounding vineyards (famous for their good wine) are rich in Roman and Iberian fragments: there is much about it in that fascinating work *Antigüedades prehistoricas de Andalucía.* Baza is splendidly built in the Moorish style on the eastern slope of a hill; its narrow streets wind and climb round close-built houses and ruined Moorish castle in a fine huddle; its Gothic collegiate church stands on the site of the Visigothic cathedral of the ancient see, of the Moorish mosque that replaced this, and the Christian church consecrated after the conquest. Immediately round Baza lies a fruitful garden of vines, olives and grain, watered by a confluence of rivers; above this fertile basin rises the conical hill Javalcón, full of burrowing cave-dwellers.

The road wound on through bare, barren hills of tufa rock and esparto grass, honeycombed with caves and grotesque with odd pinnacles—a wild African scene. Suddenly it changed: an avenue of mulberry trees swept towards a graceful city; at the end of the avenue a golden-brown cathedral rose on a height above a flight of steps; it was Guadix. The Churriguerresque façade, as one approached it along the avenue, had a more than earthly loveliness in the golden afternoon light, standing high above a wall, looking over that strange tormented country. This was Wadi-Ash, a city of the Moors; Acci, Guadix el Viejo, the ancient Iberian, Roman and Visigothic city, lies four or five miles from it (but I could not locate it). Acci was important under the Empire—Colonia Julia Gemela, station of veterans of the first and second legions; it early became a bishop's see, which continued under the first Arab centuries. When the see was put down, and when Acci was destroyed and Guadix built, no one but the Moors can tell us, and they have probably forgotten. Guadix was a Moorish city of importance; it had a mosque, on whose site the Christian church was later built. Moorish-Christian battles raged about it for three centuries; it was not finally conquered by the Catholic Kings until 1489. Dominating the city on the height above it stands the ruined Moorish fortress. The cathedral, built on the site of the earlier church, was built from 1710 to 1796; in front of it runs a broad paseo, from which one passes, by steep narrow streets, into the town. The town is delightful, winding and steep; every other shop seems to sell earthen pots and crocks. While I drank coffee, the whole of the younger population of Guadix mobbed my car; they were shooed away by a very kind man, who stood on the running-board and guided me to the best pot shop; we were pursued by the delighted children, who crowded into the shop after me while I bought a white water pot, a china fruit dish, and a row of china boxes to hold salt and pepper. They followed me also when I went to the Plaza Mayor, a charming columned market square; they were truly anxious to assist and guide me to the enjoyments of their pleasant city. It was with some difficulty that I got away, out into the extraordinary, uncanny Barrio de Santiago and all the surrounding country of tawny hills and caves. For this was the cave country of the Sierra of Guadix, and all about there were doors and chimneys in the cliffs, and behind the doors (sometimes painted blue) lived the cave dwellers. It was like a child's picture book of gnomes' houses, fantastically improbable and unreal.

The road twisted up into the Granada mountains; its zigzags sharpened. Great sierras formed the rim of a huge basin against the sultry sky; their shadows lay, in lovely pastel shades, across the evening light. On my left towered the Sierra Nevada, magenta and indigo and topped with snow. The road curled between high cliffs, steep, precipitous rocks and jags; the bends were as sharp as those on the San Felíu–Tossa road. It would not be a road to travel after dark. These were the mountains of the Granada maquis against whom I had been warned; the descendants, I suppose, of the ancient banditti, Iberian, Saracen and Christian, who had always haunted this sinister country. But I met no maquis; or, if maquis they were, these occasional goat-herds and donkey riders, they wore an innocent and friendly air.

The road twisted down from the mountains, and suddenly beneath its heights Granada spread, bosomed in its wide, high plain, climbing over its three hills, towered and valleyed, delicately shadowed in the evening light, guarded by the cold lilac peaks of the Sierra Nevada. Few landmarks were distinguishable, except the steep wooded hill of the Alhambra and the Generalife, and the broad gulf of the Darro cutting through the city. I drove down into the town. One should, of course, have found a room in one of the hotels or pensions close to the Alhambra or Generalife, such as the famous Siete Suelos; but those I tried were either expensive or full, and it seemed easier to find a hotel in the city. The happy days of a century ago, when Washington Irving, Richard Ford, Gautier, and apparently anyone else who chose, could camp undisturbed in any rooms of the Alhambra or of Charles V's palace that they liked to select, are long since over. It is a tantalizing exercise to decide which apartments one would have chosen. Washington Irving had a whole suite, and changed them when he liked. The Alhambra, for so long neglected, plundered, desecrated, turned into stables for donkeys and lodgings for gypsies, criminals and tourists, has for many years now been tidied up and made into a show place, admission so many pesetas, guide so many more. The Spanish, who for so long treated their unrivalled treasure with indifferent neglect, were at last stimulated by foreign visitors into making it a national monument; it is less picturesque than in Washington Irving's day, but better kept.

Nothing can spoil the Alhambra and the Generalife. Neglected, despoiled and partly destroyed in order to build the lumpish palace of Charles V, its pavements torn up, its arches blocked, its exquisite traceries smashed and mutilated, its treasures, its rich marbles, looted and removed by the French invaders, its towers mined and blown up when these vandals fled in 1812, the mosaic floors broken and planted with shrubs and later replaced with modern tiles, donkeys, sheep, cattle, tramps, prisoners, criminals, vagabonds and maniacs defiling for years its lovely courts and corridors, foreign tourists eating and sleeping (and doubtless plundering) for months in the rooms built so delicately for Arab pleasures and tastes—all these disasters, depredations and vandalisms make one, reading the tale of them, wonder what can be left; and, on the top of destruction, a century of restoration and reconstruction, fake tiling, mosaic and stucco work, seems to complete the ruin of this unique monument to a past civilization. Yet, when one sees it, it remains startling in its beauty and in its impact on the imagination. Here is an Arabian Nights' palace. Here are the Arab centuries delicately carved in stone, in marble, in plaster, in wood, and delicately gushing in fountains and streams. There is no need (unless you are interested and armed with copious books of information) to be curious in inquiry as to which parts of the work are Arab of the fourteenth century, which Spanish of the nineteenth and twentieth; the whole effect is enchanting, and not even its tourist air, the memory of a hundred imitations, its resemblance to the over-fastuous caskets sold in Granada shops, or the tiresome gypsies at the park gates, can spoil it. The magnificent acropolis, encircled by its adobe, burnt sienna walls and towers, set with palaces, fortresses, arches and deep green gardens, rises above the city, beautiful but uninteresting woods full of the Duke of Wellington's imported nightingales climbing up its slope. From its heights one sees old and new Granada lying, with its sunburnt *vega* stretching hazily beyond it to the cold blue limpid mountains (the Moors would never have let the *vega* get so burnt). Through the Charles V Puerta de las Granadas you enter the Alameda, and follow it up through the cool woods to the Puerta

Judiciaria, that square, solid, orange-coloured gate tower, with the Karoli Quinto fountain, and so to the Alhambra palace, passing from one lovely hall and patio after another, each a delicate fantasy of fastuous traceries, old, restored and new, graceful arcades, slender shafts, cupolas, horseshoe arches, coloured azulejos (mostly new), and richly worked plaster ornament (largely new), with religious slogans inscribed among the decoration. The mixture of the original Maghribian architecture of the thirteenth and fourteenth centuries with the Gothic of the Spanish kings, the Mudéjar decorators whom they employed in the sixteenth century, and the nineteenth and twentieth-century restorations, makes an effect insidiously and sensuously charming, continually spurious and unrooted, but exquisite. The actual architecture of rooms and patios is superb and little spoilt—the Court of the Myrtles, for instance, with its long, narrow, jade-green water tank, terminal vaulted alcoves, nineteenth-century tiled floor, and slender columns, richly capitalled and once brilliantly coloured by the Moors, as Greek temples were by the Greeks. The tank used to be surrounded by a Moorish balustrade, broken down and sold by marauders, who also stripped the azulejos dado, at the end of the eighteenth century. Against one end of the patio Charles V piled his ungainly palace, destroying the Moorish entrance and a number of lovely rooms, which were possibly for the use of the harem. Above the arcaded passage at the other end towers the square red-blown battlemented Torre de Comares, one of the piquant incongruities in which the Alhambra abounds. Between the two lies the unspoilt, though so often despoiled, loveliness of the arcaded marble myrtles court and its long blue-green water so suavely holding the summer sky and slender white colonnades in its cool smoothness.

One enters Charles V's palace armed with the disgust that such a piece of outrageous vandalism deserves. But in itself this massive example of Italian Renaissance classicism is, in its own pompous way, not unadmirable. Its colour is a pleasant warm golden; it has a fine circular colonnaded court, some rich relief carving and some good marble work; the general effect, among the Arab daintiness, is of an awkward, lumpish, showy manliness, as of a wealthy and rather philistine new aristocracy embarrassingly planted in a harem. Fortunately it was never finished, so lacks the roof and the towering cupola which were meant to dominate the Arab palace and (presumably) to give the lie to the boast inscribed on one of the Moorish cupolas, 'Here is the wonderful cupola, at sight of whose beautiful proportions all other cupolas vanish and disappear.'

Leaving the mundane palace, one returns to the Arab fairyland; here is the familiar Court of the Lions, looking much better than it did in our Crystal Palace, with its charming and amiable heraldic beasts, its great alabaster fountain bowl, its smaller fountains set round the court, its light arcades and honeycomb filigree.

> Here is a garden containing wonders of art, the like of which God forbids should elsewhere be found [runs the Arabic inscription round the fountain bowl]. Look at this solid mass of pearl glistening all round, and spreading through the air its showers of prismatic bubbles. . . . What else is this fountain but a beneficent cloud pouring out its abundant supplies over the lions beneath, like the hands of the Khalif, when he rises in the morning to distribute plentiful rewards among his soldiers, the Lions of war? Oh, thou who beholdest these lions crouching, fear not; life is wanting to enable them to show their fury. . . .

One of the attractive things about Arabic art is its enthusiastic self-applause. 'I am the garden', says another inscription; 'every morn I appear decked in beauty. Look attentively at my elegance. For by Allah the elegant buildings by which I am surrounded certainly surpass all other buildings.' It strikes a different note from any mediæval Christian utterance.

In the Court of the Lions, blue and white tiles and marble slabs now pave the floor from which the Moorish tiles were torn by the French invaders, who turned the court into a garden. Imagination cannot capture the brilliant Arab beauty of this plundered, many times whitewashed (the Spanish conquerors had a passion for 'purification' of infidel buildings) and now restored court (the ceiling is altogether modern); but its effect is still lovely. After the French had left it, and the Alhambra had been further gutted by Ferdinand VII's corrupt officials, the Court of Lions was a mass of débris, even some of the lions being broken and flung down; in 1821 an earthquake shook the palace; after that galley-slaves worked away at it, destroying Moorish work to turn some of the rooms into a store for fish. The restoration, when at last it was taken in hand, was creditable; even the fountain plays, on occasion, again. Nothing can defeat one's enjoyment of this court. Out of it open the Hall of the Abencerrajes, with its succulent stalactite ceiling and sixteenth-century azulejos, the Sala de la Justicia, with its half-orange vaulting and entrancing ceiling paintings, and the Sala de las Dos Hermanas, rich with magnificent honeycomb vaulting and more than Churriguerresque frolic of fantastic décor, like a web of petrified fine lace. 'Here,' boasts an inscription, 'are columns ornamented with every perfection . . . Columns which, when struck by the rays of the rising sun, one might fancy to be so many blocks of pearl. . . .' In this room stands the famous enamelled fourteenth-century Alhambra Vase. It is a room of pleasure and rest; round it are raised mosaic sleeping alcoves, which must, even when cushioned and tapestried, have been rather hard.

Almost as rich in ornament is the two-storied Hall of the Ambassadors, inside the Torre de Comares. The deeply recessed windows open on to great sunlit spaces and steep slopes and the city spreading westward below; the arrangement of windows and vistas and colonnaded miradors shows the exquisite æsthetic awareness of beauty that makes the whole palace such a studied elaboration of art. Beauty for beauty's sake was the Arabs' creed; it needed no such excuse as the glory of God; though theirs is a God-conscious art, and Allah in their inscriptions is continually praised, they made beauty for their pleasure. There is here no rearing of towers, vaults and spires heavenward, no ascetic emphasis on holiness and prayer, no scorn of the body; the Arab way of life was to embellish it with every lovely decoration, to seek beauty in colour, elegance, grace, perfumed gardens, and the perpetual singing of water. The bathing rooms of the palace (underground) are delightful, with the galleries above them for musicians to soothe bathers with music while they rested from the exertions of the toilet. The hot-water system was destroyed by the Spanish. What did those hydrophobes, who thought ablutions dangerously infidel, make of it all? They admired and valued the place; as Charles V remarked, 'Ill-fated the man who lost all this.' But they daubed much of the coloured ornament with whitewash, broke off Moorish emblems, and destroyed rooms and courts for their own purposes; they changed the lovely mosque into a chapel, blocked up passages, built incongruous additions. It was not an age of architectural or æsthetic principles; one cannot judge them by the standards of our own Building Preservation Societies; and some credit should be given for the preservation of the Alhambra as we see it to-day.

Close to the Comares Tower is the corridor to the Tocador de la Reina, the charming pavilion decorated by sixteenth-century Italian artists. The apartments of Charles V, next door, overlook the lovely cypressed garden patio of Lindaraxa. 'I determined at once,' said Washington Irving, 'to take up my quarters in this apartment,' and so he did. What a stunt! I visited Granada over a century too late. Irving even bathed in the tank of the Myrtles; while an elderly count shot at swallows from the balconies and held a family banquet in the Sala de las Dos Hermanas. Alas, nothing can restore the liberty of those days. Still, had they continued, one supposes that even more of the Alhambra would have been ruined or lost. As it is, ruin has been arrested, though late. One may still see the courts, the cypressed and fountained gardens, the towers of the Alcázabar, and even if the Torre de la Vela and the Tocador de la Reina have been renovated, there is still the view to be seen from them—the sprawl of the ancient and not yet wholly spoilt Albaicín, clustering beyond the dry bed of the Darro, with its tiled roofs, white arcaded houses, square belfries and narrow streets, the spread of the *vega* beyond it, the climb of the hot cactus and fig-grown hill across the ravine up to the Generalife palace; and that exquisite little summer palace itself, with its flight of brick steps and its terraced gardens and little courts full of oranges, myrtles and cypresses, its Moorish arcades and sixteenth-century brick-work, its fountains, its melodiously running waters, and its wide, shimmering expanse of view.

On the way up to the Generalife one passes the site of the great Alhambra mosque, built in 1308 out of tributes levied on Christians; a contemporary historian described its loveli-ness, its mosaics, its tracery of intricate patterns, with silver flowers and graceful arches and 'innumerable pillars of the finest polished marble . . . the building has not its like in this country.' At the conquest it was handed over to the Fran-ciscans. Nothing is left of it now but an inscription over a garden gate, and, within a villa, a tiny Moorish chapel. The beautiful mosque building was destroyed by the French, out of military exercise, spite, irreligion, and, no doubt, cupidity; they probably looted the silver flowers, the mosaics and the marble pillars, and blew up what was left. It is not surprising that the Spanish cannot forgive the French. French travellers through the nineteenth century relate how they and their families were stoned and mocked over Spain, but more par-ticularly in Granada.

The rambling, walled village of the Alhambra hill is now tidied up and largely demolished; those who go expecting to find the picturesque scene described by Washington Irving, or the squalid hovels and 'wretched population exposing its filth and rags' deplored by other nineteenth-century travellers, will be disappointed. Some fear that one day this hill may be stripped of its ancientness, as well as of its attractive later villas and gardens, and turned into a kind of fake oriental city.

What is one to think of Granada, apart from the Alhambra? It has been decried and abused for dullness, backwardness, unlovely modernity, ugly commercialism, vandalish destruction; and indeed the city as a whole is not very attractive or beautiful; it lacks the splendour of Seville, the grace of much of Valencia, the crowded magnificence of Barcelona, the picturesque aliveness of any of the seaports, and its modern and rebuilt parts are dull, smart and cosmopolitan enough. But a town cannot be dull which still, in its older parts, has so much of the Moor remaining, in which one may come on mosques, Arab patios, houses, gateways or wells, or on Christian churches on Moorish sites, or an occasional Renaissance building with a Herrara façade; a town in which one can walk through such a quarter as the Albaicín, between Arab houses and taverns and cypressed gardens, and find destroyed Arab baths; a town in which Spanish Catholic conquest superimposed itself on Arab culture so that scarcely any old building is not a mixture of both; a town girdled by violet hills snow-crowned and cooled with running waters, and surmounted by its incomparable ancient acropolis.

The cathedral (on the site, of course, of a mosque) has an imposing, heavy look outside; most buildings must look hulking beside the starry grace and sweetness of the Arab palace on the hill. Handsome is, I suppose, the word for all this sixteenth-century massiveness, and for the richly decorated exterior. The side chapels are loaded with decoration, sculpture and pictures. The Capilla Real, the burial-place of the Catholic Sovereigns, is rich in admirable Renaissance statues and tombs; the figures of Ferdinand and Isabella, kneeling beside the ornate retablo, are beautiful. There are a number of fine paintings—an El Greco, a Memling, some charming primitives.

One emerges from the cathedral into the little plaza of the
Lonja; here I was accosted by a boy of about fifteen, eager to
show me a Moorish room in the Ayuntamiento, or Casa del
Cabildo. It was a pretty octagonal room, that had been a
chapel in the university of the Moors; it was now used by the
Granada Juventud, to which he belonged; he showed me
with pride the Alhambra-like traceries and mosaics of the
arches, in such good repair that they suggested recent restoration. He was a very charming and kind boy; he apologized
for the way the Grenadino boys followed and jeered at
foreigners; he shooed them away; he shook his head over
them, telling me that such manners were 'muy descortés,' and
he had been told by strangers that the Grenadinos were particularly liable to this solecism; indeed, so had I. His *amende*
for his native city was to escort solitary foreign ladies politely
about the sights, with no thought of reward. He knew a little
English; he asked me what England, which he hoped to visit
sometime, was like. Cold, I told him. Had we anything as
beautiful as the Alhambra? No, we had not; the Moors had
never paid us a visit. We had, however, green fields and beautiful country, where we had not yet spoilt it. Had we a
Juventud? I told him about the Boy Scouts and Girl Guides.
He was a very nice, amiable, dignified boy.

I drove out to see the Cartuja (of the Assumption), which
is in a dusty northern suburb beyond the Renaissance mad-
house. It stands in a tree-shaded court up a steep road, beyond
a fine Renaissance gate; the baroque façade of golden stone,
rising above a balustraded terrace reached by steep flights of
steps, is delightful. The convent was begun in 1516; it had
great wealth, magnificence, and artistic treasures; it was suppressed in 1789, and used as a magazine by Sebastiani during
the French occupation; now only the seventeenth-century
church and the eighteenth-century Sagrario and Sacristy and
part of the cloisters remain; and even from these Sebastiani
made off with many treasures. But this celebrated sacristy can
spare some treasures. It is one of the richest, fussiest, most

restlessly opulent of Churriguerresque fanfares, with its coloured marbles and alabasters, the lavish stucco work of pillars and walls, of which not a foot of space is left unadorned ('innumerable fretted pilasters surging with delirious ornament'), the exquisite tortoiseshell, silver and ivory inlay of doors, cabinets and shelves. The whole effect is most delicately showy; for those who enjoy Churriguerresque, a feast, for those who detest it, a nightmare; but in any case a bijou marvel and glorious fuss.

A little dizzy after this surfeit of wedding-cake, I came out into the tranquil convent court, golden in the sun, blue-shadowed under the plane-trees, and so back along the dusty Calle de Cartuja into the Moorish streets of the Albaicín, and once again up the Alhambra hill to cool and delicate gardens of cypresses and playing water where the kings of Granada once took their ease.

Next day I drove down again to the coast, along a mountainy road whose bends were less like hairpins than like sharp dog-tooth moulding. It was, I think, the most zigzag road I had yet met; my arms ached with dragging the wheel round, my foot from pressing the brake. It was a great valley, guarded by precipitous mountains, silent but for the cicadas. Peaks and rocks and terraced hill slopes burned beneath the morning sun; on my left ranged the Sierra Nevada, and the Peñas del Diabolo. As the road descended, olives and figs, cactuses, aloes and sugar canes, grew round villages of balconies and tiled roofs, white villages with an occasional splash of deep blue, all with the Moorish and most unchristian heritage of dazzling cleanness. The country had a lonely wildness. The day hotted up; by half-past ten it was scorching. Suddenly between two hills I saw the sea, and Motril was only five miles off. The road descended into the Meseta de los Pelados and the valley of the Guadalfeo.

Motril is a pleasant town, over a mile from the sea, surrounded by sugar canes, vines and banana trees. In a banana grove boys were diving into a pool. I turned west to Malaga;

it was a spectacular road, running high above the sea, with sharp bends and ravines; far below were magnificent blue bays and tantalizing coves, until, about thirty miles from Malaga, the road ran down to the sea. Here, on a little beach, I bathed; the sand burnt my feet through rubber shoes, the rock I sat on through a wet bathing suit. A friendly man called down from the road, wasn't I too hot? I said I was. So was the car.

The road ran on to Malaga—seventy miles from Motril, through tropical vegetation, sweet potatoes, sugar canes, cactuses, cotton, bananas, custard apples, prickly pears. The Phœnicians marted down this coast from the eighth century B.C. or before; between the Cape of Gata and Malaga, says Avienus, 'there were once many towns, and a multitude of Phœnicians lived there.' Fortunate and wise Phœnicians. They founded (or settled in and expanded) Malaga, which, says Strabo, seven centuries later, 'bears the stamp of a Phœnician city.' The Greeks too visited this coast, and beyond it to the west, from the days when, as Herodotus relates, Kolaios the Samian was swept out of his course by the east wind and 'passed through the Pillars of Hercules and came to Tartessos, guided by divine providence,' to the time a century later (towards the end of the sixth century) when the Phocæans, 'the first of the Hellenes to make long voyages,' founded their little trading towns down the coast, of which one was Mainake, which 'lies furthest of the Phocæan cities in the west.' Mainake, destroyed probably by the Carthaginians in order to leave undisputed domination and trade to their own cities, was already in ruins when Strabo wrote, 'though it still preserves the traces of a Greek city.' And its ghost haunted my road, lying somewhere by the sea, some miles this side of Malaga. Some archæologists put it on the cliff above the mouth of the river Vélez, sixteen miles or so east of Malaga; Avienus seems to indicate this; he describes an island, a marsh, a quiet harbour, the sheer climb of the mountains up from the sea, and 'the town Mainake stands above.' Others surmise that this was the site of the Roman town which, much later, replaced Mainake, and that Mainake itself is still to seek. I would rather have Mainake in a fixed place, not a flitting ghost along these shores, so I placed it on the Peñon of Vélez, where, climbing with its markets and its temples and its arcaded colonnaded houses on this steep acropolis above a shining river estuary and limpid sea (where once lay a marsh), it looked all that could be wished, among all the ruined castles that crowned the further hills, and the African villages that fringed the shore.

The road, climbing steeply up and down above the narrow strip of coast, was backed by a precipice of mountains; the views were stupendous, the heat sweltering. The vines that make Malaga wine crept about the terraced hills and reed-thatched farm-houses; Malaga, muscatel, Pedro Ximenes, that the seventeenth-century English called Peter-See-Me; all good wines. Broad straw hats were now often worn by the men, women and children working in the fields or riding donkeys on the roads; I am not sure where the hat-line begins; I think I saw none (on women or children) north of Alicante. But in Africa the sun is too strong, and this shore is truly African, and burgeoned, as Gautier observed, with 'les formidables végétations africaines.' It began to burgeon also into the Malagueñan suburbs—villas, gardens, bathing beaches, all very gay and clean—El Palo, Miramar, El Limonar, La Caleta, which is really part of Malaga. And there against the western sky stood Malaga la Bella between its viney mountains, climbing up from its white sea front and deep blue bay, and it looked like a circular wedge of pale cheese ('pâleur dorée,' as Gautier said of the women's complexions) with blue-green veins of mould, which were trees and shrubs and gardens, winding about it; this cheesey look made it appear very beautiful to a cheese-starved Briton. And, indeed, I hold Malaga to be a beautiful town, though there is little in it to engross. 'One day will suffice,' said Ford. 'It has few attractions beyond climate, almonds and raisins and sweet wine.' The cathedral, he added, is a pasticcio in bad taste, and 'the lower orders, as at Cadiz, are bad.' Ford was a stern judge of human beings and pasticcios. For my part, I liked Malaga, that prosperous, easy Phœnician city, the opulent queen, after Cadiz, of Spanish commerce two thousand five hundred years ago; the important Roman Malaca, rich with silver mines and salt fish, invaded and plundered (under Marcus Aurelius) by covetous Africans; later the earthly paradise of the Moorish conquerors, who made it into an independent kingdom under Granada; the victim of the cruelty of St. Ferdinand, who, after long siege and assault, captured it, and enslaved, imprisoned or burnt its defenders. After that, Malaga sank in prosperity and glory. Neither has this smiling city, for all its fertile, luxuriant vegetation, golden sunshine, sweet wines, and wealth of fresh and salted fish, led through the last four centuries a life of undisturbed ease. It has been often troubled by insurrectionary activities—those of discontented Moriscos in the sixteenth century, discontented liberals in the nineteenth, angry nationalist rebels in 1937. The bombardments of these last, before they took the town, reduced half of it, according to eye-witnesses, to débris; they had better weapons than had the Catholic sovereigns in 1487. But Malaga has made a good recovery; débris is seldom so widespread as it appears immediately after a bombardment, and neither the destruction of the town by one side in that savage and pernicious dispute, nor of its churches by the other (church-burning and priest-murdering raged excessively and brutally in Malaga, which has an ancient liberal tradition; alas for liberalism beneath a Spanish sun!) is now very apparent, though valuable things perished in both, as also when the French sacked it in 1810. Malaga has always been famed for its religious tolerance; it built a Protestant cemetery (for even in Malaga people must die in the winter) as early as 1831, where, say its chroniclers proudly, burials were conducted with perfect publicity and no untoward incidents; it has also long had an Anglican church and chaplain, to minister to the large English colony. But, when Mala-

güeñans get annoyed by the attitude of their own Church,
tolerance ends, tempers explode, and up go the churches in
flames, and the clergy are fortunate if they do not got up with
them.

Before the civil war broke, Malaga was a favourite winter
resort of sun-seeking foreigners (perhaps it is so now again).
The dirty streets complained of by nineteenth-century travellers have become clean, the hotels are improved. Possibly this
is partly due to the winter visits of Queen Victoria (Ena) and
her mother Princess Beatrice of Battenberg, who stayed there
every year. I dare say even the lower orders are improved too.
In 1830 a Mr. Inglis was warned (or so he believed) by the
British consul that he could only ascend unaccompanied to the
Alcázaba and the Gibralfera, the Phœnician-Moorish forts on
the hill above the town, at risk of his life; when he did so one
evening he was persuaded that a lurking Malagueño, whose
dark face he descried watching him from the shadows of the
ruins, meant to rob and assassinate him; he only escaped this
fate by fleeing hot-foot and breathless down a path to the city.
No such dangers to-day attend the visitor to these now restored and tidied-up forts, except the dangers attendant on a
steep climb in the sun. If you brave this, you get a fine sweeping view of Malaga and its bay, the broad basin of its splendid
harbour full of the ships of the world—cargo steamers, cruis-
ing steamers, Spanish battleships, white-sailed yachts, fleets of
fishing boats—a lovely sight. Beyond it stretches the line of
coast that curves south-west to the Straits, and it is true that
you can faintly see Ceuta and the mountains of Africa.

Walking down the steep narrow streets of the old town
that climbs above the long alameda and park and modern
frontage that lie along the harbour front, one passes an occasional broken gesture from the Arab past—part of a house, a
gateway, an arch. There is, too, the cathedral, though this is
not particularly interesting. It is, as Ford observed, a pastiche,
since it was begun (on the site of a mosque and of the Gothic
church run up just after the conquest, of which only a portal

of the Sagrario remains) in 1538, and not finished until late in the eighteenth century. It was a good deal damaged in 1936, but still has a fine showy commonplace Corinthian façade and towers. I did not see the inside, which has, says Baedeker, pictures by Alonso Cano, Ribera and others (but I dare say they were burnt) and some good sculpture. There are other churches in Malaga, and an archæological museum, and a museum of fine arts, all shut. More interesting is the general lie and feeling of the town and port, this oldest Phœnician Mediterranean port of Spain, anciently so powerful and so opulent a fair for Tyre, for Carthage, for Rome, for the Moor, and now again for Spain. Malaga has its industrial quarter, its cotton mills, its sugar refineries, its factories, west of the Guadalmedina, and its port is full of ships carrying grapes, raisins, wine, sugar, cotton, and (one hopes) bananas, sweet potatoes and custard apples, out to sea.

For those who like parks (I do not) there is a handsome modern park along the sea front. For those who like nice crowded bathing beaches (I do not) there is a nice crowded bathing beach. I remembered how Mr. Joseph Townsend, visiting Malaga in 1786, had reported that all the young people bathed for hours by night in summer, and the female section of the sea, carefully segregated from the male, was defended from eager gentlemen by sentinels with loaded muskets. Deaths in such a cause were, no doubt, numerous among Malagueño señoritos. Strange things were in those days related to visiting Englishmen; Mr. Henry Swinburne, in 1775, was 'assured that it was hardly possible to breathe in summer.' This sounds like the kind of assurance made by those patriots who desire to defend their city from any suspicions of chilliness, and was probably made to Mr. Swinburne on a day when the cool *levante* was blowing from the sea, or the icy *terral* from the mountains. Malaga, when I was there, was not too hot, but breezy and pleasant.

But I felt no temptation to stay there: as Murray succinctly expressed it, 'one day will suffice.' I went on in the evening

to Torremolinos, about eight miles down the western side of
Malaga bay. The mountains had withdrawn a little from the
sea; the road ran a mile inland; the sunset burned on my
right, over vines and canes and olive gardens. I came into
Torremolinos, a pretty country place, with, close on the sea,
the little Santa Clara hotel, white and tiled and rambling,
with square arches and trellises and a white-walled garden
dropping down by stages to the sea. One could bathe either
from the beach below, or from the garden, where a steep,
cobbled path twisted down the rocks to a little terrace, from
which one dropped down into ten feet of green water heaving gently against a rocky wall. A round full moon rose corn-
coloured behind a fringe of palms. Swimming out to sea, I
saw the whole of the bay, and the Malaga lights twinkling in
the middle of it, as if the wedge of cheese were being de-
voured by a thousand fireflies. Behind the bay the dark mountains reared, with here and there a light. It was an exquisite
bathe. After it I dined on a terrace in the garden; near me
three young Englishmen were enjoying themselves with two
pretty Spanish girls they had picked up in Malaga; they knew
no Spanish, the señoritas no English, but this made them all
the merrier. They were the first English tourists I had seen
since I entered Spain; they grew a little intoxicated, and they
were also the first drunks I had seen in Spain. They were
not very drunk, but one seldom sees Spaniards drunk at
all.

I got up early next morning and went down the garden
path again to bathe. There were blue shadows on the white
garden walls, and cactuses and aloes above them, and golden
cucumbers and pumpkins and palms. I dropped into the green
water and swam out; Malaga across the bay was golden pale
like a pearl; the little playa of Torremolinos had fishing boats
and nets on it and tiny lapping waves. Near me was a boat
with fishermen, who were hacking mussels off the rocks and
singing. The incredible beauty of the place and hour, of the
smooth opal morning sea, shadowing to deep jade beneath

the rocks, of the spread of the great bay, of the climbing, winding garden above with the blue shadows on its white walls, the golden pumpkins, the grey-green spears of the aloes, the arcaded terrace and rambling jumble of low buildings was like the returning memory of a dream long forgotten. Lumpy cathedrals, tiresome modern parks, smartly laid out avenidas and alamedas, tented and populated beaches, passed out of mind, washed away in this quiet sea whispering against shadowed rocks. I climbed the ladder to the platform, and went up the vine-trellised garden to my annexe.

I had to go again into Malaga, to cash a cheque and get my exhaust pipe mended at a garage. They sawed off its end, and told me there was nothing to pay. I gave them ten pesetas and some English cigarettes, and told them how kind they were; they said I was *muy simpatica,* and we parted in mutual esteem. I like most Spanish mechanics very much; they are both clever and obliging, and often witty too. For that matter, so are most British and French mechanics; but the Spanish (or is it only the Andalucian?) negligence about payment is attractive.

Going back again through Torremolinos, I picked up a stout and agreeable woman laden with bundles and baskets, who asked me if I could take her to Marbella, twenty-eight miles on, as she had missed the bus. I said yes by all means, if she was not in a hurry and would not mind my stopping to bathe somewhere on the way. She said that she would not mind at all, but strongly advised me to wait till we reached Marbella, which had the best beach in the world. She was a Marbella enthusiast; whenever I showed signs of admiring some sequestered cove or beach she assured me, with much fervour and gesticulation, that it was nothing to Marbella, which had the best beach in the world, and that when I saw Marbella I should never again want to bathe anywhere else. She had me in such a state of pleasant anticipation about Marbella that I sped quickly on. We talked agreeably all the way about her family, the coffee she was taking them, the beauty of her married daughter, the terrible price of food, why I had come to Spain, why I was alone, why Spanish women did not drive cars nor Spanish little girls ride donkeys in the streets like their brothers; that is to say, she did not really know why, only that it was 'costumbre española,' and the other 'costumbre extranjera.' She was rather a delightful woman, handsome, stout, loquacious, beautifully mannered, comfortably off; either a peasant or a small Malaga bourgeoise; I liked her a great deal.

We got to Marbella, which had a large, hot, quiet beach with a river running into it. The house which my companion was visiting was down by the shore; she invited me into it for refreshments, but I refused. Instead I drove down a track on to the sands, undressed in the car, and bathed. The beach and sea were pleasant enough, but, after all my anticipations, I was disappointed, and did not think Marbella all it had been cracked up to be. It was once important both as trading port and coast stronghold, and in the days when, as old engravings show, it was ringed about with towered Moorish walls, gradually falling to ruin, it must have been a very picturesque city, standing before the sea with the fruitful mountains behind it. It was then full of convents and churches, had a fine alameda of trees watered by fountains; and its port was full of ships being loaded with wines, figs and raisins. But 'the present inhabitants,' wrote a traveller of the 1770s, 'bear the character of an uncivil, inhospitable people, many of them descendants of the Moors, who still seem to resent the ill treatment of their forefathers; hence the Spanish proverb "Marbella es bella, pero no entrar en ella." ' The Marbellians seem in these days to have improved in civility, so perhaps they have now forgotten the ill treatment of their forefathers. The town is guarded by two forts, but in vain, for African barbarians crossed the sea in A.D. 170 and devastated it, with Malaga and the other towns on the Bætican shore, and the Moors took it quite easily in the eighth century, and the Catholic Monarchs, though with more difficulty, in the fifteenth. It was after that peopled with Christians. The Moriscos made some trouble there later, but were expelled, and after that, says the *Cronica,* the inhabitants of Marbella devoted themselves to art, industry and agriculture, leading lives happy and tranquil, rich in the abundant fruits of their soil and sea. Fishermen drew from the liquid element nets laden with the most savoury and delicious fish in Spain; the sardines in particular are of exquisite taste. In few ports does one enjoy such beautiful sea, and such a variety of admirable objects. Opposite one may observe the mountains of the Riff, on the right the Rock of Gibraltar. The countryside (the description continues) is covered with vines and olives, oranges, pomegranates, wine presses, farm-houses, orchards. In the Plaza de la Constitución is a magnificent stone fountain. There is much trade and manufacture, and iron mines in the hills, and Marbella flourishes greatly. Obviously a remarkable place. On first seeing it, Isabella the Catholic threw up her hands and exclaimed, 'Que mar tan bella!' like my companion of the road. But the mar, anyhow the Mediterranean mar, is always bella.

I drove three kilometres on, to the half-ruined hamlet of San Pedro Alcantara, where a steep stony road turned up into the mountains for Ronda, thirty-five miles away. For the first twenty miles this track was covered with loose flints; apparently it was being mended. It climbed up in steep zigzags above tremendous ravines; a great basin of pine-clad mountains opened out, range beyond range, on my left, brown and indigo and purple and softly mauve, stretching into hyacinth-blue distance. Over the ravine great birds flew with wide wings. On my right the rocky precipice rose sheer. They were silent mountains, and a silent track, till, as I rounded a sharp bend, three roadmenders hailed me, black-a-vised, unshaven, wanting a lift to 'dieciocho,' the eighteenth-kilometre stone, ten miles on. They got in: I thought their weight would make it bad for the tyres over the sharp flints, but it proved all right. They were very kind roadmenders. One of them got out at a spring he knew of and filled my earthen pot with fresh water; they kept collecting things they had hidden behind bushes along the track. They left me at dieciocho, where a path to their village went down into the ravine. If ever in the future, one of them said, they could do anything to repay me for my kindness, I was to let them know at once. I said that I would; I hope that an opportunity may offer. Meanwhile, I went on through the mountains. The road became good for the last ten or fifteen miles before Ronda. The mountains presently levelled out into a spacious amphitheatre, in which Ronda stood high on a sheer rock.

Barbaric, emphatic, noble-looking, yet questionable city: a chasm yawns across its face and across its history. For before the Moors made it known to the mediæval world, under the name of Ronda, its existence is dubious. There have even been those who have said that the Moors built it new, quarrying material for it out of the ruined site now called Ronda la Vieja, seven miles north. But the Moors seldom built new cities; they enlarged and Arabized the Visigothic, Roman and Iberian cities and villages that they found. The present site of the Moorish half of Ronda, magnificently poised on its tremendous gorge, in the heart of that mountainous and embattled country, where peace never was, where turbulent tribes for ever warred with one another and with whatever dominant powers ruled them, cannot have been neglected either by Iberians, Romans or Visigoths. Indeed, Ronda is full of Roman relics and fragments; and the mosque on which the chief Christian church was built by the Christian conquerors was itself built on an earlier Visigoth temple. Ronda must always have been a place of importance; but under what name is unknown. Research has, I understand, dismissed Arunda and Acinipo (once held to be Ronda's Roman ancestors) from that district of Spain. One cannot enter this trodden and obscure field of controversy. Enough that before me rose the Ronda of the Moors, the Ronda of twelve centuries of known and turbulent history, famed Ronda, the

Mecca of American tourists and of many English, the Ronda of the Great Gorge. It had, said a fifteenth-century chronicler, at the time of the conquest a hundred mountain towns round it (mostly vanished long since), but Ronda was the queen of the *serranía,* and known as the strongest fort of Andalucia. Ronda, says a much later chronicler, is combated by the north wind, and also by those from east and west, by this last with so much strength that on various occasions it tears up by the roots even the most corpulent trees. Yet it is a healthy climate, the ailments in winter being mainly lung affections and constipation, in summer intermittent fevers produced by excess in eating fruit.

As I drove up into the town, a group of lads threw stones at my car; I had heard before that this was an ancient Rondeño custom. I knew of a crippled Englishman staying in Ronda who had had to renounce his walks about the town because his foreignness and his lameness drew stones and jeers. I got out at the magnificent one-span eighteenth-century bridge, the Puente Nuevo, and looked down into the gorge, which is certainly very singular and noticeable. It is, of course, the great point about Ronda: whether it improves the look of the town or not might be argued; it depends on whether one likes towns to be cleft in two by a gorge, or whether one prefers them all in one piece. Be that as it may, it is a remarkably fine gorge, very wide and very deep; a Salvator Rosa kind of gorge. It actually has some water running in it —most unusual in Spanish rivers in summer. No wonder that the romantics of the eighteenth and nineteenth centuries adored it. Indeed, it is a romantic thing to stand on a bridge and look across from an old Moorish towns of the eighth century to an old Spanish one of the fifteenth. Both towns, or rather both halves of the town, have charm. The fifteenth-century town, the Mercadillo, a good deal rebuilt in the seventeenth and eighteenth centuries, is, for the most part, regular, clean and white; many of the houses have beautiful balconies and *rejos*; there are among them some narrow

Moorish streets and Moorish houses. There is a handsome eighteenth-century bull ring, and a generally admired alameda with a fine precipitous view. But the more interesting part of Ronda is, of course, the older town, the Ciudad, with its narrow, twisting Moorish streets, and white houses with walnut doors. From one of the oldest houses, the Casa del Rey Moro (prettily restored and charmingly bijou, with terrace and patio and gorge view) stone steps cut into the rock by Christian slaves lead down into the Tajo. I did not go all the way down; after about a hundred steps I returned to the street, and followed it down past the two older bridges, the Moorish Puente Viejo and the later Puente de San Miguel. I got on to a path that wound down into the gorge and to the flour mills; the view of the river, the great bridge, and the sheer precipices on either side of the gorge, with apparently decadent houses clinging precariously to their edges, was, in the gathering dusk, intimidating in the extreme.

It takes Baedeker (who does it very well) to describe how one steers a tortuous course about the maze of the Mercadillo and the Ciudad, the Tajo and the streets. It is, to say the truth, confusing, and I made little of it that evening. But next morning I arrived, largely by chance, at the various things that should be seen—the Renaissance house of the Marqués de Salvatierra (or so I was informed, though it had 1798 above the family arms on its carved stone door); various Arab houses and arches, various pretty plazas with ochre churches and charming belfries. The best church was Santa Maria Mayor, a fascinating pastiche—mosque (of which some remains) built on Visigothic (nothing to be seen), 1485 Gothic on the mosque, sixteenth- and seventeenth-century extension on to this, very rich, spacious and plateresque, with fine jasper pillars. There are other churches; and there is the Alcázaba, begun by the Romans, continued by the Goths, and finished by the Moors, and rebuilt after the French blew it up in 1809; it was once the most impregnable fortress in Bætica. There was a strong and active resistance movement to the French in

Ronda; the Rondeños were adept at maquis methods, and the French did not enjoy their occupation of this town.

I should have liked, but had not time, to visit the ruins of Ronda la Vieja; they are said, however, to be now negligible. I should have liked too, given time, to explore the *serranía* for the sites of all the perished towns of the neighbourhood listed in the fifteenth century. And how many little Iberian-Roman-Moorish villages and walled towns are still extant in these mountains, seldom visited because too remote? Ronda is famous, because of its size and its eccentric gorge, so admirable, so picturesque, so serviceable for the throwing down of enemies and slain bulls. But the mountains and ravines of Andalucia are set with the crumbling walled villages where Moors and Christians settled, desiring to live their lives unmolested, and to molest, so far as might be, the lives of others.

I left Ronda at noon for the magnificent silence of the mountain road, where there moved only a few donkeys with loads and a few groups of roadmenders; I passed my three friends of yesterday, who waved their hats and called greetings. And so down through the great wild blue-shadowed sierras to the Mediterranean road again, smooth, easy and civilized, rich with sugar canes, orange groves, bananas and tropical plants. All along it were white villages. At Estepona ships were building on the beach, and donkeys ambled along untended with huge loads of straw and chaff. Beyond Estepona there was a pleasant beach, with a cove between two spurs of rock, one of which jutted out to sea. I thought I would bathe from these rocks, but a *guardia civil* emerged from a hut on the road above me and told me that this beach belonged to an English general at Gibraltar, who allowed no one to bathe there. People might only bathe from the other side of the further rocks. It seemed that the general owned about half a kilometre of beach. I asked if I might swim out from further down the shore and land on the rocks of the general; the guard said no, the general did not permit that

one landed on his rocks. Does the general own the sea too?
I asked. Yes, the sea also was the general's. For how far out?
For two kilometres, replied the guard—further than I would
wish to swim, and I agreed. Who, I asked him, is this general,
and how much does he pay for all this beach, sea and rock?
The guard did not know the general's name, but believed
that he paid nothing at all. The guard was a pleasant man,
and had a sense of humour. It seemed either that the cove was
a gift to the English general from the Spanish nation, which,
in view of Gibraltar, was generous; or that the general had,
with true casual British imperialism, just annexed it, and
engaged a guard to defend it. I felt my customary admiring
pride in the exploits of my countrymen, and thought there
should be a Union Jack flying over the beach. It was Sunday
afternoon; some Spanish families came presently to bathe and
picnic; we were all warned off the general's cove and had to
bathe further down. But it was a pleasant bathe, in that warm
and scintillating afternoon sea. It was, I reflected, one of my
last Mediterranean bathes, for it was only about twenty-five
miles to the Straits, the Pillars of Hercules, where the known
world ended and the dark bottomless void of the misty Ocean
began.

I drove along towards this dubious bourne, the blue of the
Middle Sea still bright and familiar at my side. A stout
woman and her three 'niños' (large creatures of about sixteen),
begged a lift, and crowded into the car, sitting on one
another's knees and on my piled luggage; they were going to
San Roque. I did not like them much; four passengers were
too many for the loaded car, and they had shoved away a
frail-looking old woman who had also wanted a lift; I had
rather that the boy had walked, and was vexed that I had
lacked the strength of mind to say so. I was glad when they
relieved me of their forty stone or so of weight at San Roque.
San Roque, five miles short of Gibraltar, is a picturesque-
looking, crowded hill town, created a city after 1704, when
many of the Spanish refugees from Gibraltar settled in the

village and in Los Barrios and Algeciras. Here the Spanish archives from Gibraltar were removed, and here the inhabitants settled down to wait for the recovery of their homes. They made, partly out of material quarried from the ancient ruins of Carteia, seven miles on round the bay, a characteristic and rather beautiful little brown Spanish town, climbing up, with flagged sidewalks and small plazas, to the Plaza Mayor at the summit. From there, and from the cañones above it, there is a magnificent view of Algeciras Bay, and the Straits with Calpe and Abyle guarding them, and Las Palmas out to sea, and, north, east and west, sierra sweeping behind sierra, lilac brown under the hot blue. In the Plaza Mayor is the church of Santa Maria de la Coronada, named after the mother church in Gibraltar, and preserving such treasures and images as were smuggled out of the clutches of the profane invaders. All about San Roque are delightful houses and patios, of the kind that were probably in Gibraltar before the British took it and transformed it, and before the guns of the Great Siege later smashed them up. Spanish Gibraltar must have looked very charming, with its jumble of tiled and patiod Moorish-Spanish houses lying between the Rock and the sea. I fancied resentful glances at my G.B. car.

From the base of the San Roque hill the road forked for La Linea and Gibraltar, curving, hot and dusty, round the blue bay. La Linea is not particularly interesting, but has a good market, and a plaza with palms. Just beyond it begins the great frontier fuss, first with the officials of Spain, then with those of Gibraltar. They confiscate all one's pesetas, and keep them till one comes into Spain again. Only English pound notes are allowed to enter; these can be changed for Gibraltar pound notes; the coins are the same. You also have to get a permit to stay. The Gibraltar frontier officials (not the La Linea ones) are, like the police, all bilingual; they speak English with a queer, clipped accent, rather like Eurasians. When at last I cleared the frontier and drove into the town, I felt that I had entered into a fantastic dream. Travellers have always said of Gibraltar that it was a piece of England set incongruously down in Spain. It is not, however, in the least like England, this extraordinary, exotic, bilingual fortress town, yielded to the crown of Britain by the crown of Spain two hundred and thirty-five years ago, 'to be held and enjoyed absolutely with all manner of right for ever without any exception or impediment whatsoever.' Gibraltar is, in fact, so far as I know, like no other place on this earth. Its lines of fortification, its bastions, moles, gates, aerodrome, batteries (named after the wife and daughters of George II), great wall (put up, with other strong defences, by Charles V), steep roads zigzagging up the fortified, galleried and intimidating great rock, all the appurtenances of a strongly guarded, highly efficient garrison fortress, make a piquant contrast with the strip of town that climbs along the Rock's western side and consists of one long narrow street and a few side streets and squares off it. The street (Main Street) is full of shops; outside most of them stand their owners or vendors, looking and talking like the Jewish decoys who stand outside shops in Soho and Wardour Street; if you pause to look, they address you in an identical strain, only in Gibraltar English instead of Jewish Cockney. It seems that a very large proportion of Gibraltarians are Jews by origin. Others are Spanish-British, Genoese, Indian, Moorish and Maltese; some are pure Spanish. The original Spanish population fled *en masse* inland when the British took their town in 1704, and no wonder. Apart from their natural distaste for living under foreign conquerors, the behaviour of the eighteen hundred British soldiers and sailors whom Rooke landed in the town after its capture was atrocious; they seem, according to the contemporary records, both Spanish and British, to have become (as always when they took towns) excessively intoxicated, and to have rushed about sacking and looting houses, violating women and churches, attacking the many shrines (such as the famed and revered Our Lady of Europa) and convents in which old Gibraltar (a religious centre) abounded, and destroying and mutilating images and relics in an orgy of drunken lust, robbery, anti-popery and anti-Spanish triumph. The diary of a British chaplain with the troops gives a shocked and shocking account of the behaviour of these men; the crews of British ships were often a disreputable and brutal set drawn from the lowest part of the population; released from their hard life on board and given *carte blanche* on foreign soil, and among a conquered enemy whom they despised, they ran riot in an orgy of drinking, raping, sacking and church destruction. Every church was sacked but that of Santa Maria la Coronada, where a courageous priest stayed behind to guard it; to the credit of the troops, they gave this priest the respect that the British are apt to feel for courage, and did not molest either him or his church. Later on, many of its images and treasures were smuggled out across the frontier to San Roque. Many churches, after being sacked, were turned to secular uses. Six thousand Spanish fled from the town, leaving behind them a good many Jews, Genoese and Moors, who were prepared to adapt themselves and their commercial activities to any régime, and a few women, whose activities were also adaptable. The houses of the refugees were taken and occupied by those who remained, and by the invading power. The poor Spanish, waiting hopefully at San Roque, Algeciras and Los Barrios, and in towns further inland, to return to their homes when the enemy should be ejected, are there still—'the citizens of Gibraltar residing at San Roque.' They still hope one day to recover the *plaza de guerra importantísima enclavada en nuestro territorio.*' But few Spanish think it possible to take Gibraltar by force, the only point of access being a narrow isthmus of land defended by such formidable batteries; and as for attrition by a long siege, that is impossible while Great Britain commands the sea.

For the restoration of this part of our territory [wrote a Spanish historian eighty years ago] we must wait the decline of British power, or for an act of abnegation, which would be a very laudable step of which we see so far few indications; the English do not seem at present disposed to repent their past sins.

What the present expectations of Spaniards are in this matter, I am not sure. There has indeed been a slight decline in British power of late years. But one has not observed that British repentance in this matter is any nearer than it was eighty years ago; indeed, recent history may have confirmed us in our sound view that Gibraltar is a useful place to hold. It played, of course, a key part in the winning of the last war. Also, we think that if we returned it to Spain some other rapacious power would soon be there, which would be more than a pity. It would be convenient to have Ceuta too, and we might one day play the Spanish for that and Algeciras against Gibraltar, double or quits.

Few Gibraltarians are pure Spanish, except those who come daily over from Spain to work. They are less handsome than the Spanish; in fact, they are, for the most part, not handsome at all. In complexion they range from the coffee colour of Indian and Moor, through the lighter brown of the Genoese, the sallowness of the Jew, the uncertain fair-to-dark of the British-Spanish (an Irish-Spanish cross is very common) to the ruddy fairness of the English. They are, on the whole, a smallish people. Such pure Spanish as there are, are many of them descended from refugees (political or criminal) from Spain. The English spoken often has a chi-chi sound; often, too, it has a touch of brogue, owing to having been learned from Irish schoolmaster priests. Compared with the Spanish, the Gibraltarians have an uneasy, rootless, rather diffident, yet amiable and animated air; in a sense they are more sophisticated and cosmopolitan; anyhow, they naturally take British visitors for granted, without stares.

Moving about among them are the garrison and their women; sunburnt soldiers, white-jacketed, simple-faced sailors, slim, sandy, long-legged English women with shopping baskets, frowning against the sun that freckles and burns their light skins, young men driving cars and trucks at breakneck

speed about the narrow streets, intimidating other road users
with the somewhat domineering air of Visigothic conquerors
or of Black-and-Tans. Gibraltar is their fortress, and they are
its privileged garrison.

The Governor and his wife were (as Baedeker says of hotels
at which he has not stopped) well spoken of; one heard of
them nothing but good, and they are popular figures. Indeed,
the thankless job of an occupying power in a corner of someone else's country seems, anyhow in these days, as inoffen-
sively performed as may be. No technique can make the
occupation anything but offensive to Spaniards; in spite of the
commercial and financial advantages conferred by Gibraltar
trade and employment of labour, they naturally want their
peninsula and their fortress back again, as we should if they
occupied Dover and commanded the Channel straits. But
there we seem likely to remain, piling defence on defence,
leading our curious British garrison life, and writing blandly
in our guidebooks, 'There are still traces of the Moorish and
the Spanish occupations.'

There are indeed. We have not succeeded in expunging the
several thousand years of the Rock's past, whereon our own
less than two centuries and a half lies like a thin but formidable palimpsest. 'The fabulous Greeks seem to have selected
this neighbourhood as the scene best adapted to their fictions,'
as Ayala, the eighteenth-century Spanish historian of Gibraltar, observed. The fabulous Greeks left on Calpe, it must
be owned, no traces but the wreathing mists of myth; if there
was a temple of Hercules, it has long since perished; nor did
the Phœnicians or the Carthaginians who had a trading settlement here, build a town to endure. There are Roman traces,
and Ayala and his predecessor, Hernandez de Cortillo, the
historian who wrote of Gibraltar in the early seventeenth
century, describe an ancient tower on the higher part of the
Rock that was 'probably used by the Carthaginians or the
Romans' as a look-out tower, from which to warn the rich
neighbouring port of Carteia of attack. The great cistern of

the Punta de Europa may also have been pre-Moor. No doubt there was always an Iberian population living round the lower part of the Rock, fishing and trading. In old Spanish plans of Gibraltar, the town lies in two parts, at the foot of the Castle; one part, says Portillo, was crowded and poor, the other, above it, had good houses and gardens and streets. The Castle, built by the Moors above the town, was a magnificent fortified and walled group of buildings stretching down the slope to the beach; of it only now remains the great square Tower of Homage, that familiar landmark seen from the surrounding seas. Portillo describes the fortress as of immense strength, capable of resisting any enemy. Apart from the fortress, the Castle ranged over the hill like a palace, with its beautiful Moorish apartments and domes, its mosque chapel, inscribed in Arabic 'To the God of Peace,' its gardens, fruit trees, vines and water tanks; they covered a space little less than that of the whole city. Below, where now is the Dockyard Fort, stood 'the Tower called Tuerto,' parts of which were possibly also pre-Moorish; it was used by the Moors, and later by the Spanish, who watched from it to ring the great clanging alarm bell when the eternally adventitious infidel foe was sighted on the sea; it was enlarged and strengthened in the seventeenth-century. The fortifications added to the Rock by Charles V were immense; that slow and patient Teuton emperor piled defence upon defence; his dreams were ever of huge works and impregnable castles of war, and in the Rock he had a fortress to his mind.

Its beauty, before we spoiled and spoilt it, must have been great. Vineyards and gardens covered the long slope to the north (wine was one of the exports of the province of Gibraltar), and all over and all round the Rock and the colony of crowded dwellings there were churches, convents and shrines. On Europa Point stood the chapel of the Virgen de Europa, a shrine to which pilgrimages were continually made, for she directed the fortunes of sailors, was held in great veneration, and performed many miracles, her chapel and image were decorated with gifts, and great silver lamps, presented by grateful or hopeful commanders of galleys, burned night and day before the holy image, serving also as a lighthouse for sailors (the present lighthouse stands on nearly the same spot). This chapel was originally Moorish, and from its tower the One God was for centuries daily declared. Till the British sacked it, it was full of treasures and saintly relics.

The principal church, Santa Maria Coronada, now the Roman Catholic Cathedral, was once a mosque, built on the foundations of a temple; Portillo refers to 'marble in the buildings, cloisters, and the court of orange trees, which resembles that in the church at Cordova,' and describes its numerous chapels. Then there was San Juan de Lateran, with a prior, priests and chaplains, and many other ancient churches, some in the Vila Vieja, some like San Juan el Verde (under the Knights of Malta), with its green glazed tiles and its neighbouring Calvary, scattered over the slopes of the Rock. There were many religious houses, Benedictine, Franciscan and others; one of these is now Government House; the others were long ago, like the churches, either secularized or destroyed. A traveller in 1772 wrote that the church of Government House was the only one in Gibraltar open for divine service,

all the other chapels and places of worship having been turned into store-houses, to the great scandal of the Spaniards and inconvenience of the protestants: the bells of the Tower, incommoding the Governor, were by his order unhung, so that the inhabitants are forced to repair to church by beat of drum.

Looking back to the Moorish centuries, to Gebel-Tarik, one sees a rich and populated promontory, beautifully adorned with marbled mosques, arcaded houses and courts, lovely fountained gardens, vineyards and orange groves, with a closely built city crowding narrowly beneath and up the steep climb of the hill, while bells rang from minarets and watchtowers, and Moorish feluccas sailed in and out of the bay, which was guarded on the south by the white stronghold of Algiers, while Tarifa jutted out beyond it, and African fleets passed to and from across the Straits, between Calpe and Abyle, their sailors noting at dawn how the Rock took the golden light from the east before the sun rose, the flame from the west after it had sunk beneath the hills, and how it shone, as an Arab writer said, as if it were on fire, a beacon to the Straits.

After the Spanish conquest, in 1462, Gibraltar dwindled in strength, in riches, in trade and in population. The inhabitants were frightened, with reason, of plundering and kidnapping raids from across the Straits; they had a tendency to seek safety inland; and in the year 1500 Gibraltar had less than fifteen hundred residents. The Spanish kings did their utmost to keep it populated, by employing men on building and road works and by using the Rock as a place of transportation for convicts and an asylum for criminals. In these days it is crowded enough, with the British garrison, the permanent residents in the town and on the fishing beaches, and the Spanish who come in daily from Spain to work. When the Rock goes into action, it is cleared; the redundant occupants are exiled, lest they be a nuisance, and because their houses are required for the military. The war evacuees had a dismal time. Those of them sent to London hated its weather and its bombing, as Londoners who encountered them will remember; as a Gibraltarian said to me, 'You see, in Gibraltar we are not used to crime and violence,' and the guns that all too often go off on the Rock are fired, normally, rather in ceremony than in anger. They had a terrible time, these poor evacuees, what with the horrors of London, and, later, the desolation of camp life in Ulster in the rain; they died a hundred deaths from fear, homesickness and cold. Now they are home again, and so happy in the familiar sunshine, gaiety and security of their Rock, that they beam on and chatter to visitors from England, exchanging memories of London.

The shops are lavishly full of gaudy trash from the bazaars

across the Straits, from India (Indian-owned shops and Indian sellers are many) and from Britain. Oriental rugs hang cheek by jowl with silk and cotton goods from Manchester; cosmetics, stockings, shoes, bright dresses, cheap jewellery, fountain-pens, Moorish boxes like those in the Alhambra shops but cheaper, everything to catch the eye of the starved visitor from austerity-ruled lands, a meretricious vanity fair of the gaudy commonplace. It all makes of Main Street a bright, fantastic nonsense, which seems to connect with no European country. Turning off it, into its adjacent squares, one finds none of the picturesqueness of Spanish plazas; they are business-like, set about with offices and with those British-looking houses built after the smashing up of the town by the great French and Spanish siege of 1779–83, which left, it seems, few houses standing, and accounts for Gibraltar's modern look. What an opportunity was here, and how it was misused! For, 'the English being a nation who, in all their colonies spread over the face of the globe, study more the useful than the grand,' the houses were replaced by these dreary-looking English dwellings of brown-grey stone, slate roofed, solid and unbalconied, called by such names as 'Cumberland Buildings,' and standing among the eucalyptus trees as if they had been transported from Margate, drab little gardens and all. Yet not altogether, for here and there there is an exotic touch, green persiennes, a verandah, a portico, or what not; some slight involuntary gesture to Spain. In the largest square, which lies off Irish Town and is called John Mackintosh, I saw on Sunday afternoon, believe it or not, two young men with a harmonium, exhorting people to accept Jesus. Their small audience may or may not have possessed enough British blood to know what they were talking about.

There are more attractive squares than John Mackintosh. There is, on the Rock side of Main Street, Convent Place, where stands the Convent, the residence of the Governor, a beautiful yellow sixteenth- and seventeenth-century Franciscan house; like Santa Maria Coronada, it was one of the buildings that survived the great siege. There is now also an Anglican cathedral (the see being held by a roving bishop); built in Moorish style, it looks common; better is the garrison church, King's Chapel, which is full of rather touching monuments. Before these churches were built 'in this sink of Moslem, Jewish and Roman Catholic profligacy,' as Ford sternly puts it, Protestant services were held in the Convent chapel. The Spanish cathedral has now little of interest in it; and restoration has robbed it of distinction; confessions are heard there in English, Spanish, Italian, French, German and Maltese. In Gibraltar all religions and all races live together in neighbourly amity.

After the long strip of Main Street and the town squares, the side of the great limestone Rock rises sheer, and up it wind the steep zigzags of road that climb, bend on bend, to the top—awkward bends for a car. At the southern end of the Rock is Europa Point, and a stupendous view of Africa and the sea. At the northern end, the ruined Moorish Tower stands high, all that remains of the citadel and palace that once covered the hill-side. Over the rugged tower now waves, incongruously, impudently, the banner of a people who, when Tarik occupied Gebel-Tarik, were fighting one another, tribe against tribe, on an island of forests and swamps in a cold northern sea over a thousand miles away. Such are the fantastic turns and tilts of fortune: poor Tarik pushed back to Africa whence he came, the Spanish pushed off the Rock whence they pushed the Moors, the northern islanders in possession. The islanders have now held it for two hundred and forty years; the Spanish held it for the same; the Moors for seven centuries and a half. Whether the Visigoths or the Romans fortified Calpe, it is difficult to tell; there is no mention of any town or stronghold there. Strabo, writing in the first century, calls it merely 'a mountain belonging to the Iberians,' which 'rises to so great a height and is so steep that from a distance it looks like an island'; he goes on to refer to the ancient city of Calpe-Carteia, forty stadia from the Rock;

Ptolemy and other geographers speak of it only as a mountain, a column in the sea; even the fourth-century Avienus refers to no dwellers on the 'Herculanæ columnæ, saxa prominentia, Abila atque Calpe.' Probably Calpe was only lived on by Iberian fishermen when Tarik took it; there is no record of his meeting resistance there.

From then on, the Rock has been attacked and besieged continually, and its fortifications and defences have strengthened year by year; it is a walled, gated and embattled fort, to which the town is a mere appendage. To live there would be oppressive: roads and tunnels are barred and guarded by armed sentries, going and coming to and from Spain is an enterprise attended by tedious circumstance and fuss; scarcely any money may be taken across, and the frontier closes after a certain hour of the night. The Rock bristles with regulations, bayonets and guns, and casual explorations about it are let and hindered. The climate is tiringly hot in summer, often with an exhausting wind, and in winter beaten by the Levanter and by chilly and damp Atlantic gales. 'Gibraltar is with reason called the Montpellier of Spain,' one reads; but with what reason is not clear. The bathing is not good; there are a few crowded beaches, and one or two for local clubs; no solitary rocks or coves. As I had discovered, some English drive down the Mediterranean coast to bathe; others bathe and stay round the bay, at Puente Mayorga and elsewhere. A pleasant, friendly, hospitable, insular social life flourishes among the garrison, which has its club house, library and other amenities. Local papers and journals are published, which have the immature provincial brightness of school or parish magazines. Could there be, has there ever been (I inquire without dogmatism, pre-judgment or enough information), art, letters or music created in Gibraltar, by any race or any mixture of races? One imagines not. The Rock is too circumscribed for the literary activities of a recording Kipling; possibly a Jane Austen might make something of its social and personal relationships (she was good at garrison life);

poetry or music would be stultified in a garrison atmosphere.

The place has an odd, fantastic charm, apart from its magnificent views; the charm, I suppose, of incongruity. If the Spanish had it, it would rapidly become more florid and more picturesque, more attractive and a great deal less efficient.

I liked the local museum, with its memories of the great siege, and its portraits of Gibraltar worthies—Rooke, looking very pleased with himself, as well he may, in a full-bottomed wig; Elliot, the commander during the great siege, looking contentious, indomitable and purple-faced in a tie-wig, and so on. The keeper of the museum, a friendly Irish-Spanish Gibraltarian, told me some Gibraltar gossip—why there were so many Irish accents to be heard; why evacuation had been necessary; how, during the war, a Spanish German agent had tried to blow up the fort by means of bombs concealed in bananas, but had been betrayed by a Gibraltarian and foiled, in fact, hanged; how Barbarossa, the Turkish pirate, had landed on Europa Point in 1540, sacked the town, and carried off a thousand captives, after which Charles V had built his great defensive wall; and how the Duke of Kent, Queen Victoria's father, had been governor for a time and had made himself unpopular with the troops by cutting down the public-houses, so they mutinied and he had them shot, and retired under a cloud.

To attempt to describe Gibraltar without describing some of the fortifications, bastions, galleries, great caves, and (I suppose) monkeys, that adorn its Rock, seems inadequate and poor of spirit; but I do not understand fortifications and do not care for and did not see caves or monkeys, so (like Spanish bull-fights and for the same reasons) I omit them. Enough for me was the magnificent galleried Rock, with its cactus-grown heights and enormous blue views, that extraordinary setting for the odd little pale-brown town snuggling in its shelter with its early nineteenth-century British houses and gardens, its eucalyptus, bougainvillæas, cheerful, amorphous population, gaudy shops, and dark-eyed, obliging, polite small policemen in British uniforms and helmets, who answer questions so kindly in clipped English and curious idiom. 'It is straight on,' they say. 'You will not miss it,' which has a sound more reassuring and prophetic than the London 'You can't miss it.' At the Post Office an extraordinary, un-Spanish briskness and efficiency reigns: if there are letters addressed to you, you get them; if there are none when there should be, it is because letters forwarded from Spain, even from places so near as Malaga, often take weeks to reach Gibraltar; as the Post Office clerks remark, 'You can't hurry the Spanish.' One could not stay long in Gibraltar; but, as a change from Spain, the masculine, efficient vigour and intelligence of the British is restful. Intelligence. Is this where our often-maligned race perhaps shines, in comparison with some others more attractive? Stupid as many of us are, on the whole we do seem to have invention, and a kind of active power of performance, of getting things done. We have also our share of courage, some sense of fair play, fairly cool heads, a not unkindly tolerance, and (in these days, though certainly not of old, but then no race had) a certain humaneness. Set against these our snobbery, our widespread philistinism and vulgarity, our often ungracious manners, our supposed contempt for foreigners (but is this greater than the contempt of foreigners for us and for one another?), our drunkenness and gluttony (we are, it is said, the only nation in the world which likes to eat five, sometimes six, large meals a day, and certainly Gibraltar was the only place in Spain where I saw bacon being eaten at breakfast, 'elevenses' in mid-morning, and sailors and soldiers drunk)—and the balance between us and the foreigners seems about even. But in the matter of efficiency, I have a notion that we tip it.

After some difficulty in getting another visa to enter Spain (the Spanish consulate is crowded all day with aspirants for this; I suppose those who live there have season permits) I left my country's fortress, passing down the long, narrow causeway that leads out by Waterport and the airfield to the

British Lines, retrieved the pesetas I had left with the frontier police, filled up a great number of forms at the Spanish frontier and customs, and found myself at last in Spain again, driving through La Linea and round Algeciras Bay. It was very hot on the shadeless road.

I was still in the Straits, still, I suppose, in the Mediterranean: I do not think it becomes the Atlantic until Tarifa, the most southern point of Spain, is rounded. But I should soon be past the Pillars, once to the Greeks the bourne of the known world, for from 500 B.C., when the Carthaginians made themselves masters of Andalucia, to 200 or so, when the Romans beat them out of Spain, Greek voyagers trespassed into the ocean beyond the straits at their peril. Even Polybius, in the second century B.C., could write, 'The channel at the Pillars of Heracles is seldom used, and by very few persons, owing to the lack of intercourse between the tribes inhabiting those remote parts, and owing to the scantiness of our knowledge of the outer ocean.' The Tartessian shores, once known, had slid gradually into the regions of myth. To the Greeks, the Pillars guarded the Mare Tenebrosum, the dark, shadowy and alarming ocean beyond the Middle Sea. It was an intimidating thought, even to me, though those far-western shores had been free of the Punic menace now for over two thousand years.

Those extraordinary Pillars—were they once joined together, one mountain, and dug through by that remarkable man Heracles, as some have supposed? 'But the traditions respecting Hercules I conceive to be fabulous in the highest degree,' said Pliny, and one cannot help agreeing with him. He was accurate, too, in his comment on the Straits—'From so small a mouth as this does so immense an expanse of water open upon us.' It strikes, as he said, as they all said, the mariner with alarm. Indeed, even on land, on the road that runs round Algeciras Bay, the approach to the great Outer Sea is faintly alarming. It has storms, strange monsters, wild tribes, mists; it is fathomless, bourneless, it runs up and down in tides, it is chill, and has great waves. So, at least, the ancients complained, and so one has always found. 'It is not easy,' said Pindar, 'to pass further than the Pillars of Heracles into the not to be trodden sea beyond. Those pillars fixed by the hero god are glorious witnesses of his furthest voyaging'; and again, 'Into the world beyond neither the wise nor the unwise may fare. I will not strive to penetrate there: I should be one of the witless if I did so.'

> From these columns [wrote Avienus's sixth-century sailing-book] going west one finds an illimitable abyss; the ocean stretches far . . . no one takes his ships through that ocean, for there are no winds to sail by . . . always mists swathe the abyss and the day is continually darkened by clouds. This is the ocean which spreads over the great expanse of the world, this is the largest sea, the sea which goes round the world's shores, supplying the inner sea with water; this is the source of our sea. . . . Many monsters abound in it, and many terrors from the wilds. . . .

These melancholy and intimidated geographers were, it seems, sometimes vague as to whether they referred to the bay of Cadiz beyond the Straits, or to the vaster and even less known ocean beyond Cadiz; when Pindar wrote, 'It is not possible to pass beyond Gades towards the darkness of the west; set thy sails back again, oh Pindar, to the mainland of Europe,' he may have believed Cadiz much nearer to the Pillars than it is; he calls them 'the gates of Gades.' But some believed (as Strabo remarked) that the Pillars were actually the bronze pillars of the temple of Hercules in Cadiz city; those who ended their voyage here 'have had it noisily spread abroad that this is the end of both land and sea.' In fact, everything west of the Straits was for three centuries obscure and dubious to the Greeks, shut from the Outer Ocean by their victorious Punic rivals after a brief eighty years or so of adventuring and trading along the Tartessian shores. Through those three centuries they only knew that ocean and its shores from the reports of such incredible romancers as Pytheas, and from intimidating Carthaginian propaganda. Heracles, Odysseus, Jason, and other epic heroes, adventure about this fabulous world, stealing cattle, and golden fleece, visiting the Hesperides and the Islands of the Blest, but only here and there a Greek sailor or merchant dares the Straits; the silver-rich Tartessian lands and trade remain a Carthaginian monopoly. 'To this day,' Strabo wrote, long after the Carthaginians had gone from Spain, 'almost all the cities of Turdetania are inhabited by Phœnicians.'

The road that rounds Algeciras Bay from Gibraltar runs past the ghosts of Phœnician, Carthaginian and Roman cities. The cities are long gone: coming to what I believed to be El Roquadillo farm on the river Guadarrante, where once Carteia flourished, I looked for the site of that noble city in vain. Unless I searched in the wrong place, every vestige of what were, as late as the present century, called 'traces still to be seen' ('some low mounds' were observed by Baedeker) has vanished. The total disappearance of a once great and prosperous city always has fascination. Carteia was founded by Phœnicians, perhaps before Cadiz; it was long famous as a mercantile port, a stronghold, a fishery, a populous and noble city. It fought for Carthage against Rome, and Carteian soldiers joined Hannibal's army; later, in the second century B.C., the Romans planted there a colony of the half-Spanish children produced by the Roman legionaries, and called it Colonia Libertinorum. Pompey, defeated at Munda, fled there and was betrayed to Cæsar; Crassus hid there for three months; it was a headquarters of the Roman fleet, as it had earlier been for the Carthaginian, and before that, says Livy, for the Spanish. The cargoes going in and out of that splendid harbour were rich and numerous. Was it founded by Heracles and called Heracleia? Was it the ancient Tartessos, or perhaps built on the Tartessian ruins, as asserted by Pytheas, Pliny ('Carteia Tartessos a Graecis dicta'), Pomponius Mela ('Carteia, aliquando Tartessos, et quam transvecti ex Africa Phœnices habitant') and most other historians, until the present century, which has placed Tartessos in or near the mouth of the Guadalquivir? Not that the classical historians were agreed; Artemidorus called the Tartessos identification 'another false statement of Eratosthenes, who made many, relying on Pytheas' (who had a notorious reputation for travellers' lies), and the argument has continued until recently. One would like to think that here, in the crook of this horse-shoe bay, stood Tarshish, in whose fairs the world traded, that from this very harbour sailed the navies that brought to King Solomon every three years gold, silver, ivory, peacocks and apes, perhaps the monkeys from Calpe round the bay, the peacocks that strut on the sierras behind Carteia, the elephants' tusks from Africa across the Straits. One would like to place here the questionable, the fabulous Tartessos, to which, as Herodotus relates, Kolaius the Samian came driven by the easterly winds through the Straits, four centuries before the Romans took it, and met there Argonthonius, the Tartessian king. One would like to, merely because here, at least, is an identifiable site, unlike the Tartessian sites in Cadiz Bay and in the mouth of the Guadalquivir; but the evidence on the whole seems against us, and we must be content with knowing that here was the great Carteia, which fell from sight, probably destroyed by the Vandals about the time when the empire also fell. It stood on the east bank of the Guadarranque river, a furlong from its mouth; above the harbour rose a noble city of marble, temples, statues, towers and walls. Its ruins lay about for centuries; they served as a quarry out of which the Moors rebuilt the destroyed Algeciras, and the Spaniards, when they fled Gibraltar in 1704, the town of San Roque. In 1771 there were still to be seen the remains of a stone quay, a mole, town walls climbing over the hill, some towers, a Roman theatre ('in a deplorable state of ruin,' but rows of seats and arches could be distinguished), a line of buildings, great blocks of carved marble lying by the farmhouse that stands on the foundations of some great building; in the walls of the farm-house Mr. Francis Carter, in 1771,

saw a marble slab carved with satyrs and boys; near it lay a
broken statue, moss-grown. A hundred and fifty years before
that, a visitor reported seeing the illustrious ruins of great
buildings and the entire mole. This was, of course, before
San Roque quarried it. Ford, in the 1840's, saw substantial
remains; I, in the 1940's, nothing, not even the large purple
shell-fish in the bay from which the Phœnicians got their dye,
nor bonitos biting fishermen, nor one of the sea monsters of
which Pliny tells, which used to raid the fishermen's yards for
fish. So far as I was concerned, Carteia was gone. I was sorry,
but did not stay to mourn in the eloquent manner of earlier
visitors, such as Mr. Carter in 1771 and Señor Ayala a few
years later.

O Carteia! [cries Mr Carter] thou once favoured and renowned
city, whose beauty captivated the merchant, drawing all nations
of the earth to thy port, can I contemplate without compassion
thy present desolate state? Behold thy noble theatre is destroyed,
thy populous streets are ploughed up and sown, thy walls are
taken away, thy sacred temples are beat down, and thy beauteous
head once crowned with turrets is now levelled with the dust.
Where are thy Senators, thy purpled Quatuor-viri, thy Aediles,
thy streets swarming with people? The port is deserted, no
fleets are to be seen in it, nor the shouts of mariners any more
heard; thy fields for want of culture are turned to morasses, the
very air over thee is become heavy and unwholesome, and the
chilling ague drives man from thine habitation; in thy latter
end, as in thy prosperity, one common fate attends thee with the
mighty Babylon!

Señor Ayala was moved to similar lamentations. 'O!' he
exclaimed, 'what does not yield to the slow workings of
numerous years; and what may not be found buried in the
depth of the ocean! Buried now in silence and ruins art thou,'
and so on.

Reflecting duly but more briefly on all this, I left Carteia
and drove on to Algeciras, the Roman Portus Albus, that
large and flashy white Moorish city which, seen from the

Rock, shines so luminously across the bay, a magnificent cluster of pale cubes, roofs, towers and gardens by day, of sparkling lights by night, all reflected in shining water.

Of the city's history, less is known than one would wish. Between the Roman period and the coming of Tarik the Moor, Gothic darkness hides it. If the barbarians destroyed it with Carteia, it must have been rebuilt, for Tarik took it from the Visigoth Count Julian on landing in Spain, and built it up into a great stronghold, fortifying it with huge walls, towers and castle, and calling it el-Gezira el-Khadra, 'green island,' from the island, now Isla Verde, which they also walled and fortified, half a mile offshore. The Moors held it, continually assaulted, teased and battered by Spaniards on land and Norman pirates from the sea, until the great twenty months' siege of 1342–4, at which Alfonso XI of Castile was assisted by Christian chivalry from all Europe (Chaucer's much-campaigning knight was there). Seldom have so many members of the nobility assisted at a siege; seldom have they besieged so ineffectually for so long. At last, however, the city yielded; Alfonso marched in with his great cosmopolitan procession of knights and prelates, purified and consecrated the mosque, christening it Santa Maria de la Palma, repaired the fortifications, and rewarded his warriors with the beautiful Moorish houses and gardens of the city. Alfonso was so delighted with his conquest that he added to his titles that of King of Algeciras.

The infidels, however, had not done with Algeciras; in 1369 it was almost completely destroyed by an attack from the King of Granada; a century later its territory and ruins were given to Gibraltar, which quarried fortifications out of them. It lay ruined for three centuries and a half, until many of the inhabitants of Gibraltar fled there from the English; after that it was gradually rebuilt (partly out of the Carteia ruins), and its population quickly grew. Convents were built, plazas and streets laid out; in the largest plaza, the Plaza Alta, the cathedral of Santa Maria replaced the ancient parish church; it was a companion cathedral to Cadiz, and has a dull look. In 1760 Charles III began to enlarge the town; the process has gone on ever since. The old Moorish town had been on the right bank of the river that divides the city; the eighteenth-century town was built on the left, with broad streets and three fine plazas; the symmetrical Plaza Alta, with cathedral, trees and fountain; below it, close to the mole, the Plaza Baja, with its lively market, where Moors in fezes from Morocco chaffer with Moors without fezes from Spain; the smaller Plaza San Isidoro in the north-east quarter. The town, which has nowhere a characteristically eighteenth-century look, for it was rebuilt in the Arab manner, is handsome and spacious, full of fine Moorish-looking houses with patios, fountains and roof gardens. The Hotel Cristina is a de luxe model, like the Rock Hotel at Gibraltar, white and rambling, with fine gardens and magnificent views across the bay; the British see it from the Rock, and stay in it when on holiday. Algeciras is a city of pleasure, luxury and beauty, with its harbour of little ships and fishing fleets and steamers crossing to and from Africa, which lies, a grey-blue shadow, across the way. The superb horseshoe of tossing blue sea, with the picturesque island moored outside the port, the crouching Rock to eastward, the jut of Tarifa to westward, the great ocean expanding beyond the Straits, and the mountains rising behind, make a fine setting to this handsome and lordly city. It seemed suited rather to rich British and Continental tourists and oriental sultans than to me in my battered, dust-smeared car; I felt no temptation to linger, but took the road to Tarifa.

This ran through wild moorland country, desolate and bare; the August afternoon burned on the arid, thymey, cork-forested hills, where the cicadas hoarsely sawed; the shadowless road wound and bent, framing in its angles what I feared must, now that Algeciras Bay was behind me, be called the Atlantic; anyhow it was not the Mediterranean. It was blue enough; the shadowy, mist-cloaked Outer Ocean, monstrous with intimidating creatures, still wore a civilized air.

Not so Tarifa, the southernmost point of Europe, whose square-towered castle rose before me, guarding the white, entirely Moorish town, with its long narrow winding streets, flat-roofed houses, and quiet, idling, Arab-eyed groups of natives. Leaving my car on the road outside the walled city, I entered its streets through one of the round arches that open into them, and braced myself to ignore the mob of stalking savages that would, I supposed, in a moment collect. But I was for once fortunate; down one of the streets that crossed mine I saw a dense crowd of children stalking, and before them went, in embarrassed haste, another female foreigner. She had drawn the hunt, and, taking another turning, I evaded it, and was able to explore Tarifa unpursued. It is a fascinating town; perhaps the most Moorish in Andalucia, and the first to become so, for Tarif the Arab arrived there from Africa and wrested it from the Visigoths the year before Tarik the Berber got to Gibraltar. Tarif proceeded to make of Tarifa a strong fortress, which was besieged in vain until Sancho el Bravo took it in 1292, and Alonso de Guzman, defending it against counterattacks, got himself into legend as the dutiful commandant and callous parent. The fortress still stands at the eastern end of the town, with its thick embrasured walls set with small towers, early Moorish work, of which century is uncertain. In the city walls are round-arched gateways, through which one dives into the narrow streets, where beautiful oriental women, black hooded, stand at their doors, and sweet oranges are driven behind tiny donkeys by little boys. The *parroquial* is mainly fifteenth century; it has three broad naves, a magnificent door, and a poor tower. The houses are low and white; the iron balconies bright with flowers and blue pots; below the streets and above the sea an alameda runs. Beyond the town is a long isthmus with an island at the end, the Isola de las Palombas, now connected by a narrow causeway running very beautifully between two small fishing harbours and beaches, where copper-skinned children bathed, and ending at gates beyond which passage was barred, for a fortress and lighthouse have been built there. Here is the Punta Marroquí, the southernmost point of Spain; the Phœnicians called it Josa, which is Phœnician for passage, the Romans Julia Traducta. From it one sees the Mediterranean to the east and the Atlantic to the west; for now we are really come to the Outer Ocean.

Returning to my car, I met the hunt in full cry; their quarry had emerged out of the streets into the road outside, the pack at her heels. She looked distressed and cross as she came towards me, seeking protection in the company of a fellow-victim. The pack, sighting me, gathered round their double quarry and the car, nudging and pointing, 'Mais, c'est formidable!' the flustered lady exclaimed, trying to laugh. She was a nice-looking French-woman, at the moment flushed with heat, embarrassment and annoyance. I told her it was wiser to take no notice, for this made them worse; one should go on one's way as if they did not exist. She, it seemed, had turned and protested, a fatal mistake. She told me that she had not been long in Spain; she was married to a Spaniard; they were staying at the Cristina in Algeciras and she had come to Tarifa in the car of an American friend, which was to return and pick her up presently. She had not known, she said, what it was like to walk about Tarifa alone, or she would never have tried it. It was *incroyable,* the manners of these children and young people, and that no adult called them off. I told her that it was just Spanish curiosity, and that one got used to it in time. 'And you go about alone, madame?' she said. 'You are very brave. I confess that I could not face it.' It was a bore, I agreed, but if one wanted to see Spain, it was worth it. Her husband, she said, did not like her going about alone; he had told her that Spanish ladies never did it. Were he here, he would box the ears of the children; he had done so the other day in Algeciras when one of them was rude to her. I began to understand why the stalking children ducked if one looked round.

At this point the car of her American friend arrived; she

hurried to its shelter with the relief of a traveller in a wild country rescued from savages. These, I reflected as I drove away, were the Turdetanians, of whom Strabo wrote, 'The Turdetani not only enjoy a salubrious climate, but their manners are polished and urbane.' They had, he said, gentleness and civility, had forgotten their own language, and lived in the Roman manner, having become, for the most part, *togati*. That was two thousand years ago. And Strabo was never in Spain. The present inhabitants of Tarifa were perhaps more like the *feroces Libyphœnices* who lived across the water.

A fresh wind blew about Punta Marroquí; the sea outside the little sheltered harbour broke in waves on the beach as I drove north-west along the shores of the Atlantic towards Cadiz. The fabulous shores of Turdetania, of the ancient rich Tartessian land where the Phœnicians traded and founded their cities, where Heracles adventured and drove cattle and took legendary possession of the whole fabled sea and shore, where Odysseus too voyaged, where Homer placed the abode of the blessed and of the damned, where lay the lost Atlantis, were bloomed the Hesperides with their golden orchards, and (more historically) the golden and silver wealth with which Tyrians trafficked down all the coasts of Europe and of Africa. I wished that my road ran closer to the sea. It bent inland, through a wild dry mountain land, smelling of hot prickly pears, cactuses, cork trees; on my left ranged the Silla del Papa, shutting out the sea, on my right the Utreras, with higher sierras rearing behind. Between two rocky heights spread the marshy Laguna de Janda, which Avienus says was called in his day Herma; round it Tarik fought Roderick the Goth, whom he was to beat finally at Guadalete. If the lagoon had more water, it would be a good lake. A little way beyond it, above the bridge over the Barbate, rises the precipitous hill on whose summit stands the fortified Moorish-Iberian town of Vejer de la Frontera. Vejer must be a very fine and interesting town; it looks, anyhow, very well from below, and I had

been told by someone who had seen it that it had a good
Gothic Mudájar church. But it stands at the top of a very
high hill, and few travellers seem to get near enough to it to
describe it. I was sorry to join the unenterprising herd, which
includes Ford, Baedeker, Muirhead, and most other tourists
in these parts; but evening was approaching, and I wanted to
get to Cadiz, and it was hot, and the road looked both steep
and bad, and at the foot of the hill was a little centa where I
stopped for a drink, watched by an absorbed family group,
who, I believe, had not seen a foreign woman since
Alfonso XI fought and beat the Kings of Granada and Fez
in that neighbourhood six centuries before. They fed me with
sandwiches and inquired after my family, whom I seemed to
have unaccountably left at home in France; or perhaps, they
suggested, hearing that I was bound for Cadiz, my husband
awaited me there, too ill to come and drive me. I found myself soon committed to transporting as far as San Fernando
two large young soldiers bound for Jerez with two large
wooden chests. I hoped that they might tell me something
about Vejer as we drove, but they could not; it was to them
just Vejer, or Vélez, and of no interest; they were uninformed youths, and knew nothing about anything we passed
on the way, only that, if I could not take them all the way
to Jerez, they would like to be dropped in the San Fernando
plaza in time to get the bus. So Vejer I still only know by
hearsay. Photographs I have seen show very white patios and
interiors with wells, and donkeys standing by them, and
Moorish-robed women on ancient stairways. Someone had
mentioned to me the parish church; a Spanish encyclo-
pædia adds that Vejer has narrow streets, old houses and
picturesque and wide views (which one can deduce by looking at it from below), is one of the oldest towns on this
coast, contains many churches of unspecified dates, was conquered by Ferdinand in 1284, and that the French climbed up
and occupied it in 1811, which does them great credit. Next
time I pass that way I shall follow their example. This time I

drove on, getting impressive glimpses of the mountain-top city as the road twisted past it.

The hampering presence of my soldiers prevented my turning aside to see Medina Sidonia, twelve miles away in the hills to my right, or the mouth of the Sancti Petri channel across the salt marsh country to my left, where lies the fortified island of Sancti Petri, in which I did not feel that my companions would be interested. The one advantage of transporting these young men was that their chaperonage seemed to check the usual hoots and yells at a female driver from those we passed on the road; perhaps it was not apparent as we drove by who held the wheel.

We drove on through the salt marshes, which were dotted with upright salt pillars, as if hundreds of the wives of Lot, fleeing long ago from the wicked city of Gades Jocosæ, had turned to look back wistfully at the gay goings on there, and been salted in their tracks.

The Sancti Petri channel was very beautiful; it formed a harbour of green water beneath the San Fernando bridge, where large fishing boats lay. San Fernando itself is a pretty town, though a naval headquarters and arsenal. It is the capital of the Isla de Leon; it has a spacious street and plaza, and most of its pleasant low white houses with their charming bright green *rejas* and balconies were built in the late eighteenth and early nineteenth centuries, after Charles had made the place a naval arsenal. The naval buildings and the iron foundry are fortunately in a suburb away from the main town, which has a nicely civil and leisured air, standing so whitely on the green channel among the wide salt plains.

Across the channel is the Isla Leon, the Erytheia of the ancients, where Geryon lived with his cattle that Heracles drove off, 'the island called Erytheia, near Gadeira outside the Pillars of Heracles by the Ocean,' as Herodotus describes it. Strabo says there was good grass on it, and its cattle grew fat. On it stood the temple of the Phœnician Heracles; it was probably the earliest Phœnician settlement, before Gadir. The road ran smoothly across it, past the eighteenth-century observatory, to the long narrow isthmus that pushes out to sea holding Cadiz like a great lily bud at a stem's end. It is one of the lovely wonders of the world, this long causeway road, built on arches, thrusting an arm between the smooth blue circle of Cadiz Bay and the dancing silver immensity of the Atlantic. On the mainland side of the bay, the peninsula of Trocadero curves, shutting the deeply indented harbour of Puerto Real from the Atlantic winds and waves. At the end of the isthmus Cadiz and its pale domes lie like a spray of water-lilies on a gleaming turquoise lake under a peach-bloom sky. No city can have a lovelier approach than Gades Jocosæ, now Cadiz la Joyosa. It is perhaps, says Pliny, a fragment of the lost Atlantis, that, as we know from Plato, lies sunk somewhere off that coast. It was, says Avienus, in his muddled way, formerly Tartessos—'Ipsa Tartessos prius cognominata est.' It was a common confusion, this between the long-destroyed Tartessos and the great Phœnician and Carthaginian city that was heir (if Tartessos indeed was ever a city at all) to its magnificence. Even many fifth-century Greeks made it, and, later, nearly all the Romans except those who ran Carteia-Tartessos as a rival claimant. When Avienus wrote his enigmatic, and surely (in the fourth century) premature lines on the fallen state of Gades, 'that great and rich city, ancient in age, now poor, small, destitute, a heap of ruins, "*nunc destituta, nunc ruinarum agger est,*" in which there was nothing left to admire but the temple of Hercules,' his identification of Gades with the ruined Tartessos may have led him into exaggeration. Gades in the late empire had declined in importance, but can scarcely have been ruined yet.

That the Tyrian hero founded Cadiz we can believe if we choose: though the stories of its oracle-guided founding Strabo dismisses as Phœnician lies. One would like to keep for it the traditional date of 1100 B.C.; but historians tend now to take three centuries from this, which seems a pity. Anyhow, to found Gadir was one of the first things the Phœnicians did when they reached Spain; it became the rich mart and centre of their trading in Europe, as Carthage was in Africa. It grew in size, opulence and authority; it became a fabulous exporter and importer of wealth. Silver, tin, amber, sailed in and out of its deep harbour. Extending, one would suppose vulnerably, for miles into the sea on its slender stem, it yet seemed impregnable. In it Phœnician and Carthaginian merchants dwelt and traded; and to it doubtless Kolaios the Samian came when his seventh-century ship was blown westward to the Tartessian shores; and a century later the Phocæan Greeks traded there until the ocean west of the Pillars was shut to them. Cadiz may always have been the chief Tartessian port; for was the fabled Tartessos a city, or only a region and kingdom? Herodotus leaves it open: he never uses the word 'city' of Tartessos, though his loose translator Rawlinson gratuitously throws it in whenever Tartessos is mentioned. When Herodotus speaks of 'they who discovered the Adriatic and Tyrsenia and Iberia and Tartessos' (not 'the city of Tartessos,' as Rawlinson has it) Tartessos would seem more reasonably in line with the others if it were not a town but a region. Yet the tradition has persisted and persists of this opulent city port, on some undiscovered site between the Pillars and the Guadalquivir, which was destroyed by Carthaginians about 500 B.C., in order that their town of Gades might reign without a rival. The Greeks, as has been observed, always tended to think of a State in terms of a city, and would scarcely have been content without their vanished Tartessos, whose ghost still haunts the Tartessian shores, as the drowned Atlantis haunts the ocean, while her great successor lies, a spray of white blossom, across the deep blue Tartessian Gulf.

To walk the white streets of modern Cadiz, that sing and breathe of the sea, is to be companioned by the ghosts of nearly three thousand years. Here, after Phœnician and Carthaginian merchant navigators and merchant princes had

piled city and harbour with wealth and grandeur, and Hamilcar had used it as his base of operations against Rome, and
Gades had deserted Carthage and become, as reward, a
favoured Roman city, Romans and Greeks came and enjoyed
its amenities with Italian and Grecian zest for five centuries.
They loaded and adorned it with marble, they built their
villas and gardens all about and around it, learned and
curious inquirers came to watch (as had Pytheas long ago) its
extraordinary Atlantic tides, rich and luxurious livers to enjoy
its dancing girls, its erotic music, its delicious potted meats
and rich varieties of fish, its fabulous oriental luxury, its sea
air and hot sun, its public entertainments, its mystic religious
miracles and rites, its ebbing and flowing wells, its temples
and altars to the god Hercules or Melkarth, to the maritime
Aphrodite, to the forces of nature and time, life and death.
All the religious and social amenities, commercial opulence,
gaiety, luxury and vice, attracted a great cosmopolitan con-
course of merchants and citizens; it was, says Strabo, second
only to Rome in population. It was Urbs Julia Gaditana; it
had, under Augustus, five hundred *equites*; the rich Balbus
uncle and nephew enlarged the city, made the harbour of
Puerto Real, built the bridge over the Sancti Petri. Visits to
Jocosæ Gades were cheerful, riotous, opulent affairs; Gaditan
slaves and dancing girls would be trafficked about by the disreputable slave masters of whom Martial speaks; music and
entertainments and delicious banquets, admiration of the tides
and wells and mystic trees that gave milk, voyages about the
bay and along the warm Bætic shores, pleasure with lovely
golden-skinned long-eyed gaditanas and gaditanos, so much
more beautiful than Roman girls and boys, fleeted the Gades
season happily away. Gaditans had an immoral reputation in
Rome; Gades was to Romans what Paris once seemed to
Britons, but far better, because of the sun, and the beauty of
its citizens.

Gades dwindled during the later empire, and before the
Goths broke into Spain was inconsiderable, even though

Avienus's 'nunc ruinarum agger est' was probably picturesque over-statement. There is no record of any catastrophe having overtaken it before Rome fell, a century after Avienus wrote. For whatever reason, we hear nothing of it under the Visigoths, and not much under the Moors, who used its port and may or may not have rebuilt its town; they admired it, called it Kadis, and compared it to a silver dish. For centuries it was strewn with wreckage from its Roman pride; to-day nothing but a few ruins are left of the richly marbled and villa'd Roman city, or of the Moorish Kadis, or of the mediæval and Renaissance Spanish town, suddenly and splendidly enriched by the treasure fleets from the New World, so that it became once again Cadiz la Joyosa. That Renaissance city perished almost as completely as the Roman; this time the destroying barbarians were the English raiders under Essex in 1596, who sacked the town of everything of value and burnt most of it with an efficiency which our scientific destroyers of to-day have scarcely excelled. Having easily taken the city, which put up a remarkably poor resistance, the invaders rushed round it, looting houses, churches and public buildings, taking away anything they could carry, including church images, and destroying the rest, then set the town alight; flames raged through it for days, and when the English weighed anchor and sailed off with their plunder and their hostages (on orders from their government, which fortunately forbade them to advance into the interior, as Essex wished, and treat Seville in a similar manner) only a few houses were left whole. The unhappy hostages were taken to England and flung into loathsome dungeons until the agreed sum was paid for their release.

Avienus, had he visited Cadiz in 1597 or so, would have repeated his lament for the ruined city. But rebuilding quickly began. A handsome seventeenth- and eighteenth-century city gradually grew up; what was left of the Phœnician and Roman ruins that had, in the sixteenth century, still lain strewn about the ancient temple of Hercules on the Sancti

Petri shore, was used in the building. Cadiz flowered up again, snowy white, straight streeted, terrace roofed and towered, on its rocky limestone isthmus behind its great sea walls. It looks now so new a city that some visitors (Hans Andersen and others) have found it dull. 'Perfect cleanliness, neat, white-plastered houses . . . nothing to attract a stranger . . . Cadiz did not interest us . . . only one charm, the sea.' Others have found it 'mournful.' But that is the last thing it is. White and beautiful, sea circled and sea walled, with its shining domes, flat roofs gay with shrubs, pots and miradors, green balconies and *rejas,* often glassed, plazas bright with flowers, straight streets, and at the end of each street blue sky and sea, Cadiz has a gay elegance that charms; as Gautier remarked, it is a city lively and luminous, with no remarkable architecture. The two cathedrals are dullish; the *vieja,* built after the English destruction, the *nueva,* of the eighteenth and nineteenth centuries. Both are neo-classic, richly adorned, heavily domed, crowded with decoration and pictures.

A long, rather dull, suburban-looking road, lined with houses, hotels and bathing beaches, leads through the district called the Extramures to the town proper, which begins at the Puerta de Tierra. I entered the town at about nine-thirty, and looked about it for a room, with the help of a pertinacious little boy and the advice of helpful and encouraging policemen; no room, however, was to be had; Cadiz la Joyosa was full. So I slept in my car on the road behind the shore, in the Extramures. It was a cramped kind of night; I rose at dawn and went on to the beach, and looked along the long isthmus to where Cadiz lay, a pale dream of towers and domes, thrusting out into a dawn-blue sea. The tide, that Pytheas and Polybius and Artemidorus and the other learned Mediterranean inquirers had come so far to gaze at, ran up the smooth beach in waves and broke about my feet as I waded. Young men in yellow shirts cantered on horses with long flying tails at the edge of the ocean. I got some coffee at the Playa hotel, a fine new place with terraces and glass roofs,

which was full of Spanish bathing visitors. Then I saw Cadiz
—the cathedrals, some other churches, the port, the quay, the
castles, a lot of pictures in various places. The Academia de
Bellas Artes, which contains the picture museum and the
archæological museum, is now in a charming little plaza
which took me some time to find, owing to a patriotic change
of name; it was once the garden of a Capuchin convent, and
the name of the revolutionary general suits it ill. The museum,
after all, was shut for the summer. It contains some pictures
which might be worth seeing, and the tombs from the
Phœnician necropolis.

Unusually, I suppose because it was in the morning, I
found some churches open; the Carmen and the Oratory of
San Felipe Neri (both Churriguerresque), San Agustin, the
Capuchinos, all with Murillos. The Women's Hospital, which
has an El Greco and a beautiful mosaic court, was shut.
Against the Spanish shutness, especially impregnable, I suppose, in August, I lacked energy to battle. Anyhow, the outside of Cadiz (perhaps of any town) is better than its interior;
I spent the rest of the morning going about the streets and
plazas and market (silver and scaly with fish) and seeing the
fragmentary remains of the old walls and the castles. The
Temple of Hercules, the only thing Avienus liked in the
ruined Cadiz of his time, is not now to be seen, though its
foundations are said to be discernible when the tide is very
low. Finally, I climbed the Torre de Vigia (a hundred and
fifty-one steps) and looked down on the gay, terraced roofs of
Cadiz, at the luminous white city cut deep with blue shadows,
at the Tartessian gulf crooked in the isthmus's long arm, at
Puerto Santa Maria (the Port St. Mary of English sherry
shippers for centuries), on the opposite shore, with the marshy
salinas behind it and the ships (were they full of sherry?)
swimming about its port, at the lilac-blue, shimmering spread
of the Turdetanian coast round the massive shoulder from
Rota to Chipiona point. It all looked benign and inviting
enough, and the Atlantic in the afternoon sunshine was blue

and dazzling, not the murky, mist-cloaked gulf of darkness, the shadowy sea full of monsters, of Mediterranean imagination and Carthaginian propaganda; nor did those shores seem the regions inhabited by barbarous tribes described by Polybius, who, however, admits elsewhere that the climate and fertility of their land had on them a civilizing effect; and by Strabo's time they lived in great wealth and civility and ate and drank off silver. They were, he adds, the most intelligent of the Iberians; they had an alphabet, and ancient writings. The reports are contradictory, and show the rashness of generalization; no doubt some natives, then as now, there as elsewhere, were civil and polished, others wild and rude.

And there off their shores, sunk beneath the ocean, lies, it is clear, the lost island of Atlantis; and the life lived on it, as described by Plato, had been, surely, the life lived on the Tartessian shores, prosperous with precious metals dug out of the earth, luxurious with abundance of fruits and foods, watered by sweet fountains, with a rich city (vanished Tartessos) built with temples and palaces, crowded with inhabitants, set in a great plain, where rivers ran down from the mountains, wonderful mountains full of wealthy villages and many lakes and woods. As to the Atlanteans, they were, being partly divine by inheritance, for many generations so good, so gentle, so wise, that they despised everything but virtue; but presently their human nature got the better of them. . . . And one suspects that this is what occurred also to the Tartessians. Atlantis, as we know, sank beneath the sea; from the Torre de Vigia I could discern blue shadow that perhaps indicated its whereabouts.

One must not believe all one hears. It is not likely, Strabo assures us, that those are right who say that in the Outer Ocean the sun sinks into the sea with a hissing noise as of hot metal plunged into cold water. We may not hope to see that: but we shall see continual beauty and fertility, and we might also see Tartessos city, though we should not know it if we passed through its rich, invisible streets and trod its once chaffering and crowded quays beside whatever deep bay or great river's mouth it lay.

In earnest hopes of this unwitting find, I left Tartessos's triumphant successor, so luminously, translucently, whitely poised on its rock, and drove again down its long causeway round the bay, through pretty San Fernando, across Sancti Petri and out of the island of Leon, to Puerto Real a few kilometres on; a pleasant white town built after the reconquest on the ancient remains of Portus Gaditanum, whose harbour Balbus of Gades so greatly improved. It is now a bathing resort, and full of the villas of visiting Gaditans. The road on from there runs through salt marshes and among broad rivers to Puerto Santa Maria, Portus Menesthei to the Romans, to the English sherry merchants of Jerez simply the Port. The sherry firms of all nations have bodegas and wine ships there, though it is less used for shipping now that a railway runs from Jerez to El Trocadero at the end of the peninsula opposite Cadiz. Puerto Santa Maria is a very beautiful town, on the broad green Guadalete's mouth, which is spanned by a boat bridge. In the river ships and boats lie, and the sea runs up and down; the streets are bordered by arcaded shops; the wine bodegas (mostly British) are built along the river; a ruined castle stands in the plaza of the fish market; some say it is Moorish, others that it was built by Alfonso el Sabio, in memory of the appearance of the Virgin, the same miracle commemorated by the Iglesia Mayor, the lovely parish church once almost destroyed (perhaps by the English, who dreadfully sacked and desecrated the town) and rebuilt in the seventeenth century; it has a sumptuous and richly carved pillared façade. There is great grace and elegance about the broad streets and beautiful white houses (many of them belonging to wine merchants) in the Puerto. The Calle Larga, in particular, is spaciously beautiful. The town is full of what once were convents. From its port, in the old rich days, ships of adventurers and merchants put out to and came in from the New World. Now the wealth of the Puerto comes mainly from wine, with fishing as a subsidiary industry. Vineyards stretch behind it; they do not, say the Jerez firms, produce the best sherry. But Port St. Mary was once the centre of the sherry trade, before it shifted to Jerez; as was Viana of the port trade before it moved to Oporto. Its vineyards also make sweet wines, muscatel and Pedro Ximenes. Sherry from the Jerez vineyards is largely shipped from it; most of it goes, in normal times, to Britain. The Port was one of the earliest Phœnician settlements; destroyed by the Goths, neglected by the Moors, it was reconquered and renamed by Alfonso el Sabio. From the fifteenth century on, expeditions sailed thence to conquer the Canaries, the Indies, Portugal. Its fortifications were destroyed by the French in 1810. To-day it looks the pleasantest town and port imaginable, though it has no striking architectural features except general beauty and grace. I saw no place I liked better between the Pillars and Portugal.

Jerez, indeed, runs it close; finer in buildings and lovelier in plazas and trees, it lacks the great green river and the sea. Between the Puerto and Jerez there is a long, dull road, through the flat, dull plains of the Guadalete, where the Moorish invaders under Tarik fought for three bloody days the hosts of Roderick the Goth, four times themselves in number, and thereby won Andalucia, for the Crescent. But Jerez and its vineyards, so carefully cultivated by the Romans, and the golden wines of Bætica that the Spanish and Goths and the Romans had enjoyed, were for some time wasted on these teetotal infidels, who, whether or not they rooted up the vines to avoid temptation, or retained them and ate the fresh grapes in season, had, before the five and a half centuries of their occupation of the Jerez country came to an end, fallen from the pure principles of the Prophet, for when Alfonso the Wise won back Jerez he found its vineyards flourishing and gave each of the forty hidalgos who settled there a piece of vine land for his own, and from that time down to this present, sherry wine has flowed from Cadiz bay to every part of the world, and most of all, from the fifteenth century on, to Britain.

Jerez, the Roman Cæsaris Asidonia, the Arab Cæris Sidonia, is a most pleasant city. It has been called white; but it seemed to me to be for the most part sherry coloured. The palacios, the churches, the plazas, were mostly of the local apricot sandstone, and very charming and mellow they looked in the afternoon glow. The bodegas are mainly white, very beautifully and cleanly white, with red-tiled roofs and arcaded forecourts green with orange trees. They are scattered about the town; the largest bodega establishments cover several acres, and form (like that of Manuel Misa, close to the station) a whole *barrio* of white walls, roofed and pillared arcades opening on paved courts, and long white red-tiled bodegas with bright green shuttered windows and doors. Others are on the sites, or in the converted buildings, of old churches or convents. One of the largest stands on the hill of the old Moorish Alcázar (now converted into dwellings). Inside, they are cool and dim, and aromatically delicious with the smell of wine; they are divided into aisles like a church nave, and the great casks lie in them, tier above tier, full of sherry of all dates, all colours, from rich brown to pale amber. One is shown round by kind hosts and offered samples to taste; the result is very agreeable, and Jerez, when one emerges again into the sunlight, seems more than ever a pleasant, golden, sherry-coloured town. Indeed, it is a very charming town, with an air of elegant opulence, fine manorial houses (like the sherry, of all dates) standing among palms and orange gardens, with coats-of-arms over their sculptured doors; some descend from the hereditary hidalgos, others were built in the prosperous nineteenth century by rich wine merchants of all nations. You can see the white *casas de viñas* on the vine-grown hills that stretch for many miles behind and round the town. Jerez is, of course, full of British wine firms; wherever wine is to be got, the British come and get it, and ship it to their thirsty and wineless land. Great Britain imported before the war incomparably more sherry than any other country. The Spanish themselves drink it a little. One agreeable effect of the presence of British residents in Jerez is that visiting British are more taken for granted than elsewhere in Spain, and do not get so followed about; the breed is familiar. Even female car drivers have doubtless been seen. The English have always been in and out of this country, sacking the ports, getting, no doubt, gloriously drunk on these delightful wines. Sherry sack, so popular in England in the sixteenth century, was to give place a little in the seventeenth and eighteenth to French wines, madeira and port; but in the nineteenth century the tide of sherry flowed again, and Jerez grew really rich.

It is a town of spacious, tree-bordered streets, and charming fountained plazas embowered in acacias and oranges and plumbago vines and palms. The houses, whether white or apricot, are pretty, with their emerald-green balconies and *rejas* and cool patios. There is not much of the old walls left, and the Alcázar has been almost demolished since a century ago, when Ford pronounced it 'very perfect.' It belonged to a ducal family, who sold it in the present century to a company who made houses of it. Either Jerez has changed out of all knowledge in the last hundred years, or Ford wrote of it in one of his worst fits of churlish ill temper; he called it 'a straggling, ill-kept Moorish city' (Port St. Mary he described as 'a dull vinous town'); Gautier, however, who was there a very little later, liked it, though less than Cadiz. Indeed, it is full of lovely buildings—the Colegiata, with its blue dome, detached bell tower, and engaging Churriguerresque façade ('vile,' groans Ford), the rich plateresque façade of the Cabildo Viejo (built by Andrés de Ribera), with its crowded popula-tion of sculptured beings—Hercules, scowling gorilla-like with his club, a dominating but anonymous military man, said to be an emperor, the four cardinal virtues (female, intoxicated, and perched precariously on the cornices of the side portals) and a charming frieze of satyrs, vases, garlands and boys. Then there are the churches of all styles, some built by Alfonso out of mosques, others later Gothic, Mudéjar, Renaissance, plateresque and baroque. They are scattered about the town, which, now that it has lost most of its ancient walls, is, as has been said, girded about with the great bodegas like a rampart.

But the glory of Jerez lies outside it, two and a half miles south-east, along a dusty country road through vineyards—the magnificent fifteenth-century Cartuja, secularized in 1836, for long used as a stud and now become a national monument, falling into ruin and decay, thistles and flowers and tall weeds pushing up in the cloisters, the walls and doors scrawled over with names, unswept rubbish scattered about the broken paved floors. The lonely and derelict beauty of the place, standing among farm buildings in the hot, silent siesta of the afternoon, is indescribably haunting. I was let in by a little girl, presumably the child of the caretaker; no one else was there, except some soldiers lounging in the forecourt in the sun. The rich classical façade and portal of the convent, sculptured in tawny stone by Ribera in 1571, is very good, with eight great Doric fluted pillars, balustrades, and statues in niches, topped by St. Bruno and, above him, God the Father. Inside the convent there is a wealth of mid-sixteenth-century plateresque. Beyond it are three grassy patios and cloisters; the largest (sixteenth century) has twenty-four marble columns and is grown with cypresses and other trees; the pond and fountains are gone, but the old cross is still there. The other cloisters are Gothic, very lovely and graceful. The weeds and shrubs are all uncut, the whole place mouldering gently into decay, hot and silent, haunted, dreaming and desolate. The refectory and sacristy and chapter hall are beautiful and dignified. The Gothic church, built earlier than the convent, has an exquisite baroque façade of 1667, gracefully and lavishly pillared and pinnacled. The tomb of the founder of the convent, Alvaro de Valeto, is in the church.

A Spaniard wrote in 1868, 'How long will the Cartuja last, in this century of movement, when one sees so many historic buildings turned into factories? One fears for it.' It has not been turned into a factory, and there seems a chance that it may one day be occupied again by Carthusians, as Porta Coeli has been. It was once the great monastery of these regions, and its vineyards had wide fame; it should be restored to its original use. Meanwhile, it is mouldering into ruin. It has perhaps, in its forlorn grandeur, a stranger charm than it would have were it an English national monument, all tidied and swept and cleaned, the weeds cut, and a caretaker to mind it. But it will fall to pieces sooner.

The vineyards, still called 'las viñas de la Cartuja,' lie some distance to the north, and a great bodega stores the wine. At vintage time those lonely dusty roads are full of carts and oxen, and donkeys with their panniers piled high with grapes. On the August afternoon that I was there, the vine country of swelling hills lay hot and dusty and quiet above the Guadalete and its plain, creeping round the great Cartuja with a slow, stealthy patience that must surely, in the end, engulf.

Leaving Jerez next day, after an agreeable morning seeing bodegas and churches and buildings, and a pleasant lunch, I took, before going north to Seville, the bad secondary road that went to Sanlucar de Barrameda at the mouth of the Guadalquivir, about fifteen miles away. I decided to spend the night there, going on to Seville next day. I wanted to see not only the silver-bedded Guadalquivir, but the site, according to the learned Dr. Adolf Schulten, who has written a German treatise on it, of the vanished Tartessos, which, he opined, had lain on an island in the river's broad mouth. I had with me a fascinating but somewhat confusing little French monograph on this engrossing theme; confusing because it insisted on shifting the mouth of the Guadalquivir all about the coast as it rolled down the ages. I dare say he was quite right.

My bad road ran through plains, salt marshes, vineyards and orange groves. The flat, sandy shore was some miles to my left. Sanlucar, when I reached it, did not seem particularly interesting; a town surrounded by sandhills, vineyards, palms and pines, with a good beach half a mile away, where the river opens into the sea; it is a popular bathing resort for Jerez. In the evening I drove down not to the sea beach but to the river, and there bathed; the water was warm, smooth, and twilight green; it lapped on the sand dunes and rustled back, for the tide ebbed. I swam up-stream, between flat, distant, piney shores; there was no island, and I failed to locate Tartessos. It was a dreary country; in the distance herds of cattle wandered, and mosquitoes skimmed the warm surface of the river. Its shores seem to have deteriorated since Strabo wrote how well they were cultivated, how thickly populated, how their groves and gardens delighted the eye, how precious metals—silver, copper, gold—lay about them—'and besides that there is the charm of the scenery.' No; the shores of the Bætis are definitely not what they were, in the old days when the *divites Tartessii* flourished there so prosperously, and once every three years the fleet sailed from Tarshish to Solomon, bringing him gold and silver, ivory, apes and peacocks. But to swim in the Bætis, the great river of Tartessos, which bore the silver ships down from the silver mountains, had at least historic interest. Further up it lay Hispalis-Seville; and all the way up to that great city the river was navigable; for once, I wished my car away, that I might go up to Seville by river, as the treasure fleets returning with their spoil from the New World used to do;

and if he [the traveller] be there at the arrival of the Plate-Fleet, he shall see such a *Grandeza* [wrote James Howell in 1642], that the Roman monarchy in her highest flourish never had the like, nor the Gran Signior at this day. There he may converse with Marchants, and their conversation is much to be valued. . . .

In the green sky stars began to candle. I left the warm green Guadalquivir and returned to Sanlucar, where, after some hunting, I got a room for the night. The town was not unattractive; above the lower, newer town where I stayed rose the higher old town, with its square-towered Moorish castle, once the dwelling of Guzman el Bueno, who became Duke of Medina Sidonia, for his war services were rewarded by Alfonso the Wise with the gift of this town just captured from the Moors. The dukes reigned in Sanlucar for several centuries with the firmest tyranny, until it was taken over by the crown in the seventeenth century, having become important as a navigation centre. The magnificent castle is now used as a barracks. English sailors were such frequent visitors to Sanlucar in Henry VIII's reign, and so often far from well, that he founded a hospital for them there in 1517; it looks a fine building, is called the Colegio de San Francisco, and I do not know what it is now used for. The Spanish, in some ways more but in others less conservative than ourselves, seldom use buildings for long together for the same purpose, they like to change them about, which all helps to make sight-seeing confusing.

Sanlucar lives, like so many Spanish ports, on fish and wine, which always sounds a pleasant life; the wine is mostly manzanilla, which grows all round it. I left it early for Seville, via Jerez; from Jerez to Seville it was a long hot drive of sixty miles. Seville is too far inland to come into this book, which is just as well. My journey re-enters Ora Maritima a few days later, when I drove through the dull, fertile plains of Bætica, the Garden of Hercules (how the Romans, who loved fertility and olives and disliked wild hilly country, over-praised these regions!) and crossed the Rio Tinto at the ancient town of Niebla, the Roman Ilipla, standing finely on its Roman bridge over the coppery Tinto, still partly Moorish, partly Spanish reconquest and chivalric, with its broken walls and towers and magnificent castle. Niebla had been a Gothic, then a Moorish kingdom; after the reconquest it had great riches, political dominance and a ruling colony of bullying knightly chivalry, and was cock of the walk in the *conado*. The Guzman counts built themselves, out of the old Moorish fortress, a grand palace on the scale of a royal alcázar, and threw up a tower almost the height of the Seville Miguelete. Niebla was then and for long afterwards a splendid mediæval city, with its forts and fine seigniorial houses and churches; after the fifteenth century it fell from power and wealth, suffered from royal vengeance after a dispute with the Castilian crown, and dwindled into unimportance and poverty; its place in the *condada* was taken by Huelva, with its port and rich trade. Niebla is now a fine-looking ancient city, but what guidebooks call decayed. It was once, and I dare say is still, full of Roman inscriptions and remains.

The road, crossing the Tinto, ran flatly on to San Juan del Puerto; before I reached it a road for Palos and La Rabida branched left, running down the river's left bank, through a plump-looking country of vegetables, corn and fruits. This is the Columbus country; one passed Moguer, castled and Moorish, where he said his prayers in the Convent of Santa Clara the night before embarking from Palos to find America. Palos is further on; a small ancient white town (Roman), standing on the cliff above the Tinto, which is here very broad, and rolls beyond a stretch of marshy shore; it must have receded since the day Columbus came down from the high, steep little town to where his little fleet waited in the river's mouth. The rebuilt church of San Jorge, where he heard read the king's proclamation that gave him leave to voyage, stands in a small plaza at the top of the town. It was to Palos also that he returned, the New World in his hands; it is to Palos and La Rabida that good Americans make pious pilgrimage, to honour him who found them such a fine home. The Franciscan convent of Santa Maria de la Rábida is ten kilometres down the river, on the broad estuary where the copper-coloured Tinto and the Odiel, meeting, flow together into the sea. The fourteenth-century convent, whose prior so encouraged and helped Columbus, stands high on the wooded hill above the estuary; it is now restored from its long dereliction as a national monument, and occupied again by monks.

Much of the restoration is as bad as one would expect; I did not go inside. In spite of modernization, the convent and its gardens and woods, above the broad green flowing estuary full of sails running down into the wind-touched sea, have a romantic beauty, partly historic, partly of to-day.

To get to Huelva, one has to go back to the San Juan del Puerto bridge and down the river's right bank. Huelva stands on the Odiel, just above its join with the Tinto; it fishes for tunny and exports ore from the Rio Tinto mines, and flourishes. It was the Roman Onubo, and through the Gothic and Moorish periods was under the domination of Niebla; as Niebla declined, Huelva grew in power and wealth. Huelva citizens are immensely proud of their town, which has given its name to a province. Some of them say that Huelva was the place where the Phœnicians first landed in Spain and the first city they founded; others put its foundation back before the Flood. All say that it has every qualification for a great maritime port, standing on its estuary in fertile country covered with timber for ships, and with the ore cargoes coming down the Tinto for shipping. What no guidebook seems to say of Huelva is that it is a beautiful and interesting town; they pass it by with a reference to its prosperity, and perhaps to Columbus. But Huelva is beautiful, standing among its woody hills on its broad deep estuary. Above the more modern town, the old town, the original early town, climbs a hill, crowned by a splendid four-towered castle, probably built after the reconquest by the Dukes of Medina Sidonia, who left it later for their new palace in the middle of the town. The other magnificent work is the ruined Roman aqueduct. There are several churches; the oldest, San Pedro, in the old town, near the castle, was built out of a mosque; it is a fine solid building with three large naves, which stood up firmly to the earthquake of 1755 that destroyed much of the town, and to all the Atlantic storms that have always blown over Huelva, a town which gets, though sheltered from the north, plenty of ventilation. Its port, full of ships and boats of all sizes coming and going up and down the green water, its shipyard loud with building, its soft salt air, its surrounding wooded hills, make it a very pleasant town, though there is little to see in it, and it lacks the exquisite grace of Puerto de Santa Maria. I had coffee on the quay, looking over the estuary, then took the road for Portugal.

The road does not cross the Odiel (here a tremendous many-branched river) before Gibraleon, ten miles north. If, by the way, one should want to travel along the sea coast between Sanlucar and Portugal, one would have to walk, or ride a horse; there is no driving road. It is a desolate, flat, deserted *marisma* shore—*inhospitales nunc harenas porrigit deserta tellus*—though it would be pleasant, I dare say, to see the various kinds of crab and shell fish and seaweed left at low tide, and the *atalayas* set along the coast from all time to guard against pirates, invaders and smugglers.

Inland, the country is beautiful. The *marisma* of the Guadalquivir left behind, small hills begin, and pinewoods. Gibraleon, with its high ruined fortress, stands imposingly on its hill (Gebel, Arabic for hill, was added to its Roman name by the Moors). It has a good conquest church (Santiago), some convents in disrepair, a good bridge, and was obviously once a fine little *plaza de armas,* important in mediæval wars against Portugal. Just beyond it the road to Ayamonte crosses the Odiel and turns south-west, running through pinewoods to the frontier. I went through Cartaya, some of whose historians have put up claims that it is the ancient Roman colony of Carteia, whose ruins, it has generally been believed, have lain for centuries in Algeciras Bay; further, they say that Cartaya may have been Tartessos. Anyone wanting to read a great deal about this can do so in the works of several Spanish historians, which cite various Roman sources to buttress their dubious case. But it is less trouble to ignore these speculations, and to note only that Cartaya is a small ancient town, lying between a hill and a ravine, surrounded by rivers, mostly dry, with a Moorish castle now used as a cemetery, a good plaza, where once stood a beautiful Casa Consistorial, now ruined, a convent, now turned into dwelling houses, and several churches, some of them out of use. This all sounds decayed; but Cartaya has not a decayed air; it is a pleasant and thriving little town, and all kinds of fish and occasionally a sea monster, as occurred in 1630, swim up its river. The country round is fertile and pretty and agricultural, and all these towns live on selling fish, figs, wine, olive oil and wheat, or so I was informed. The next ancient castled town was Lepe, in the valley of the Rio Piedras, rich with wine, olives and figs. I bought plump black figs in the plaza for about sixpence the kilo; they were bursting and sweet, and delicious to eat as I drove through the warm pinewoods to Ayamonte.

Ayamonte, lying at the Guadiana's mouth, the last town in Spain, is amazingly beautiful. The old upper town on the hill above, where the Moorish kings lived and where tournaments are held, I did not visit; the lower town lay, white and marine, on a great breadth of blue water. The Guadiana deltas out eastward, between the mainland and the large Isla Canela, flowing into the sea on either side of the island, and Ayamonte is half circled by water. On the island traces have been found (they say) of Phœnician occupation, so Ayamonte historians like to believe that the Phœnicians founded a town there when looking about the coast for somewhere to build a temple to Hercules. However this may be (and, after all, the Phœnicians were everywhere on the Iberian seaboard), and whatever Ayamonte's age, it is an enchanting place, with the river a league wide and salt as the sea, and the hills of Portugal rising beyond it. A broad quayside, with customs sheds and harbour works, borders the river port, which is full of ships and boats. I left my car in the plaza, and was immediately mobbed by a horde of wild natives, who followed me about with shouts as I looked for an inn. Having got a room in a tiny fonda, I crossed over to the island in a ferry boat; as many of the younger population as could crowd into it did so, and followed me about the island until I crossed back again;

my return was greeted with yells from a dense crowd of young people now assembled in the plaza. I dined in the fonda café, with the mob yammering and beating the door, which was guarded by a policeman. 'It is strong; it will hold,' the café proprietor said to him. I asked the policeman if they never saw foreigners in this frontier town, and why they were so excited; for I half supposed myself come to a colony for those not right in the head. He replied that few foreigners except Portuguese entered or left Portugal by Ayamonte, but that when señoras did so they always caused excitement. And a señora alone, and driving a car too. . . . He shrugged his shoulders, apologizing for the manners of his young compatriots; he said it was 'the new Spain,' in which he was wrong; it was probably the same Spain that the Phœnicians, landing at Ayamonte, had found; possibly this was why they did not stay there very long. The policemen were kind, courteous and helpful men; as indeed I found the police all over Spain; however they behave to their compatriots, they are to foreign visitors all that is amiable and polite.

I had to leave my car and luggage in the street outside for the night; it was locked, but would, I believe, have been un-robbed even if not; I was only stolen from once in Spain, and that was in Madrid. Even the *improbi Gaditani* do not seem to rob foreigners.

Next morning I went to the quay, got through the customs, and waited while they telephoned to Portugal for the boat, which did not arrive till twelve. It was very beautiful on the quay, with timber being loaded on to barges from mule carts, ships and boats with coloured sails lying in the harbour, and the strong green sea river flowing by between Spain and Portugal. I sat in the car, while the young Ayamontese swarmed over it, staring in at me: every now and then a customs officer hit them over the head with a bundle of passports.

The ferry boat arrived, and I drove on to it. It was a pic-turesque crossing, with the hills of Spain behind and the hills of Portugal ahead. We went downstream, for Vila Real, the Portuguese port, is nearer the sea than Ayamonte. The green Guadiana tossed and rolled, the Atlantic running up it, the river running down. I was not sure at what point in midstream it became Portugal.

## CHAPTER FIVE

## ALGARVE SHORE

THE river had become Portugal: its green waves lapped at the quay of Vila Real de Santo Antonio, that mushroom town thrown up in five months by Pombal to be a fishing centre, close to the site of an older town drowned by a stormy sea a hundred and seventy years before. It took me two hours to clear the customs, and some more time to borrow some escudos from the British vice-consul, since the banks were shut. Vila Real is a quiet, neat white town, built in the regular Pombaline manner, rectangular, round a large smooth square called Marqués de Pombal, with an obelisk in the middle and seats and trim little trees all round. The houses seem all like one another, and the effect is dull. The remarkable quietness of Vila Real is nothing new; a German visitor in 1798 commented on the deadly stillness of the streets. It is an important port, where they catch and preserve tunnies. It has neither a beach nor other amenities. I drove out of it at half-past three.

It was cool in Portugal; much cooler than it had been in Spain. My road ran delightfully between white walls and cactus hedges in golden flower. The houses were small and white, with doors and windows painted deep blue. Fig trees, olives, carobs, aloes, almonds, pomegranates, melons, oranges and lemons, all the fruits imaginable, grew in groves along the way. For this was Algarve, the orchard of Portugal. It is, I know, often hot in Algarve in summer; on this end-of-August afternoon it was coolish, with a breeze blowing in from the Atlantic. It was different from Spain—gentler, softer, less vivid. The people were different, less handsome, smaller and squatter, with faces more round and undefined, more of the negro, less of the Moor (even though Algarve was for over five hundred years a Moorish kingdom).

Many of the women wore men's bowler hats, tied under the chin with scarves; there were straw hats everywhere; men and women rode on donkeys with umbrellas up against the sun. There was the familiar Portuguese spitting, and the endearing Portuguese nasal twang. It was charming to be in Portugal again.

I came to Tavira, the Roman Balsa, once Algarve's capital, lying beautifully on either side of the river Gilão, or Sequa, with its ancient bridge. A delightful Moorish town, with palmy arcaded praça and white houses. The church of Santa Maria do Castelo, once a mosque, is thirteenth century; it has the tomb of that Correa who won Tavira from the Moors in 1242, and of seven knights slain by Moors while hunting. The sixteenth-century church of the Misericordia has a fine Renaissance door and manueline windows. Having briefly admired these and other charming details, I drove on along the coast road, past carob and olive groves and small clean white Moorish villages, to Olhão, more white, more Moorish and more cubically built than any town in Portugal; it is a little like Tarifa, but trimmer. It is a charming and remarkable town, looking very Moroccan: crowded, low-built houses, all with flat terraced roofs, many of them paved with red bricks, contrasting vividly with the white roof parapets and chimneys. There are steep outside flights of white steps running up to the roofs; gardens in boxes and birds in cages hang on the dazzling white walls. The streets are deep and narrow; some are paved with black and white stones in patterns and stripes; arcaded shops and balconied houses border them. The whole effect of Olhão is exotic, beautiful, oddly modernist, with its square houses and rectangular parallel streets. The population looks Moorish, and the children chase strangers with the eager curiosity of those in Spain. The church is charming, with a good azulejos-decorated façade and tall tower. The main praça is adorned with tiles illustrating the tale of the eight enterprising local fishermen who sailed to Brazil in 1808 to give John VI the news of the expulsion of the French. The port, like all these Algarve fishing ports, is a little way from the town; it is crowded with sardine fishing boats, a jostle of masts and sails; at low tide it smells. Olhão is famous for its spring tunny massacres; these must be a dreadful and bloody sight, hugely enjoyed by the males of the neighbourhood and from abroad. The tunnies off Algarve are fine fat fish, perhaps acorn-fed, for Polybius said that 'in the sea off Lusitania acorn-bearing oaks grow, upon which the tunnies feed and fatten themselves, which may well be called sea hogs, as they feed like hogs on acorns.' Myself I saw neither sea hogs nor sea oaks.

The coast road runs well back from the sea, with turnings off it going steeply down to the ports and beaches, so that for most of the way the sea is hidden from the road. A little way on from Olhão is Faro, the present capital of Algarve. Faro is not, on the whole, an interesting-looking town; it has been too greatly and too often destroyed and rebuilt; but it lies finely round its great blue harbour basin, full of small ships and bordered by palms, and with two low sandy islands lying in the bar. It has in it some beautiful things; the Carmo church, called by Algarvians the most beautiful building in Faro, with its lovely baroque façade and portal and elaborate gilded retablo and altar; S. Francisco, beautifully and coolly dressed inside with blue and white tiles; the tiled walls of the nave and transepts, and some of the chapels, of the cathedral, which was first a basilica, then a mosque, then a Gothic church, then burnt by English raiders in 1596, then destroyed by the great earthquake and rebuilt in the eighteenth century; but, after all that, the thirteenth-century bell tower still remains; one of the chapels is a reliquary of fragments of saints. Then there is the tiled court of the bishop's palace, and some charming ruined cloisters, and the view of the town and bay from the chapel of S. Antonio do Alto above the town. Faro has had a catastrophic career since it grew up, as Alfaro, from a colony of Mozarabic fishermen after the destruction by the

Moors of the ancient Roman town of Ossonoba, which had used it as a port. The Moors later heavily fortified Faro, but it could not stand up to the siege of Alfonso III; it passed to him in 1249, its fortifications knocked to bits, to be built up again as the years went on. Then there was Essex's raid of 1596, when Faro was stormed, sacked, and burned to the ground, its inhabitants having wisely retired inland on sighting the intimidating fleet that approached Faro creek. Modern Portuguese and some English writers are apt to complain that Essex stole the town library and archives and presented them to the Bodleian; but contemporary records do not mention anything but his theft of the private library of the poor Bishop, in whose palace Essex quartered himself; probably the archives were burnt with the town, of which little was left; it was built again, in seventeenth-century style, and very charming it must have looked, only to be destroyed again by earthquake. It now has a modern air, with some dull large praças and gardens; but some of the smaller streets and market squares, and the palm-grown alameda, and the harbour quays, are agreeable. It is full of the attractive Algarve chimneys, that stand like gay little latticed castles on the roofs. There is the eighteenth-century Arco da Vila, with its statue (I forget why) of St. Thomas Aquinas, and two or three museums, which I did not visit, and a few fragments of the ancient walls and gates, which I did not see. I drove five miles inland to Estoi, and saw the ruins of Ossonoba, the Roman city destroyed by the Moors; nothing much there but a few tessellated pavements and a reconstructed bath-house. At Estoi I was shown a charming little eighteenth-century palace and garden by an amiable inhabitant (and the Algarvians are very amiable, in spite of the opinion of the German Professor Link, who called them, in 1798, 'less refined and polite than the other Portuguese'). I drove back to Faro, had coffee in the praça by the Sé, went on to Loulé, through the delightful undulating olive country, that grew hotter as one went inland and out of the Atlantic air. I was now in the half of Algarve called Barlavento, or windward; from the Guadiano to Faro it is Sotovento, or leeward, and the coast is more sheltered. But Loulé seemed sheltered enough, and, in fact, pretty hot. It is the largest town in Algarve, but still not very large. It stands among cork and carob woods. It is very white, very Arabic and prettily castled all over with the fascinating open-work Algarve chimney-pots. It has some remains of Moorish walls; the white houses have charming balconies, bright with flowers; there is a market piled with pomegranates, oranges, figs, golden cucumbers and white pots. There are sad indications of industry in parts of the town, but much of it is unspoiled and delightful. There are several good churches—a beautiful manueline portal, with looped cables and rich capitals, in the Misericordia, some attractive cloisters in the disused Graça convent, and the parish church is Gothic on Moorish. I strolled about the hot white streets, bought green figs and a white pot in the market, and drove back through the pretty cork-wooded country to the coast road. It was evening; herds of black goats, driven by little boys and girls in great straw hats, tripped along the dusty road; small donkeys ambled home, their panniers full of water pots or vegetables or turf; the smell of flowers and sticky fig leaves drifted on the warm air. But soon the warm air met the Atlantic breezes, as I drove into Albufeira, a pleasant old town on the cliffs, above a crescent-shaped beach, to which you go down through a rock tunnel. I went down to the beach to bathe; there were rocks and caves, and a few other bathers, Spanish and Portuguese, on the sands. It was not a really warm bathe; the Atlantic coast of the Barlavento is draughty and cool. The days of perfect bathing were far behind me, beyond the Pillars of Hercules, on the shores of the blessed Middle Sea. At no point is the Atlantic like a warm bath; it has that disagreeable quality called invigorating. Still, I bathed on Albufeira beach, and scrambled about its rocks and caves, trying to get warm, then climbed up to the town again, got a room in a pensão (which, at the end of

August, was lucky) and looked at the Moorish castle. Albufeira is a picturesque and charming town. My pensão was
very pleasant, and my fellow-guests (all Portuguese) friendly
and kind.

Next morning I left the coast, to go by the main Faro–Lagos
road. It was definitely cool; at nine a.m. the thermometer
stood at only 75°. There was bright sunshine, and a windy,
chilly-looking blue sea, beautiful without allure. My road ran
three miles or so from the coast; roads turned off it at intervals, running down to the fishing and bathing beaches. I
did not take these turnings; it was a day on which the interior
of Algarve was definitely better than the coast, with its rocks
and caves and splashing waves. Inland, it was lovely country,
smelling sweetly of thyme and figs and aromatic shrubs, with
gentle hills and cork and olive woods, and plantations of sugar
canes and almonds and carobs, and the little white towns had
a dream-like charm—Alcantarilha, with its manueline church
and ruined castle; Lagoa, a charming village whence the sea
road runs down to Carveiro, which has the best grotto and
bathing beach on the coast. A few miles further on the sea
runs up an estuary to meet the road at Portimão, where a
long bridge on stone piers spans the broad harbour—blue
water at high tide, an expanse of wet marsh when the sea is
out. The town lies beautifully round its port. On either side of
the estuary, where the river meets the sea, a sixteenth-century
fort stands—St. John on one side, St. Catherine on the other.
St. Catherine has a chapel, and once a year her image is
carried down to the sea, in full procession, to bless the fishing.
Up the estuary of the river, which is the river on which, some
miles up, Silves stands, the fleet of foreign crusaders, English,
French, Norman, German and Danish, came in 1189 to help
King Sancho I to take Silves, the capital of Algarve, from the
Moors. Portimão must have been noisy with the revels of
these tough, intoxicated, barbarous Christians landing on her
quays, aflame with anti-Saracen zeal, dazzled with the violent
Algarve sun and white town. Portimão was deserted, for the

Moorish inhabitants of country and towns for miles round, seeing the formidable fleet (these visitations of crusaders had long been too bitterly familiar on the Portugal shores) swimming again into the bay, had fled to the walled stronghold of Alvor, where the Christians pursued them, destroyed and sacked their castle and town, and massacred six thousand persons before proceeding on their way to the Holy Land. A few months later another fleet of them arrived in Portimão bay, to help in the Silves siege, and sailed up the river Arade to encamp outside the walled city and castle, where the fleeing inhabitants had shut themselves as into a sure defence. Portimão, Alvor, all the rocky bays and luxuriant countryside, deserted of fishermen and peasants and rich Arab landowners and merchants, lay lonely and empty and untilled in the eye of the July sun.

Portimão, no longer the Roman Portus Hanibalis, no longer the rich, arcaded, mosqued Moorish port, no longer the mediæval Spanish town that succeeded to this (for the great earthquake left little of old Portimão), is to-day a cheerful, charming sardine and tunny fishery, the best port in Algarve, but with a sandbar across the estuary that keeps out the large ships. Along the harbour lies the Praça Bivar, tree-grown, busy and gay, with its public garden, its shops and banks, its fish market, cafés and pastellerias. Most of the present town is post-earthquake; the Gothic church is rebuilt; azulejos, with illustrations of Portuguese history, run delightfully along one of the praça walls, and along the backs of the seats round the square. There are trees and shrubs and bright flowers everywhere, and in the town they can sardines, preserve figs and almonds, and do whatever is done in factories to cork. The harbour is full of cargo boats and fishing boats, coming and going or lying at anchor, gazing coolly at the brimming sea with their painted Phœnician eyes.

From Portimão it is two kilometres on to Praia da Rocha, the favourite bathing resort of Algarve, with its smart villas and two hotels and a casino on the cliff, and an esplanade, from which steep paths go down to a sandy beach strewn with great fantastically-shaped rocks, arches, columns and caves, of all shades of tawny orange and grey and black, carved by centuries of battering sea into a city of gnomes' castles, uncanny and strange. Bathing among these rocks must be delightful in hot weather; I bathed, but the sea was cool and windy and broke in frisky waves on the beach. The English go to Praia, one hears; I saw none myself, but the two hotels look as if they might. One is a very pretty white, red-tiled pensão, with blue paint decorating its white walls and a charming garden. I thought Praia too windy and unsheltered; a local guidebook says the wind keeps the place 'beautifully cool in summer,' which is what I suspected. It also recommends Praia as a winter resort; I should think it would be cooler even than the mistral-blown French Riviera.

I left it for Portimão again, and drove up the river to Silves. A mediæval bridge turns off the road nine miles from Portimão, crossing the broad Arade, and beyond it and high above it stands the splendid town, crowned by its huge red-walled Moorish castle. The sight of Silves from the bridge is stupendous. So, seven and a half centuries ago, the crusaders from the north must have stood and looked up, through the sweltering July heat, at the rich strong infidel city of Chelb, the residence of Moorish kings, described by contemporary chroniclers as of shining whiteness, climbing its hill in three tiers of great guarding walls, for there was the high citadel, the lower city spreading under it, and a suburb below that, and each was girdled by broad moats and towered walls. All about the white city were rich arcaded and terraced houses, arcaded streets of shops and small dwellings, mosques, climbing, twisting, narrow streets, and cool patios with cisterns and wells, and everywhere were gardens, orchards, orange groves, palms. It looked impregnable, but how worth, thought the avaricious crusaders, the sacking!

Silves held out through July and August, surrendering at last from thirst, the water conduits having been cut. The exhausted Moors, promised their lives, filed out through the town gates, and were massacred and stripped of their clothing as they came. The atrocious deeds committed by our crusading ancestors in Portugal, against both Moors and Portuguese, do not bear thinking of. The garrison thus liquidated, the city was sacked; it proved richly rewarding, and the crusaders sailed away with their loot. The infidels were to recapture Silves later, and it was not finally held by the Christians until the mid-thirteenth century. It was after that that the Gothic church was raised on the foundations of the old mosque; the ghost of the mosque still haunts the ruined and restored building that was once a cathedral.

The view of Silves from the hilly country outside it is magnificent, even now, as it stands high above its river surrounded by woods, most of its ancient walls and towers gone (and very noble they must have looked, the three lines of defence, the towers outside the citadel walls, joined to them by flying buttresses, the moats, the great gates), but the Arab city still proudly climbing and dominating its rock. I crossed the bridge, drove up the rough road below the town, turned steeply left up to the cathedral, left the car outside its dark Gothic west front and square flanking towers (the earthquake, which ruined most of Silves, left some of the cathedral standing) and, looking about, was greeted by an Englishman on a bicycle, the manager of the great cork factory that I could see below. He showed me the steep flight of steps that led up to the citadel; climbing them, I was at the massive gate of the keep that guards the huge red sandstone enclosure. I was followed by a kind and courteous young Portuguese; he was a clerk in the cork factory, had seen me speaking with his manager, and had followed me to show me the citadel. He talked good English, was a student of English literature and of Portuguese history; he knew all about the citadel, and guided me round the ramparts of its tremendous walls. It was a ghostly place, this great empty fortress which had once been a close-packed city holding thirty thousand besieged Moors;

237

which had been underlaid with cellars, granaries, subterranean passages and cisterns; which now lay an empty waste in the sun, grown with almond trees and loud with chirping cicadas. There is a huge Moorish cistern left; it still supplies Silves with water; there is a deep well; there were, when I was there, still the mattresses of those who had been imprisoned in it, for, till quite lately, it was used as a gaol. We walked round the walls and told the towers; beneath us and round us spread the white, flat-roofed city, the shining river winding by, the shimmering sweep of wooded and gardened country, the great range of Montchique, transparent lilac against a luminous pale sky. The place smelt faintly of mortality; perhaps of long-dead Moors, perhaps of lately incarcerated Portuguese, perhaps only of almond trees and cicadas in the dusty burnt grass.

We came down from the citadel; my guide showed me the cathedral, which was, of course, shut, but he roused someone who came and let us in. The west front is pointed Gothic; it is said to be like Alcobaça. Inside it is cool and dark and broad naved; there are charming carved capitals, some good woodwork, and pleasant, florid altars and choir. Silves was a Sé cathedral until 1579, when the see was moved to Faro. I could not find the old episcopal palace; my guide did not know of its whereabouts, and it was probably destroyed, with most Silves houses, in 1755. Poor Silves, once so rich, has been desolated and laid waste ever since it was first attacked by the Christian armies; the Moors lost it, re-took it, lost it again, raided it at intervals till the eighteenth century; plague and pestilence swept it, earthquakes tossed it down, prosperity left it; under a century ago travellers wrote of it as desolate, deserted, ruinous. Now it thrives again, largely on cork; it has several cork factories, and boats carry cargoes down the Arade to be shipped at Portimão. One might spend a long time in Silves, climbing about its steep, winding Moorish streets among its flat-roofed houses, its gardens, its walls, its little squares.

My Portuguese friend and I exchanged names—I found that he knew at least one of my books—and parted, he to return to his cork factory, I to Portimão, so different from Silves, so gay, so busy round its blue basin of ships. I lunched at the pastelleria, the Casa Inglesa, in the praça; then took the road to Lagos, twelve miles away.

Lagos, where the railway ends, is an exciting place, once the Algarve capital, very ancient (the Roman Lacobriga, whose ruins lie a mile away), its bay of great renown; it has sheltered in its spacious harbour the fleets of many nations—Phœnician, Carthaginian, Roman, English, French—and the Portuguese fleets which Prince Henry the Navigator assembled there in the fifteenth century to voyage to new worlds, and King Sebastian in the sixteenth for the luckless expedition that never returned from Morocco. It is Prince Henry whose dreaming Plantagenet spirit still dominates Lagos; Prince Henry, whose first home it was in this province of Algarve that he governed, whose tomb it for a time was, who lived there with his legendary, if now disallowed, navigation school, his observatory, his charts and cartographers, planning and equipping voyages, receiving travellers from all the world, talking with them of distant seas and shores, dreaming his wild, rich, careful, hazardous dreams of African and Indian seas that came true. He lived in the Governor's Palace (it still stands, as a hospital); from the castle of Penhão overlooking the harbour he could see his ships coming in again from Madeira, Africa, India and the Azores, fraught with their cargoes of amber, sugar, ivory, gum, strange woods and Guinea and Canary blackamoors. In the arcaded market square these mournful black men and women were sold to bidders, sent to plant sugar canes and till vineyards, olive gardens, fig plantations and corn fields in the fertile red soil of Algarve.

Lagos Bay, as one comes to it along the Portimão road and the stone bridge that crosses the long, thrusting inlet of sea, is a lovely sight: the huge blue spread of harbour, full of ships, between two enclosing promontories, and above the harbour and the earthquake-ruined church, the steep town rising, narrow-streeted, difficult for cars, twisting and climbing about from praça to praça. You pass the arcaded slave market; the descendants of those terrified, weeping Africans and Canarians walk the streets to-day in blithe liberty; their piccaninnies, with little white shirts and great shining black eyes, goggle at strangers with the same merry astonishment with which the Lagos children gaped at the poor blackamoors five hundred years ago. In the highest praça is the little church of S. Antonio, very pretty, charmingly rebuilt after the earthquake that ruined most of Lagos, decorated gorgeously within with gilt carving and lovely blue and white azulejos running all round the walls below the gilt. There is a pretty white belfry tower, and in the church is a museum, which treasures among other interesting objects a little eighteenth-century statue of Major-General S. Antonio in a field officer's crimson sash over his monk's habit. From this height one looks down on the harbour and the long coastline of sandy beach, strewn with fantastic coloured rocks, for south of Lagos stretches the most beautiful and famous beach in Algarve, where the rocks are a labyrinth of marine castles, arches and grottoes and communicating tunnels; a fairy city, stretching out to the lovely grotto and green bathing pool at the Ponta da Piedade. To these beaches and grottoes visitors go to bathe; Prince Henry and his friends did not do so, and nor did I; they thought bathing an infidel perversion; I thought the Outer Ocean swept too coldly among the pierced and tunnelled rocks and that the beaches were already too inhabited. Besides which, I wanted to go on to Sagres and Cape St. Vincent.

There are charming corners in the narrow streets of Lagos; some are pre-earthquake, and here and there one comes on a manueline carved window or doorway. The houses are not all of the uniform white of some Algarve towns; some are a delightful rose colour, canary yellow, or deep blue; some have gardens and terraces of bright flowers and shrubs, and flights of stone stairs outside. The streets are sharp-angled and steep, and full of donkeys.

It is twenty miles to Sagres, about ten to the village of Raposeira, 'a place remote from the tumult of men, propitious for contemplation and study,' where Prince Henry had a country house, half-way between Lagos and Sagres. The house, or inn, must have perished; Raposeira is now a post-earthquake village of white houses and tiled roofs, blue azulejos and blue paint, with a pretty church tower. Prince Henry must have ridden continually along this Lagos–Raposeira road, through this hilly country planted with sugar canes, almonds, olives, figs, vines and maize, his African slaves working among them, shivering in the wind that blew from the sea and filled their master's mind with dreams and charts.

After Raposeira the country becomes less cultivated; the Algarve garden lies behind; bleak moorland and mountains begin. At Vila do Bispo, a tiny earthquake-ruined hamlet, women in men's felt hats did the washing in a large stone tank, and a few houses spared by the quake (none looks later) stood round them. After Vila do Bispo the desolate road bends south down the rocky promontory which ends in Sagres and Cape St. Vincent and the ocean.

The cape of Sagres, as one comes down to it across that windswept jut of massive limestone rock, is startlingly Europe's end; the end, said the ancients, of the whole inhabited world (for who was going to believe Marseilles liars like Pytheas, with his tales of strange seas, dense like the air, like jelly-fish, and remote shores and islands round and beyond the Lusitanian coast? Strabo considered him very misleading, and did not believe that he had ever got so far).

There is a village of Sagres; a road of small cheerful houses, a tiny praça, a church; beyond it, at the end of a narrow neck of land, is the treble-walled, ramparted fortress, that was stormed and burnt by Drake in 1587, built up again, overwhelmed by the great earthquake seas in 1755, later repaired, and now stands formidably within its massive gates, with a huge geometric circle, a *rosa dos ventos,* drawn in white stones on the ground inside the gates (said, but not by scholars, to have been used by Prince Henry; it was discovered in 1921, on the site of an ancient church, and the best informed Portuguese do not think it very old). On the cape's end there stands a lighthouse, and a high-ramparted view-point. The whole cliff plateau is a jumble of limestone boulders; thyme and saxifrage and cistus thrust up among them. I walked over them to the cliff's steep edge, looked down the frightening precipice into the clear deep bay where fishing boats rowed and sailed, saw how the wild coastline stretched west, point beyond point, with narrow green gulfs between the points, all round the great bay of Beliche to where the tremendous bluff of Cape St. Vincent stood out to sea four miles to the north-west. The Promontorium Sacrum: it is not clear whether they gave the name to the whole promontory, or which of the two great capes was the Sacred Mount. Probably Cape St. Vincent. On old Portuguese maps one reads 'Cabo de S. Vincente. En outro tempo Promontorio Sacro.' 'From there,' wrote Avienus, 'the sacred mount of Saturn rises jagged with rocks. The sea boils, and the rocky strand stretches far. Many shaggy-haired goats belonging to the natives wander always over the rough turf.' And Strabo: 'But as to the Cape itself, Artemidorus, who says that he visited the place, likens it to a ship.' There is no temple or altar to Hercules, Artemidorus said, but only stones. And it is not lawful to offer sacrifice there, or even to set foot in it at night, because the gods, the people say, occupy it at that time; those who come to see the place spend the night in a neighbouring village and visit the Cape by day, taking water with them, for there is no water there. 'Now these assertions of Artemidorus,' say Strabo, 'are allowable, and we should believe them; but the stories he has told, in agreement with the common multitude, are by no means to be believed.' As, for example, that the sun sets in the ocean beyond the Cape with a noise of sizzling.

But, standing on that great fissured cliff of Sagres, with those wild rocks and bays running out to the western cape, and the limitless Atlantic heaving beyond, I can, with Artemidorus and the common multitude, believe that anything might here occur. The waves thrash at the craggy rocks far below. It was in the Bay of Beliche that Drake, having retreated foiled from Lagos, landed eight hundred troops and led them scrambling up the cliff to the assault of the great castle of Sagres, piling faggots and pitch against the gates, firing them until the castle surrendered, and with it the forts and monastery on Cape St. Vincent. All Prince Henry's fortresses, and his two towns, the Vila do Infante and the Vila de Sagres, were burnt and blackened heaps of stones.

Discussions have been carried on by scholars for many years as to how much the Navigator ever lived at Sagres, whether he had a school of navigation, and if so where, and where he died. Anyhow he had two towns, one on each cape, the Vila do Infante on St. Vincent, the Vila de Sagres on the other. There are letters written by him from Sagres about both these; the town 'which anciently was Sagres, for long depopulated and destroyed by Moors' was ordered to be repeopled as of old, for the furnishing of expeditions to Guinea; and on 'the other cape, called Terçanabal,' was to be built 'my town of Vila do Infante,' and from there provisions and water were to be supplied to the ships which sheltered in the bay. There was to be a chapel of the Virgin, and a church to St. Catherine, and masses were to be said every Saturday. There was a fortress and a monastery of St. Vincent. It was probably in his Vila on Cape St. Vincent that Henry died in 1460.

All the Infante's town, fortresses, monastery, church and chapel, are now desolate in ruin. Sagres has been restored, but not the buildings on the other cape. The earthquake seas broke off great chunks of the Sagres cliff, wrecked the fortress gates and much of the walls, and nearly all the houses, including those of the governor and prior. Sagres town was never rebuilt on its old scale; in 1798 a traveller saw only a couple of houses outside the fort; the present little town is nineteenth century; all its houses are said to be built on the ruins of earlier buildings. All about the promontory lie shattered fragments of masonry. The boulders over which we walk are perhaps parts of ancient vanished dwellings. Prince Henry's own house at Sagres, which used to be shown, is said to be a nineteenth-century myth; so is his Sagres observatory, by those who peer more closely into history than is seemly or wise. Still, Henry did stay at Sagres, and also in his town on Cape St. Vincent, where he died.

There was a Portuguese picnic party seeing Sagres fort and being photographed and enjoying the view. I left them there, and drove to Cape St. Vincent, round the four-mile curve of Beliche Bay, among the rocks and the shaggy goats that strolled about the turfy borders of the road. It was like a road in the Highlands, and smelt of thyme and sea, and the Atlantic winds blew down it.

The other cape, when one arrives at it, is even grander than Sagres; a bleak, tremendous bluff, jutting out to sea like, as Artemidorus said, a ship, with a tall lighthouse on the prow. There is no house, except that of the lighthouse keeper (which is said to be built on the ruins of the old monastery). The Infante's town is a desolation of ruins; chapel-shaped, roofless buildings spread about the cliff; the silence and solitude are eerie. I do not know when the monastery was finally abandoned. There were Capuchins there in 1798; they related to Dr. Heinrich Link 'particulars of the engagement between the Spaniards and Lord St. Vincent, which they distinctly saw from the monastery. Such incidents alone can render a residence on this remote point of land interesting.'

Indeed yes. But such incidents are sadly rare, though less so off Cape St. Vincent than elsewhere. What engagements have been fought there, what fleets captured, what tyrant powers o'erthrown! Had the Capuchins abandoned the monastery too early to have watched Dom Pedro's small all-British Constitutionalist fleet (of which they cannot have approved), under

Admiral Sir Charles Napier, capture the navy of Dom Miguel in 1833? If so, they must have foreseen in that victory their coming doom, for they were probably victims of the Liberal Constitution.

Besides the monastery and the town and fortress and chapels, Henry built on Cape St. Vincent a great palace and park; eighteenth-century maps show remains of the walls still standing, stretching from the Fort of St. Vincent to the Fort of Beliche; in the palace wall were balconied windows. Little of it is now to be seen.

The wind sighed over the thymey boulders of the royal sea town; where sailors had once climbed up from their ships in the rocky roadstead, seeking food and water, now only goats scrambled. The evening darkened; the sun had long since sunk sizzling into the sea; it would soon be night, when no one might be on the Sacred Cape, because it would be occupied by the gods. It was time to seek a bed. My guidebook had assured me that there was an inn at Sagres, unpretentious but well spoken of. 'Recommended by those who know it,' said another guide, cautiously; the *conhecida e afamada Pensão de Sagres,* a Portuguese book called it, and Hachette told me it was a *petit hôtel très propre et accueillant.* Even the disdainful Murray (in Portugal the Reverend J. M. Neale), who thought Sagres 'beyond all question the most wretched and barren place in Portugal,' and that 'church, houses, fortifications and inn are all the picture of wretchedness,' at least agreed with the rest that there *was* an inn. But, as so often occurs in the Peninsula, there was no inn; there had not been an inn for years. It is time (as I have probably remarked before in the course of this book) that someone produced up-to-date guides to Spain and Portugal. I am weary of these inns, so unpretentious, so well spoken of, so vanished into the questionable limbo of past years, which leave me stranded, supperless and roofless, at the world's end, to sleep in a moonlit pine forest among mosquitoes at the gate of a monastery in the mountains of Valencia, or on a windswept

cape at the end of the inhabited world, among the dark and
ghost-trodden ruins of Prince Henry's town.

I made my bed in the roofless apse of what must have been
once a chapel; all night the wind whispered and moaned
coldly about the Sacred Cape; the long beams of the lighthouse, and of that of Sagres, speared and shafted the desolate
wastes of the sea which bounds the known world. Turn back,
oh Pindar, to the mainland of Europe. . . .

My journey was over. I had come to where the Outer Ocean
sweeps darkly northward round the Cape. 'There are the
springs and the ends of dusky earth, and of misty Tartarus,
and of the unharvested sea, and of starry heaven, dark and
terrible, which even the gods abhor: a mighty chasm . . .
And there stand the terrible habitations of murky light,
shrouded in dark clouds. . . .'

Into this I was to drive northward to-morrow, leaving Ora
Maritima behind me, its blue Mediterranean waves, its silver
Atlantic tides, rustling among the ghosts of wrecked Tyre,
Greece, Carthage, Rome, Gothia and Islam, on its two
thousand miles of sun-soaked shore, where still, as through
the long bright centuries before the first Tyrian ship swam
into Gadir bay, Iberians and Lusitanians sailed and fished
and fought and grew the olive and the vine.

# INDEX TO PLACES

OXFORD

## MORE OXFORD PAPERBACKS

Details of a selection of other books follow. A complete list of Oxford Paperbacks, including The World's Classics, Twentieth-Century Classics, OPUS, Past Masters, Oxford Authors, Oxford Shakespeare, and Oxford Paperback Reference, is available in the UK from the General Publicity Department, Oxford University Press (JH), Walton Street, Oxford, OX2 6DP.

In the USA, complete lists are available from the Paperbacks Marketing Manager, Oxford University Press, 200 Madison Avenue, New York, NY 10016.

Oxford Paperbacks are available from all good bookshops. In case of difficulty, customers in the UK can order direct from Oxford University Press Bookshop, 116 High Street, Oxford, Freepost, OX1 4BR, enclosing full payment. Please add 10% of published price for postage and packing.

# ABROAD

## British Literary Travelling Between the Wars

*Paul Fussell*

A literary and cultural study of the period between the two world wars in which Paul Fussell distinguishes between yesterday's 'travel' and today's 'tourism'. He contends that genuine travel is a lost art. His book is both an elegy for this art and a celebration of British writers who, in their travel books, memorialized the last age of real travel.

'an exemplary piece of criticism. It is immensely readable. It bristles with ideas . . . It admits a whole area of writing—at last!—to its proper place in literary history.' Jonathan Raban, *Quarto*

'All readers interested in the period between the wars and the art of travelling will derive great pleasure from *Abroad*.' Michael Ratcliffe, *The Times*